KUBRICK:

Inside a Film Artist's Maze

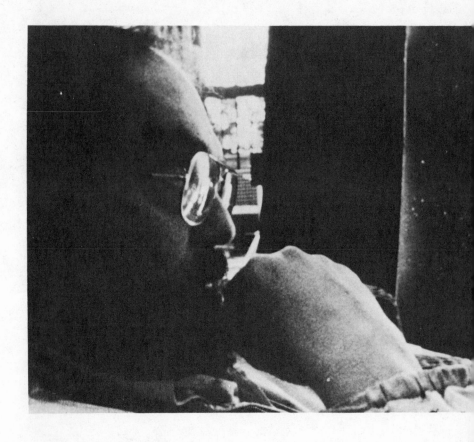

The Palace is not infinite.

The Library is limitless
and periodic.

—BORGES

KUBRICK:
Inside a Film Artist's Maze

Thomas Allen Nelson

 INDIANA UNIVERSITY PRESS • BLOOMINGTON

Manufactured in the United States of America

Library of Congress Cataloging in Publication Data
Nelson, Thomas Allen, 1940–
    Kubrick, inside a film artist's maze.
    Filmography: p.
    "A selective Kubrick bibliography": p.
    Includes index.
    1. Kubrick, Stanley. I. Title.
PN1998.A3K743   791.43′0233′0924   80–8845
ISBN 0–253–14648–8   AACR2
1 2 3 4 5 86 85 84 83 82

With appreciation, I dedicate
this book to K. N. CAIBRSBHUAK

Contents

The author wishes to thank Mr. Kubrick and his legal staff for their kind permission to use the photographic material found in this book. In addition, appreciation is extended to many others—in Los Angeles, New York, and London—who helped in the selection of stills.

KUBRICK:

Inside a Film Artist's Maze

1 REPUTATION & RHETORIC

Stanley Kubrick's reputation as a film maker remains curiously anomalous. His eleven feature films constitute a near-encyclopedia of cinematic *exempla* for film critics and theorists fascinated by both the structures of film rhetoric and the complexities of communicating with light and sound to an audience in the dark. No matter if the responsive vocabulary is generative or receptive, intrinsic or extrinsic, formal or humanistic: Kubrick's films embody such a stylistic and conceptual density that they are capable of stimulating even the most parochial of critical tastes. An updated revision of Pudovkin's *Film Technique* (1929), the film book that has had perhaps the greatest influence on Kubrick's private aesthetics, could be written with reference only to Kubrick's work. What better examples in recent years do we have of the difficulties of film adaptation—from novel to script to screen—than *Lolita, A Clockwork Orange, Barry Lyndon*, and *The Shining*; of the plasticity of film time than in the clockwork precision of the editing of *The Killing* and *Dr. Strangelove* and the match-cut linking bone and satellite in *2001*; of a dynamic and subtle use of camera and composition than in *Paths of Glory*; of the innovative use of lenses and color than in *A Clockwork Orange* and *Barry Lyndon*; of the complex manipulation of cinematic point of view—subjective, omniscient, "mindscreen"[1]—than in those films adapted from novels using the convention of the first-person unreliable narrator, namely *Lolita*, *A Clockwork Orange*, and *Barry Lyndon*; of the expressive use of film space, what Lev Kuleshov once called "creative geography," than in the three settings of *Dr. Strangelove*, the spatial poetry of *2001*, the mise-en-scène of *A Clockwork Orange* and *Barry Lyndon*, and the internal mazes of *The Shining*; of the imaginative use of asynchronous sound than in almost all his films? To be sure, critics agree, these are brilliant technical achievements. But . . . . And that, my friends, is a word which must give us pause.

Thus begins a biographical/evaluative litany that by now must sound familiar even to those unschooled in the politics and polemics of film criticism. It goes something like this. Born on July 26, 1928, of American Jewish parents of Austro-Hungarian ancestry and raised in the Bronx, Stanley Kubrick was an indifferent student who displayed an early aptitude for physics, chess, still photography, and movie-watching. After a modest success as a staff photographer for *Look* magazine, in 1950–51 Kubrick launched his film career with two short documentaries (*Day of the Fight* and *Flying Padre*) and by 1955 had made another documentary (*The Seafarer*, 1953) and two privately financed features, one a hothouse/arthouse existential allegory (*Fear and Desire*, 1953) and the other a poorly written but visually promising *film noir* (*Killer's Kiss*, 1955), which led to a partnership with an independent producer named James B. Harris. Over the next six years, Harris-Kubrick released *The Killing* (1956), *Paths of Glory* (1957), and *Lolita* (1962). Between the last two films Kirk Douglas hired Kubrick to take over the direction of *Spartacus* (1960), an ultimately unsatisfactory assignment for Kubrick, since he had no control over the script. By this time, Kubrick's promise as Hollywood's *wunderkind* of the Eisenhower era had been fulfilled. With *Dr. Strangelove, or How I Learned to Stop Worrying and Love the Bomb* (1964), Kubrick achieved at once an extraordinary success for a thirty-five-year-old director and the kind of economic control as producer that would guarantee the creative integrity of his future work. At this point Kubrick's critical reputation began to take an equivocal turn that has trailed after his work ever since, during which time he has made four remarkable films: *2001: A Space Odyssey* (1968), *A Clockwork Orange* (1971), *Barry Lyndon* (1975), and *The Shining* (1980).

Since the mid-sixties Kubrick has worked out of a studio complex in the London suburb of Boreham Wood, and in the process has cut himself off from the influential centers of film criticism. Popular critical opinion has drawn from bits of biography and inspiration a distorted portrait of a man with the temperament of a hermit—a withdrawn auto-didact, intellectual and misanthropic—so obsessed by fear of life's contingencies that he has sought and achieved an extraordinary degree of control over every detail of his life and art. We have read stories about his supposed fear of flying (even though he holds a pilot's license and has put in at least 150 hours in the air) and his refusal to travel faster than thirty miles per hour in an automobile; we know about his painstaking supervision of every financial and creative aspect of the film-making process, from script to publicity, to the publication of one of his own screenplays (*A Clockwork Orange*).[2] Especially since the mixed critical reception, particularly in New York, of *2001*, Kubrick has allowed others to carry his banner into the film marketplaces; unlike Francis Ford Coppola or François Truffaut, he does not bring his films to Cannes or engage in creative exchanges with his contemporaries. He has never been the subject of a "special issue" in a single film journal, although his reputation as a brilliant film craftsman has quietly but steadily developed, as is evidenced by the attention paid to his work in a variety of texts and anthologies devoted to film study. And yet the anomaly persists: Stanley Kubrick, who unquestionably ranks as one of the most important film directors in the generation after that of Kurosawa, Antonioni, Welles, Bergman, and Fellini (all born between 1910 and 1920), remains an enigma to a popular critical establishment which demands that those in the pantheon not only display the requisite technical skills but develop in their collected work a complex and unified vision of the world.* And here is where the real subject of this study begins.

Those who have expressed admiration for Kubrick's films—mostly

---

* See *Notes* for a listing of secondary sources as well as additional comments on Kubrick's critical reputation. Throughout this book, I use the *Notes* both to document quoted or paraphrased material and to extend my analysis and description into relevant but tangential areas.

academic critics and college audiences—have argued that they exhibit
what Gerald Mast has called a "deep thematic conviction."[3] These
critics point out two essential characteristics of Kubrick's work which
for many stand as a roadblock to understanding and appreciation:
that is, a wide diversity of subject matter and what appears to be a
general rather than specific thematic and tonal consistency. Kubrick
himself has remarked that he does not think of film making in cate-
gorical or generic terms but in broad conceptual outlines:

> I have no fixed ideas about wanting to make films in particular cate-
> gories—Westerns, war films and so on. I know I would like to make
> . . . a contemporary story that really gave a feeling of the times, psy-
> chologically, sexually, politically, personally . . . it would be the hardest
> film to make.[4]

These comments, from 1960, suggest a mind that works on more than
one level of feeling and idea, intuition and intellect, and they point up
the futility of one critic's attempt to squeeze Kubrick's films into the
generic straitjacket of the *film noir*.[5] A more informal and revealing
classification of his films could be worked out along the following
lines: (1) The *Noir* Films (*Killer's Kiss, The Killing*); (2) The His-
torical/Philosophical Films (*Paths of Glory, Barry Lyndon*); (3) The
Speculative/Science Fiction Films (*Fear and Desire, 2001*); (4) The
Contemporary Satiric Films (*Dr. Strangelove, A Clockwork Orange*);
and (5) The Psychological Films (*Lolita, The Shining*). What such
an exercise in critical taxonomy reveals is the difficulty of defining
with precision the thematic unity of the work of a film director whose
conceptual concerns are as varied and complex as Kubrick's. Alexander
Walker has best expressed this challenge in his opening description of
what he sees as Kubrick's *modus operandi*:

> Only a few directors possess a conceptual talent—that is, a talent to
> crystallize every film they make into a cinematic concept. It is a skill
> that goes far beyond the mere photographing of a script, however cine-
> matic the script may be in itself. It transcends the need to find a good
> subject, an absorbing story, or an extraordinary premise to build on.
> Essentially, it is the talent to construct a form that will exhibit the
> maker's vision in an unexpected way, often a way that seems to have
> been the only possible one when the film is finally finished. It is this
> conceptual talent that most strongly distinguishes Stanley Kubrick.

Overall, those critics, whether popular or academic, who are most

Games of chance and games of love in the candlelit formality of *Barry Lyndon.*

interested in theme, see in Kubrick's films the sensibility of a detached, ironic artist interested more in human nature than in issues of autonomy, in the broadly speculative implications of research in such scientific and socio-scientific disciplines as physics, astronomy, anthropology, and psychology. Most seem to feel that Kubrick's short-term view of humankind is skeptical at best, despite a note of evolutionary affirmation at the conclusion of *2001.* More trenchant, however, is Hans Feldmann's insight into Kubrick's profound interest in how human beings create complex extensions of instinctual and psychological conditions through a variety of cultural, technological, and aesthetic forms.[6] Feldmann, for instance, describes *A Clockwork Orange* and *Barry Lyndon* as films that "study the relations between the individual man and the cultural forms through which that individual must achieve the expression of himself." What Feldmann's excellent essay touches on but does not fully develop is the recognition that Kubrick's conceptual universe contains more than a simpleminded belief in human corruption, or, as one critic so acidly put it, a "message that people are disgusting but things are lovely."[7] The polarity between those critics who admire his technical prowess but either deplore or misapprehend his thematics, and those, like Norman Kagan and others, who seemingly equate great film art with a ready glossary of themes, exemplifies a dilemma especially prevalent in film criticism.[8] Neither position, for instance, fully acknowledges the difference between a moral or intellectual intuition expressed in film and the traditional platitudes of systematized ethics; nor does either group seem to realize the logic of that first critical insight which says that Kubrick's films are impressive experiences that stimulate a complex range of emotional and intellectual response: a logic which requires that we work out his film "content" aesthetically rather than thematically. What follows will be a definition of how this study plans to approach these and related issues.

On the question of his personal aesthetics, Kubrick may be his own worst enemy. Throughout his career, in published comments, he has appeared to denigrate the importance of style and form in order to stress his view that film should assault an audience's emotional and subconscious expectations. He believes, for instance, that good writing starts with a "writer's obsession with his subject, with a theme and concept and a view of life and an understanding of character. Style is what an artist uses to fascinate the beholder in order to convey to him his feelings and emotions and thoughts." Discussing the problems of film adaptation, Kubrick describes the perfect novel as not being, as some believe, the novel of action,

> but, on the contrary, the novel which is mainly concerned with the inner life of its characters. It will give the adaptor an absolute compass bearing . . . on what a character is thinking or feeling at any given moment of the story. And from this he can invent action which will be an objective correlative of the book's psychological content . . . without resorting to having the actors deliver literal statements of meaning.[9]

This comment provides a signpost, instructive but subtly misleading, pointing the way toward a critical definition of Kubrick's working aesthetics. It expresses his obvious commitment to the importance of film as narrative art. Kubrick's work, in fact, embodies what some see as a nineteenth-century addiction to the well-made plot, overly rationalized characterization, and a thematic/emotive cohesion. Critics at times have responded to these statements of intention as though they were digging for the mother lode, searching his films for those veins of great thematic import which many believe essential to a definition of a great artist. Some have come away from this enterprise satisfied that what they have found can be translated into true currency, others have not. One unfortunate consequence of this confusion has been a tendency to accept at face value Kubrick's comment that a "preoccupation with originality of form is more or less a fruitless thing" and that if he had to choose between a film maker like Eisenstein ("all style, no content") and one like Chaplin ("all content, no style"), he would take Chaplin. Because Kubrick has been so insistent about how he approaches the content/style issue, one ever present for a narrative artist, critics may have been too quick to define his exceptional accomplishments as a film stylist as examples of mere technical virtuosity, as tricks to "fascinate the beholder" while he is being injected with a dose of emotional or thematic content. One also must not neglect the importance of Kubrick's final words on the subject: "Obviously, if you can combine style and content, you have the best of all possible films."

To confront this problem, and its significance to the formulation of a sound critical approach, one has to read more carefully what Kubrick has said in print and to consider the difference between the experience of responding to a film as a member of an audience and responding, as a critic, to the quality of both that experience and the work that stimulated it. Many of Kubrick's comments suggest a receptive theory of film making (how films should affect an audience), while others point to a private, generative aesthetics (how *his* films spring from an attitude about the interpenetration of art and reality). When he says, as he frequently has, that an audience should respond to a film through "its feelings, not through any conscious analysis of what it has seen," and that to deprive them of an intensive experience would be a sin, Kubrick speaks as a public artist working in a commercial medium. When, however, he discusses how all art involves a to and fro between conception and execution, with the "original intention being constantly modified as one tries to give it objective realization," he addresses an issue basic to the workings of film form.[10] Kubrick has repeatedly insisted that film can only achieve the ambiguity and "subconscious designating effect of a work of art" by communicating visually and through music rather than words. But, paradoxically, that seems only to have encouraged critics to continue their thematic pigeonholing of his films or else to dismiss the films as being perversely obscure, when one would have thought that Kubrick's clearly expressed beliefs would have stimulated the critics to examine just how the film maker achieves that "subconscious designating effect" through his impressive command of film rhetoric. Only when we appreciate the *how* of Kubrick's art (what he calls "style") can we fully apprehend the *what* ("content"), and then perhaps we can answer that inner voice which follows hard upon with the inevitable *so what?*

A widely known but uninvestigated source for an understanding of Kubrick's aesthetics can be found in Pudovkin's theoretical and practical handbook on the film making art.[11] Kubrick has called *Film Technique* the "most instructive book on film aesthetics I came across." For Pudovkin, two essential factors elevated film from a photographic process to a cinematographic art: an artist-director's controlling vision and editing, the "creative force of filmic reality." Pudovkin's most famous principle maintains that a film must be "built," not shot, and in this construction process, the director must strive to achieve a "compulsory and deliberate guidance of the thoughts and associations of the spectator." Kubrick has said that the "writer-director is really the perfect dramatic instrument" and that the combination of those two functions has "produced the most consistently fine work." And his films stand as testaments to a meticulous architectonics in the organization of their temporal rhetoric. The carefully orchestrated and classical structures of *2001*, *A Clockwork Orange*, and *Barry Lyndon* serve as overt and grandiloquent extensions of a Kubrickian trademark that can be traced back to the organizational precision of *The Killing*, *Paths of Glory*, and *Dr. Strangelove*. They leave no doubt that for Kubrick the working out of shots into scenes, scenes into sequences, and sequences into consciously modulated cinematic wholes, involves an essential creative activity both during the preparation of the script and in the final editing. Significantly, Kubrick in the course of his career has gained an increasing control and mastery over these two distinct but related phases in the temporal aesthetics of film. He has scripted without collaboration two of his last three films and, of course, he has expressed on numerous occasions his fondness for the editing process as the most "reasonable environment" for creative work.

That Kubrick, like Pudovkin, exercises the maximum directorial control and, indeed, conceives of his role as that of Master Builder is self-evident; but those facts, in themselves, do not separate his work from that of a number of other directors. What does distinguish Kubrick's films from most others, including Pudovkin's, is his ability to convert cinematic form into complex cinematic meanings. Pudovkin, especially, envisioned the director as an inspired and benevolent despot whose aim it was to guide an audience toward a clear understanding of theme and to produce a prescribed feeling in them. "One must try to express one's concepts in clear and vivid visual images," Pudovkin says, so that the "psychic guidance" of the spectator can be realized through an awareness of how a film's "searching glance" reveals a truth beyond the casually and superficially apprehended surfaces of reality. Like Eisenstein, Pudovkin trafficked in the thematic and psychological implications of a simplified Marxist aesthetics—a necessary strategy, he felt, for expression in a medium not far enough advanced to deal with large and complex themes. Thus Kubrick's judgment that Eisenstein's films (and by inference, Pudovkin's) are more sophisticated stylistically than thematically seems sound enough. Kubrick's own films, as well as what we know about the care with which they are conceived and planned, demonstrate working principles very close to those recommended by Pudovkin. Kubrick, too, believes that a director must, first and foremost, formulate a conceptual understanding of his subject, what Pudovkin calls "theme"; that he must next move from concept to the construction of what Pudovkin calls "action" or "treatment," but which Kubrick extends to include the complex rhetoric of cinematic adaptation, point of view, narrative, and character, through which the emotional and thematic content of a film achieve objective (temporal) realization; and that the director's final task must be the challenging one of working out what Pudovkin calls the "cinematographic" or "filmic representation" of the action, which, for our purposes here, might better be designated as the total spatial/musical rhetoric of Kubrick's films.

What this comparison reveals is not that Kubrick shares with the Soviet film makers of the 1920s a film aesthetic based on montage and a didactic interest in certain historical assumptions; much of what has been described, after all, applies as well to what we know of the working habits of directors as disparate as Hitchcock, Bresson, and Bergman. Indeed, Kubrick's thematics are far more complex than Pudovkin's, but significantly his find expression through a methodology that shares Pudovkin's passion for an exactness of temporal and spatial directorial construction. That such a schematic approach to the construction of the scenario exemplifies the workings of a didactic temperament is obvious, especially if one understands Pudovkin's preference for thematic clarity and a total psychological guidance of the spectator. To surmise, however, that Kubrick's intentions are equally didactic because he follows an organizational exactness would be to equate methodology with aesthetics, politics with creative vision. Kubrick's comments on the question of audience manipulation reveal an attitude more in tune with the tradition of Wellesian ambiguity than the so-called "analytic" and "undemocratic" (to paraphrase André Bazin) tendencies of Soviet expressionism.[12] Rather than a blending of ideological clarity and an overt manipulation of cinematic form, Kubrick's films, as the diversity in the critical response to their thematics would suggest, embody Kubrick's belief that "truthful and valid ideas are so multi-faceted that they don't yield themselves to frontal assault. The ideas have to be discovered by the audience, and their thrill in making the discovery makes these ideas all the more powerful."[13] He thinks that film should communicate its concepts as subtext, "obliquely, so as to avoid all pat conclusions and neatly tied up ideas."[14] His view of plot and character, from early in his career, suggests a desire to challenge an audience's awareness through indirect and covert means rather than manipulate it toward a set of didactic intentions:

> I like the slow start, the start that goes under the audience's skin and involves them so that they can appreciate grace notes and soft tones and don't have to be pounded over the head with plot points and suspense hooks.
>
> . . . .
>
> . . . you let the character unfold himself gradually before the audience. You hold off as long as possible revealing the kind he is. He comes in like a nice guy, and when the audience finds out, they're trapped. You cast a person as the opposite of what he's really trying to do, so the audience will find out only later.[15]

His avowed fascination with games of deception like chess and with fantastic, surrealist literature characterizes an artist who prefers to unsettle an audience's comfortable acceptance of the familiar, of "life as it is," to quote Kubrick, and to require that it deal with his films in complex emotional and psychological ways. Hardly anything could be further from Pudovkin's didactic clarity than Kubrick's belief that "there's something in the human personality which resents things that are clear, and conversely, something which is attracted to puzzles, enigmas, and allegories."[16]

Between Pudovkin's time and Kubrick's, there is a great gulf, epis-

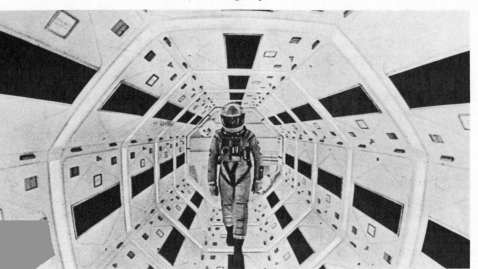

David Bowman (Keir Dullea) of *2001* moving through a Kubrickian corridor on his way to a confrontation with his double, HAL.

temological as well as aesthetic. Pudovkin and his contemporaries inhabited an intellectual and artistic environment that still had faith in man's ability to break down the world into tidy rational units and thereby to understand it. Film practice and theory by 1930, for instance, had split into two convenient stylistic and epistemological camps: (1) the realist tradition of Lumière-Griffith-Flaherty-Stroheim, which developed narrative and documentary styles consistent with the nineteenth-century belief that an organic, autonomic reality existed in history and nature; and (2) the expressionist tradition of Méliès, German expressionism, and Soviet montage, which affirmed that "reality" was best represented in such hidden areas as poetic imagination, the unconscious mind, or the dialectics of history. Stylistically, this polarity was defined and distinguished by a fondness for principles of continuity and illusory verisimilitude on the one hand (invisible editing, synchronization of image and camera movements, realist mise-enscène), and on the other an expressive and obtrusive manipulation of the spatial and temporal content of what was photographed (decor, lighting, angle, montage). By the 1950s, this polarity had been validated by the theoretical essays of Rudolph Arnheim and Béla Balázs for expressionism, Siegfried Kracauer and André Bazin for realism.

Yet even while this consolidation was taking place (which can be conveniently dated by the publication in 1960 of Kracauer's *Theory of Film: The Redemption of Physical Reality*), the secure status of both "facts" as a conclusive measure of truth and the dominance of Freudian psychology, with its humanist concept of an internally organized self, had suffered further erosion from the impact of discoveries and theories in several investigative disciplines. Quantum physics now buttresses Einstein's rejection of the absoluteness of time and space in its demonstration that attempts to map a completely ordered cosmos are futile. Psychologists more often than not tell us that the self lacks internal coherence and can best be described as a series of identities, splintered into separate roles and masks, seen respectively as either a performer skating across the moving surfaces of life or a Proteus ready to "flow" and embrace new possibilities. R. D. Laing, in particular, has popularized the notion that traditional concepts of madness and sanity cannot deal adequately with contemporary psychic conditions and that, in fact, certain schizophrenic tendencies are signs of health rather than dysfunction. In literature, the early modernist reaction to what was perceived as this century's metaphysical crisis, namely the creation of private mythologies by such writers as Yeats, Pound, Eliot, Joyce, and Lawrence, has been ridiculed in recent years by John Barth and a group of writers identified by a variety of prefixes (*meta-, par-, sur-, trans-fictionalists*) as "mythotherapy." Today, in fact, the interpretive impulse of any discipline or activity that stems, like Pudovkin's, from inclusive or total assumptive systems has been so devalued that large numbers of college-educated people prefer the "truth" of such pseudoscientific and paranormal fads as psychokinesis, astral projection, precognition, pyramid power, and astrology.

At the same time that film realism and expressionism developed separate stylistic identities—and that is the way we usually distinguish between, say, Eisenstein and Stroheim—they mined what Kubrick disparages as their "content" from a similar set of assumptions. Both testify, despite their differing ways, to the durability of nineteenth-century epistemological thinking, which believed in a system of rational correspondence between the structures of phenomena and the structures of the human mind, between private experience and the facts of temporal reality, an equipoise between the self and the world, between depths and surfaces.[17] Eisenstein's and Pudovkin's expressive renderings of film space and time, therefore, share an unlikely epistemological kinship with both the Teutonic stylizations of Murnau and Sternberg on the one hand, and the naturalistic rigors of Flaherty and Stroheim on the other. Although the stylistic modes differ, that is, each can be defined by a distinct film language, traditional realist and expressionist films have this in common: They assume the existence of "total" or inclusive answers to life's apparent contradictions. Keaton's *The Navigator* (1924) and *The General* (1927), two masterpieces of American silent-film realism, are as "scientific" and logical in their own way as Stroheim's *Greed* (1924), although Keaton posits depth in the sentimental self while Stroheim favors the determinisms of nature and society; yet both film makers shared the assumption that surface reality attains significance, or depth, through an observable system of laws and correspondences and that in their films' *total* spatial and temporal structures a facsimile of the world was represented. Pudovkin's stylistics may distinguish his films from those of his more realistic contemporaries, but his commitment to a totalized world view does not. As we have seen, he merely assumed that his cinematographic "reality" attained a thematic clarity by reaching farther beneath photographed surfaces than did the films of the realists. Similarly, German expressionism's preoccupation with subjective worlds comforts rather than disorients us with its assertion that distinctions between sane and insane are still valid. Witness the psychological dualisms of Wiene and Mayer's *Caligari* (1920), Murnau's *Nosferatu* (1922) and his American *Sunrise* (1927), and Sternberg's *The Blue Angel* (1929). All retain the High German admonition that excesses of the libido must be curbed if psychic and social order are to prevail. While these film traditions express differing political and psychological values, and in so doing adopt appropriate styles, they are unified in their faith in totalized, didactic assumptions and therefore are appreciated by today's viewer as much for their styles of presentation and performance as their substance. In that respect, Kubrick's evaluation of Eisenstein as "all style" and Chaplin as "all content" could be construed as indicating at once his rejection of Soviet didacticism and his belief in performance (in this case, Chaplin's) as an extension of substance. But more of that later (in chapters 3 and 6).

André Bazin's seminal essay on "The Evolution of the Language of Cinema," with its contention that depth of focus in the films of Wyler and Welles, and the absence of montage effects in Italian neorealism, gave back to cinema "a sense of the ambiguity of reality," would seem to possess the kind of critical clarity and relevance necessary for an analysis of how Kubrick's aesthetics express a conditional rather than dialectical world view. Bazin, for instance, described the dangers in those films (mostly examples of film expressionism) that presuppose a unity of meaning in any dramatic event, and therefore by their very nature rule out ambiguity. Yet, as I have argued in the pages of *Film Criticism*, Bazin's humanist aesthetic remains consistent with a belief in the "wholeness" of reality—admittedly in this case one that values "complexity" and "ambiguity"—and in the film maker's role as a Moses mediating between medium and subject.[18] He believed that for every film subject, from Flaherty's explorations of primitive societies to Welles's Charles Foster Kane, from the complexities of dramatic space in Murnau to the theatrical ambiguities of Renoir, an appropriate (that is, an *a priori*) range of stylistic techniques either was available or would be created. Dudley Andrew, in his excellent biographical study, illustrates how Bazin's preferences for certain films and film styles reflect a coherent metaphysical orientation:

> Beneath such concepts as the limitation of perception and the integrity of space lies a belief in the signifying power of nature. When a film-maker puts a situation under the pressure of a controlled gaze, he forces "it to reveal its structural depth, to bring out the preexisting relations."[19]

Bazin's often-stated belief that film should "reveal" the order of nature rather than "add" to it becomes a focusing aesthetic principle only in the assumptive context of the sort of dualistic epistemology of the actual and imaginal found, paradoxically, in the film masterpieces of both realism and expressionism. And while Kubrick feels strongly that the visual powers of film make ambiguity an inevitability as well as a virtue, he would not share Bazin's mystical belief that the better film makers are those who sacrifice their personal perspectives to a "fleeting crystallization of a reality [of] whose environing presence one is ceaselessly aware." For Kubrick, the old-fashioned division of film into the categories of "realism" and "expressionism," now relegated to a lower-case and qualified identity, merely represents stylistic options for the embodiment of far-reaching speculations about life as it is experienced today:

> I have always enjoyed dealing with a slightly surrealistic situation and presenting it in a realistic manner. I've always liked fairy tales and myths, magical stories. I think they are somehow closer to the sense

of reality one feels today than the equally stylized "realistic" story in which a great deal of selectivity and omission has to occur in order to preserve its "realist" style.[20]

Could it be that the informational glut created by the communications media since Bazin's death in 1958, a media that Kubrick understands and shows a continued fascination with, has eroded all authoritative visions that pretend to encompass what we must describe, in quotation marks and with equivocation, as "modern reality"? Kubrick's films, in fact, reflect one writer's belief that reality itself has become "so extravagant in its contradictions, absurdities, violence, speed of change, science-fiction technology, weirdness, and constant unfamiliarity"[21] that the traditional division between imagination and fact seems neither definable nor relevant. Perhaps no more accurate description exists for the "normal" experience of film viewing enjoyed today: one where our emotions are constantly assaulted by mixtures of visual/ aural style and technique (short- and long-lens perspectives, deep and shallow compositions, naturalist and impressionist colors, the incorporation of wild sound with complex sound mixes); one which demands that we respond with intelligence and understanding to a content that, more often than not, implies that *combinations within the surfaces of reality* (of objects and actors, of sight and focus, of color and shape, of sounds and mood) may be not only more immediate but more "real" than an older faith in *rational correspondences in the depths of reality*. Films today present us with a totally contingent universe, where images and sounds mean both nothing and everything, a world of total probability and zero signification. And this cinema of contingency finds no fuller expression than in the films of Stanley Kubrick.

If Kubrick's work cannot be appreciated through the conventions of film realism or film expressionism, or as illustrations of a Bazinian séance between an anthropomorphic universe and human meditation, Jean Mitry's encyclopedic and pluralistic approach to film aesthetics may provide a revealing although admittedly synthetic model to work from. In his *Esthétique et Psychologie du cinéma*, Mitry says the following:

The process of film joins a deep psychological reality and satisfies our desire to understand the world and each other in a powerful yet necessarily partial way. The aesthetics of film is based on this psychological truth and need. And so cinema is the greatest of the arts because it meets this need by showing us the *process* of the transformation of the world. The other arts can show us merely the end result of such transformation, the humanized art world. In cinema human beings tell each other what reality means to them, yet they do so through reality itself, which surrounds their work like an ocean.[22]

If I understand Mitry correctly, he believes that all narrative films both reveal reality (the humanist view) and organize it into significances (the modernist view); that, to use an important distinction popularized in recent studies by Louis Giannetti and Leo Braudy, film by its very nature is "open" (realism's window on the world) and "closed" (expressionism's framing of the world).[23] Mitry contends that while the film maker cannot rid his work of reality, he must of necessity insist upon his manipulation of it. Reality has no "totality" that film must serve and represent; rather than possessing a natural order of surfaces or depths, as both Pudovkin and Bazin assumed, reality, in Mitry's view, stands in a state of contingent readiness for the enrichment of human intervention. As a result, film cannot avoid the aesthetic consequences of the concreteness of reality, its *thereness*, nor can it deny the presence of man the signifier. Mitry's synthesis of the humanist (*psychologie*) and modernist (*esthétique*) traditions is the kind of eclectic but coherent discourse needed to inform our general understanding of a period of stylistic transition and our particular understanding of a film maker of Kubrick's aesthetic complexity.

An awareness of contingency arises whenever there is a loss of faith in teleological explanations, in the received or discovered validity of meaning, in the rational structures of nature or the signifying power of mind and language. Once meaning has lost the authority of teleology, we then perceive how many different ways there are to create meaning through the expressive extensions of language and form. Yet even while we are acknowledging the subjectivity of perception and the fictiveness of language, our senses continue to record the reality of a sensate and inchoate universe. And if the alliance of modern science and technology can be trusted, one which depends upon the machine's capacity for verifying the objectivity of the universe in ways impossible for the human mind alone, we inhabit a world which is incredibly complex and vast in its dimensions. No matter if you conceive the universe—its creation or eventual demise—as collapsing, expanding, or oscillating, you are dealing with a temporal and spatial fact that renders puny by comparison the duration of our existence, both individually and as a species.[24] Only with such a recognition can one discover the full meaning of contingency, not only as a burden that justifies a retreat into the existential self, but as a challenge to imagination and its potential for humanizing rather than anthropomorphizing the universe. Anthropology and history, two expressions of that potential, have chronicled our struggles with contingency in their record of the human effort at extending a dominion over a universe far more complex than an urge for meaning could possibly hope to embrace. For at least four million years, our race has projected its conscious and subconscious minds onto nature in an attempt to share its concreteness and its infinitude through forms and artifacts—including the creation of identities, civilizations, the arts—which, like the intelligence behind the monolith in Kubrick's *2001*, survive and define us amid the engulfing silence of the universe.

To say, therefore, that Stanley Kubrick's films reflect a preoccupation with this cosmic and psycho/aesthetic drama would be an understatement. His films, from the efforts of Johnny Clay to control the exigencies of time and space in *The Killing* to Barry Lyndon's entrapment within the psychological and historical forms of his ambition or Jack Torrance's journey in *The Shining* through the mazes of a collective unconscious, repeatedly investigate the human and aesthetic consequences of contingency. They explore the complex extensions of human imagination—its history and its emotion, its forms and its fictions, its grandeur and its triviality—for what they both disguise and reveal about an existence without recognizable purpose amidst the myriad stars and worlds. On this subject of our cosmic transience, for instance, Kubrick has said the following:

> If man merely sat back and thought about his impending termination, and his terrifying insignificance and aloneness in the cosmos, he would surely go mad, or succumb to a numbing sense of futility. Why, he might ask himself, should he bother to write a great symphony, or strive to make a living, or even to love another, when he is no more than a momentary microbe on a dust mote whirling through the unimaginable immensity of space?[25]

For Kubrick, contingency has provided both a stimulus for filmic expression and a perspective on a wide range of potential "content" embodied in human history and imagination within a variety of forms and

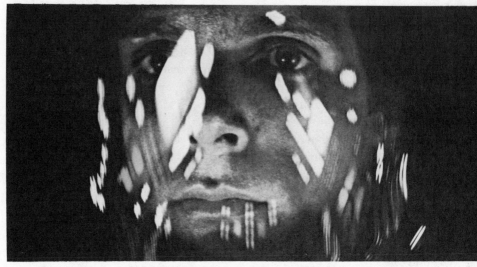

In *2001*, Bowman undergoes an "awakening" in
deep space.

ritual activities, visual and abstract structures, the shapes of societies
and histories, the struggles of individual consciousness and articulation.
Significantly, Kubrick's films stand as complex illustrations of their
creator's acceptance of the "challenges of life within the boundaries of
death" and as an affirmation of how "our existence as a species can
have genuine meaning and fulfillment."

To understand how Kubrick converts an epistemology into an aesthetics, something which will be of practical rather than theoretical
concern in subsequent chapters, we might pause to consider his films
through a concept known to readers of science-fiction as "conventionalization." Kubrick has been quoted as saying that he views the storytelling requirements of film as the initial step in creating an "objective
correlative" for a psychological and emotional content: which means
that for him a film's most basic temporal and spatial realization (Pudovkin's twin notions of "action" and "filmic representation") provides the
audience with points of reference, the panoply of "conventionalization"
we associate with the Aristotelian verities of time and place, while covertly it undermines its own didactic authority and asserts its contingency as a work of art. The relationship that an audience experiences
with a Kubrick film, beginning with *Paths of Glory*, resembles Bowman's confrontation with the extraterrestrial intelligence in *2001*. He
wanders around in an eighteenth-century room without doors—a tem-

poral and spatial "conventionalization"—while he is being subjected to an experience that will transform him from *Homo sapiens* to Star-Child. Kubrick's films aesthetically embody an analogous principle: They provide us with the familiar terrain of a temporal/spatial coherence—all the features of organizational exactness alluded to earlier, what I prefer to call an overt rhetoric—while they suggest to us, as the room does to Bowman, that viewed from another perspective, one developed through a covert rhetoric, their cinematic corporeality represents an illusion of sorts, something to "fascinate the beholder" while his awareness is being subtly altered. We must remember that the bone which Moon-Watcher, the hominid of *2001*, tosses into the air in a moment of evolutionary victory functions not only as a practical instrument at a given moment in filmic time, but as an artifact, a *ur*-HAL, for it externalizes and expresses a paradox in human nature—it is both a tool and a weapon, at once creative and destructive. For Kubrick, the aesthetics of his medium likewise are tools of expression, mythopoeic extensions for the inner complexities of his vision, an opportunity for converting cinematic form into cinematic meanings. It will be for us to determine whether or not he has used this opportunity for purposes worthy of our attention, and particularly of that precious commodity, time, which, in a contingent universe, we all hold so dear and so briefly.

2 IN THE BEGINNING

By the time he had completed his fourth feature film, at the age of twenty-nine, Stanley Kubrick had confronted and resolved a series of complex aesthetic and thematic problems. He had achieved a startling success early in the first decade of his career, largely through a process of trial and error. He learned his craft in the 1950s by doing rather than by being shown how: He served no apprenticeship in either the studios or the classrooms of academe, and in fact, his early history more closely resembles the histories of the French cinephiles than it does those of his predecessors and successors in Hollywood. Like the members of the New Wave, Kubrick moved from watching and discussing films to making them. Truffaut and Resnais, like Kubrick, began in the documentary before turning to the greater technical and conceptual challenges offered by feature films. Significantly, *The 400 Blows* (1959) and *Hiroshima, Mon Amour* (1959), two films that, among others, signalled the end of Italian neorealism's influence and the beginning of a more "personal" brand of film making, were quietly predated and, from the vantages of hindsight, preempted by Kubrick's first work of consummate skill, *Paths of Glory* (1957). Taken together, Kubrick's first four features contain several vital signs of the range of stylistic and thematic interests that were to be more fully realized in the films of the next two-plus decades.* *Fear and Desire* (1953) and *Killer's Kiss* (1955), in their best moments, admittedly few in number, achieve some arresting surrealistic imagery and suggest the first indications of the plot and character ideas that were to be worked out with more precision in the next two films. *The Killing* (1956) and *Paths of Glory*, both adapted from competently written but easily accessible novels, show significant advances in artistry as well as in budget and overall production. *The Killing* demonstrates Kubrick's skill at handling a complex temporal structure, while the spatial organization of

---

* For helpful plot summaries of these early films, see the appropriate chapters in Norman Kagan, *The Cinema of Stanley Kubrick* (New York: Holt, Rinehart, and Winston, 1972), and Gene D. Phillips, *Stanley Kubrick: A Film Odyssey* (New York: Popular Library, 1975).

Paths of Glory exemplifies a sustained control and brilliance not found in his previous work. And these two films show Kubrick departing from the overly poetic and allegorical styles of *Fear and Desire* and *Killer's Kiss* (which he has condemned as "pretentious" and "amateurish") and developing a total aesthetic capable of assimilating a level of philosophic abstraction into a rhetoric characterized by a realistic exactness of time and space.[1]

Fear and Desire and *Killer's Kiss* lack the narrative coherence and intricacy that distinguish most of Kubrick's work. The scripts are original work (with Kubrick co-authoring *Killer's Kiss*) by Kubrick's friend from high school days Howard O. Sackler, a poet-playwright who later wrote *The Great White Hope* and a clever, surrealist one-act play about American suburban impotence called *The Nine O'Clock Mail.* Both films show a jejune fondness for exploring states of "fear and desire" within loosely conceived and allegorical structures, which, however, provided Kubrick opportunities for technical experimentation and a thematic overreaching not untypical of 1950s underground film. (Joseph Burstyn, who distributed films to American arthouses and who was the first to import the work of Rossellini and other neorealists, handled the release of *Fear and Desire*.) *Fear and Desire* begins with a Conradian-sounding poem in voiceover, continues with an array of subjective devices as we watch four soldiers wander through an imaginary forest, and concludes with a penetration out of a collective heart of darkness into a dawn of new understanding. Lieutenant Corby (Kenneth Harp), the intellectual, discovers the fictitious nature of rationalism as he symbolically "kills" himself by killing his double, a Nazi general officer (also played by Kenneth Harp), while Mac (Frank Silvera), the primitive, fights through his rage and paranoia in a misty raft trip downriver. The themes of the film are out of a grab-bag of 1950s bohemian negativism (the film attacks war and other social institutions, and it shows the failures of reason and the dangers of an unexplored unconscious) and existential self-congratulation. (When James Mason as Humbert in *Lolita* pretends to be going to Hollywood to make a film about existentialism, which, he ironically tells us, was a "hot thing" at the time, Kubrick may be telling us something about his early work.) Visually, *Fear and Desire* shows Kubrick's talent for creating mental landscapes that alternate between grotesquerie and surrealistic beauty: trench knives assault the camera just before a view

In the forest of *Fear and Desire*.

of mangled corpses on which are scattered the leftovers of a meal, a scene that, among others, is briefly recalled in a series of double exposures as the four men flee in a nightmare-like frenzy; in the dreamy appearance of the girl (Virginia Leith) washing in the river; and later in the raft floating in a state of fog-shrouded suspension. And because *Fear and Desire* was a low-budget, independent, and private operation, Kubrick was able to deal firsthand with many of the problems that would later multiply in scope more than number as he advanced toward commercial and artistic success.

In *Killer's Kiss* Kubrick continues to explore internal states of nightmare and doubt, but he does so through a commercially viable, derivative narrative form. The story and style of the film evoke both the darkly romantic atmosphere of *film noir* and the melodramatic realism of such popular street films as *The Naked City* (Jules Dassin, 1950) and *Panic in the Streets* (Elia Kazan, 1950). On the one hand, the first-person account of Davy Gordon (Jamie Smith), boxer on the run,

The *noir* atmosphere of *Killer's Kiss*.

shows Kubrick's continuing interest in a psychological subject matter that traffics in basic emotional states (fear and desire, loneliness and entrapment) and allows for a surrealist visual exposition; while on the other, its street locations and neorealist flair for random detail (objects and faces in subways, and on the streets and in the shop windows of Times Square) create a chaotic public backdrop at odds with private worlds.

Killer's Kiss contains several plot and character ideas that superficially resemble a sentimentalized version of a *noir* film like Billy Wilder's *Double Indemnity* (1944). Davy Gordon's first-person flashback account lacks the bite and irony of the tale of sexual attraction and murder Walter Neff (Fred MacMurray) tells in *Double Indemnity,* and Davy begins his story in the spacious and brightly lit environs of New York City's Penn Station, an early assurance for the audience that he and his girlfriend Gloria (Irene Kane) will answer the call of the train whistle and escape to the West. Yet within these unconvincing fairy tale bookends, no doubt prompted by the hope of commercial reimbursement, the film delineates a world no less menacing than Wilder's. Frank Silvera (as Vincent Rapallo) is again Kubrick's choice to play the bestial man, a kind of modern-day Stromboli who fends off loneliness and feelings of inadequacy by subjugating and torturing others; he controls the shabby dancehall world of Pleasureland, which Kubrick's camera in two horizontal tracks characterizes as a languid movement of shapes and shadows, a tableau of faceless people lost to the somnambulant cadences of a tawdry dream. Such scenes merely express in another way Davy's premonitory nightmare of rapid movement down a vertical corridor of city buildings (done in negative image) and suggest that he and Rapallo are psychological doubles, each the other's secret sharer. The dream merges with the reality, as Davy's nightmare is penetrated by Gloria's screams from across the courtyard as she resists Rapallo's sexual assault. And while Davy awakes to save her from the ogre, Kubrick has implied a deeper psychological nuance than one normally finds in either the more popular *noir* films or the type of sentimental melodrama *Killer's Kiss* pretends to imitate.

Much of the psychological and visual logic of the film anticipates the kind of indirect assault on an audience's expectations found in later and more accomplished films like Welles's *Touch of Evil* (1958) and Hitchcock's *Psycho* (1960).[2] Those films at first set up the conventional scenario of young lovers unwittingly ensnared in an evil more complex and profound than their capacity for understanding, and then each film in its own way forces the audience to qualify its identification with the characters by a series of maliciously contrived reversals. In Welles's film, for instance, Vargas (Charlton Heston) and his innocuously named wife, Suzie (Janet Leigh), become so hopelessly lost in the borderline area between good and evil, light and dark, that an audience can only experience an unhappy confusion in its own inability to separate itself from the manic obsessions of Welles's Hank Quinlan; and in *Psycho* Hitchcock not only teases us into identifying with Marion Crane's fear that her theft of money will be discovered but also teases us, especially the males in the audience, into a voyeuristic longing to gaze with Norman Bates (Anthony Perkins) on the erotically inviting body of Janet Leigh, which Hollywood in *its* prurience had enticingly hid from view for many years. Hitchcock withholds that satisfaction from his audience and instead confronts it with the horror of its own hidden fantasies in the famous knife-rape attack on Marion in the shower. (In *Touch of Evil*, Welles had her symbolically raped.) Both these films, more expertly than *Killer's Kiss*, outwardly work within the popular conventions of an American genre, while covertly they question and even satirize the very values that provide an audience with a familiar bearing and orientation.

The best moments of *Killer's Kiss* combine a voyeuristic and narcissistic definition of character with a surrealist relish for subverting an audience's ready willingness to accept sentimental and commercial film pablum. In an early scene, we watch Davy in his apartment preparing for a fight by examining his face in the mirror (which in its detail recalls *Day of the Fight*), and right after that, we see it distorted through a fish bowl; and, while he continues this activity, we watch from Gloria's perspective across the courtyard where she, too, goes through the rituals of preparing for another bout with the daily drudgery of her existence. While this scene deftly executes some necessary exposition, and shows a command of visual storytelling not present in *Fear and Desire*, it likewise anticipates later episodes with a voyeuristic content. As Davy waits for a boxing match in a nondescript dressing room, we see Gloria in a black brassiere before a mirror getting ready for a night's work on the dance floors of Pleasureland, a setting not unlike the boxing ring as a place where an army of lonely people vicariously achieve a private coitus. Next, Kubrick takes us to Rapallo's curiously decorated office (family pictures, which recall Davy's room, are mingled with circus advertisements) where a television screen illuminates his and Gloria's faces as they watch Davy's fight. Kubrick cuts back and forth from the low angles, zooms, and hand-held action of the ring to Rapallo's increasing sexual excitement as he simultaneously watches the fight and mauls Gloria. This suggestion of parallel and doubling actions carries forward something more than the entanglements of a highly contrived and melodramatic plot; it subtly intimates that in the next sequence, when Davy watches a mirror reflection of Gloria undressing as he talks on the phone to "Uncle George" in Seattle, Kubrick would have us believe that his attraction to the girl in the window is not that different from Rapallo's. Kubrick's wit is especially evident when he shows Davy struggling with the telephone cord in his eagerness to see Gloria directly through the window; his frustration is matched by the audience's, as its attention wavers between Davy on screen right talking on the phone and Gloria undressing in mirror re-

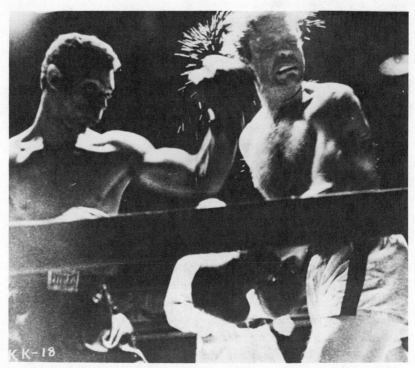

A neorealistic moment from *Killer's Kiss*.

flection on screen left. The apartment light goes off, the mirror image
turns to black, and the camera holds on Davy, standing and waiting
as if he expected that dream in the mirror to magically reappear.

   More forcefully depicted than irony is an atmosphere of poignancy
and unarticulated emotion that the film visually explores in a series of
slow-paced vignettes. In one scene, Davy inspects Gloria's room while
she sleeps and discovers both a world of feminine mystery (stockings,
a music box, a doll) and a mirror image of his own loneliness. The
camera holds back and interferes only slightly with the almost magical
mood of the scene: We see Davy walking between Gloria sleeping in
her bed and the image in her mirror of her sleeping; this is followed by
an intimation of her childlike innocence in close-up, and then a shot
of the doll dangling from above. Such a scene demonstrates Kubrick's
early talent for capturing emotional states through an interaction
of pace and atmosphere, actors and setting. And the emotion is
unmockingly rendered, even though within the film's larger narrative
ambitions this scene continues an undertone of sexual fetishism and

voyeurism. But we must not forget that Professor Rath's fascination with Lola and articles of her clothing in Sternberg's *The Blue Angel*, one of Kubrick's favorite films, contains as much poignancy as it does irony. The atmosphere of Rapallo's office, more sinister than the dreamlike rooms of the two lovers, likewise manages to capture the pathos of someone trapped in the tensions of a divided self; one brief scene shows him expressing self-loathing and disgust as he tosses a drink at his mirror image. This ability to communicate a latent emotional depth through mise-en-scène and performance will be a distinguishing trademark of Kubrick's best work, one especially important to an appreciation of his *Lolita*.

Killer's Kiss also reveals early signs of Kubrick's skill at developing narrative lines of conflict that at once intensify and work in opposition to the concerns of character. The early paralleling between Davy and Gloria, for instance, not only binds them together psychologically but initiates a pattern of narrative crisscrossing through which Kubrick, for the first time, expresses a fondness for the disparities of contingency. The two lovers begin in separate but conjunctive worlds: A high-angle shot records their paths crossing in the courtyard as they leave their apartments, Gloria to Rapallo in his car, Davy walking alone down the street. In one of the film's more inventive scenes, the camera watches, again from above, this time down a flight of stairs going from the dancehall to the street, as Kubrick weaves a pattern of fate and mistaken identity that will result in the murder of Davy's manager, Albert (Jerry Jarret). Below we see Albert left and Gloria right, each ignorant of the other's identity and both framed in the windows of a swinging double door. The camera remains stationary and ironic as one of Rapallo's hoods goes down and entices Gloria back upstairs while taking her place in the frame opposite Albert, whom he mistakes for Davy. This stairway shot precedes the backlit, shadowy murder of Albert in an alley and finds an ironic punctuation in a written warning overhead that reads WATCH YOUR STEP. Kubrick says that the sign was a fortuity of location shooting and, interestingly, is an example of the intriguing lure of coincidence which finds its most imaginative literary expression in the novels of Vladimir Nabokov. Kubrick, however, does not wait until his *Lolita* to explore and develop such possibilities, as the temporal and spatial aesthetics of both *The Killing* and *Paths of Glory* will testify.

The film's most memorable episode, a fight to the death between

Davy and Rapallo in a storeroom full of mannequins, illustrates Kubrick's habit of mixing realist and surrealist imagery. This scene is preceded by an extended chase across rooftops with an early morning New York City skyline as background, reminiscent of *The Naked City* and countless other urban crime films. Then suddenly the action drops into a nightmare environment of dismembered and chaotically arranged torsos, heads, and limbs. Rapallo follows his quarry into the room and immediately feels threatened ("I gotta get out of here," he mutters), as if he had unexpectedly stumbled into a private nightmare where the puppets turn on the puppetmaster, while Davy, on the other hand, blends in with and uses the mannequins for cover. In a tracking movement that recalls the film's visual definition of the dancers of Pleasureland (the same warehouse was used for both sets), the camera forces us to consider Davy's alignment with a world without dimension or substance, one where dreams of happiness with the doll-like Gloria may resemble little more than the pleasant but empty stasis of shop-window dummies. We see Davy's head poking up in the frame as if unscrewed from its body, while arms and hands dangle overhead. He and Rapallo then engage in a struggle of primal intensity, with one wielding a pike and the other an ax. Mannequin heads are severed, torsos punctured, until finally Rapallo falls into a scrapheap of body parts and lets out an animal squeal as Davy drives the pike through his body. This sequence contrasts with the more traditional, photo-journalistic handling of the boxing match seen earlier (which recalls Robert Wise's *The Set-Up*, 1949, and Kubrick's short, *Day of the Fight*) and defines a sensibility that continues to thrive on the creation of unsettling visual juxtapositions. Are we to interpret the mannequin scene as Davy's struggle with and liberation from destructive forces within, or as an example of Kubrick's irony and wit? As Rapallo's death cry merges with a return to the present and the sound of a train whistle, a hackneyed device as old as Hitchcock's *The 39 Steps* (1935), we are left to choose between the flat surfaces of a happy ending and a faint but unrealized satiric distance. It could be that *Killer's Kiss* intimates that in their own unique way Kubrick's intentions always have been closer to the surrealism of Buñuel than to either the baroque excesses of Welles or the sentimental realism of Kazan.

Lest my analysis leave the impression that I consider *Killer's Kiss* an undiscovered classic, let me say that it is not a very good film and, all in all, contains more weaknesses than strengths. At the time, Kubrick admitted to the difficulties of writing dialogue, and this film illustrates his point when verbal exposition is required; consequently, for *The Killing*, his first novelistic adaptation, Kubrick employed the services of action writer Jim Thompson for additional dialogue.[3] The use of fifties "jive" music, punctuated by loud blasts from a saxophone, has a low-budget desperation about it and severely dates the film; the acting, except for that of Frank Silvera, is pedestrian (further hampered by post-synchronization), even though Kubrick's camera and eye for visual detail make it tolerable; the ballet sequence performed by Kubrick's second wife, Ruth Sobotka, is gratuitous and offers neither a satisfactory motivation for the character of Gloria nor a visual coherence for the film. If *Killer's Kiss* were Kubrick's highest achievement, it would not merit much more than a cursory inspection, let alone carry the interpretive weight placed on it by this discussion. But because it is the early work of a film maker with Kubrick's credentials, such consideration seems not only justified but illuminating. Kubrick, we shall see, very quickly overcame most of the shortcomings present in *Killer's Kiss*: A year later he released *The Killing*, made on a budget of $320,000 (still below average for a "low-budget" studio film in 1956), which allowed him to hire a cast of superb Hollywood character actors and for the first time to enjoy some of the benefits of financial certainty; but more important, he resolved the confusions of cinematic point of view that were responsible for much of the tonal inconsistency in the earlier film.

By choosing to adapt Lionel White's *Clean Break* (1955) for his next film, Kubrick seems, at first glance, to have opted for a commercial future rather than following the more abstract "art film" direction of *Fear and Desire* and the surrealist elements of *Killer's Kiss*. Superficially at least, White's novel and the outward form of Kubrick's *The Killing* display the fictional incorporation of pseudodocumentary techniques that had been popularized by producer Louis de Rochemont of *March of Time* fame in films like *The House on 92nd Street* (1945), *13 Rue Madeleine* (1946), and *Boomerang* (1947). These films conferred on the public world of process (i.e., FBI investigative procedures, military commando training) and fact such an aura of epistemological urgency that the basic concerns of individuals were made to appear both trivial and irresponsible. White's novel is as clean and lean as its title—precise, economic, transparent—and contains only a few embellishments of style and tone. The characters are clearly defined and, once set in motion, stay on a psychological course as relentless in its logic as Johnny Clay's robbery plan. *Clean Break* is a neat storytelling package, but more important for this study is the part it plays in Kubrick's development as a writer, as well as director, of film adaptations.

Beginning with *The Killing*, Kubrick's progress as a film maker moves straight and upward, sidetracked only briefly by the *Spartacus* assignment, and it can be measured in part by his success with adaptation. Unlike Bergman and Fellini, Kubrick is not, strictly speaking, an autobiographical or "personal" artist. With few exceptions—one is the use of his Greenwich Village chess-playing friend Kola Kwariani (as Maurice) in *The Killing*—Kubrick's films do not draw directly on persons and events from biographical experience. They embody a turn of mind that is more speculative than romantic, where an interest in how human beings give form to those emotions and desires that throb for release inside all of us commands far more attention than what such experiences actually feel like. In *Fear and Desire* and *Killer's Kiss*, Kubrick tried to capture the look and feel of psychic worlds, but at the expense of narrative and tonal coherence. The right novel, therefore, provides Kubrick with a framework of action and character, a kind of ready-made objective correlative, within which he can integrate his own formal and psychological ideas; and more often than not, this process creates a tension between exterior and interior space, the demands of novelistic and cinematic form. We shall see that the choice of *Clean Break* and Humphrey Cobb's *Paths of Glory* (1935) reveals not just that Kubrick in the late 1950s went "commercial," but the adaptation of these two novels accelerated a process of discovery in which a complex personal vision found its own expression through the development of an equally personal and distinctive film aesthetic.

Kubrick screws the novel's story even tighter than White had, producing a vise of parallel and doubling actions that lend the concept of plot philosophic and reflexive meanings. *The Killing*, unlike the novel, begins and ends on a Saturday. It introduces each character as a piece in a temporal jigsaw puzzle and concludes one week later by showing how these separate human elements come together in time and space to execute Johnny Clay's "foolproof" robbery plan.* Beginning with

---

* Johnny Clay is played by Sterling Hayden, whose most notable film before this was, of course, *The Asphalt Jungle* (John Huston, 1950), which superficially resembles *The Killing* as another "caper" *noir* film; Hayden's performances in both

the credits, the film builds on an involuted structure of simultaneity and repetition. There, we see documentarylike footage of the Bay Meadows Racetrack and preparations for what will turn out to be the Landsdowne Stakes; later, these shots are repeated three times as they are synchronized to the start of the robbery itself. Thus images that at first lack a specific temporal meaning—but instead are generalized stock shots of a racetrack—are given significance by virtue of an alignment within the context of both Johnny's plan and Kubrick's film. Similarly, each of the film's principal characters, neatly divided between the inside participants and the outside intruders, attempts through the logic of the robbery scheme to give purpose to an otherwise fragmented and desperate existence. We realize, for instance, that at least two of the five insiders must suppress disorderly psychological factors if the plan is to succeed. The fatherly and homosexual attachment Marv Unger (Jay C. Flippen) feels for Johnny remains latent even though exacerbated by the presence of Clay's girlfriend Fay (Coleen Gray); and George Peatty (Elisha Cook, Jr.) controls his sexual jealousy until after the robbery. In each case, Kubrick extends the novel's implication that the predictable nature of Johnny's plan runs contrary to indeterminable human forces.

Important outside complications described in the novel remain almost intact in the film: Randy Kennen (Ted de Corsia) has troubles with a loan shark, Mike O'Reilly (Joe Sawyer) worries about his invalid wife, Clay has a history of being a small-timer and loser, and George is enslaved by his wife, Sherry (Marie Windsor). Kubrick, like White, shows how the parallel plot of Sherry and boyfriend Val Cannon (Vince Edwards) represents the one element that endangers both the robbery and getaway; as the members of Johnny's gang come together to finalize the plan, Sherry and Val initiate what will be a counterplot dependent upon the success of the other. Converging very early in the film, therefore, is the reflexive interaction of schemes within schemes, plots within plots. Kubrick gives the race itself an importance not found in the novel, an activity that focuses visually, aurally, and conceptually the film's complex structure: The Landsdowne Stakes envel-

are very close. And Elisha Cook became a famous American character actor after his role as Wilmer the gunsel in *The Maltese Falcon* (John Huston, 1941), although his portrayal of Harry Jones in *The Big Sleep* (Howard Hawks, 1946), as the "little man" victimized by a typical *noir* bitch, is a better comparative source for the characterization of George Peatty.

ops the workings of chance in a closed system—one measured in time, organized in space, and presided over by an offscreen deity (Saturday afternoon at 4:25, a mile and a quarter, on a circular track, and responsive to the track announcer's control)—and as a result it can be exploited or disrupted by an alien force not part of its logic. All of which means, of course, that Johnny's plan is equally vulnerable to the unknown activities of Sherry and Val; and analogically, that all three are servants to the temporal/spatial schematics of Kubrick's film, reminding the audience of an artistic design that guarantees its own success at the expense of the others' failure.

Kubrick departs from White's narrative when he magnifies in importance the role of coincidence and chance. Regrettably, he invents a scene where Nikki (Timothy Carey), the sniper, is victimized by a "good-luck" horseshoe that punctures his automobile tire and leads to his death. In the novel, by contrast, Nikki escapes cleanly without the interference of poetic justice, indicating perhaps that Kubrick's solution was practical (a gesture to the Production Code) as well as an example of the film's movement toward a total closure. More significantly, the film changes White's ending, which has George Peatty, bloody from wounds, staggering into the airport terminal and pumping several bullets into Johnny Clay at the moment when escape appears imminent. The final passage of the novel explains the irony of its title— an unnamed policeman pulls a bloodsoaked newspaper from under Johnny's body and reads a headline that says: RACE TRACK BANDIT MAKES CLEAN BREAK WITH TWO MILLION. Psychology destroys Johnny's plan in the novel, not, as is true in the film, the fateful turns of a contingent universe. Once he is thrown off his timetable, Kubrick's protagonist must accept with resignation the fortuities and reversals of chance. At first it appears that luck may save him in the absence of a plan: he arrives at the assigned meeting place fifteen minutes late and thereby avoids the film's second and more grisly "killing," namely the shootout between his gang and Val's. But in the end he must flee into the shadows of an accidental world, where a faulty lock on a suitcase and a stranger's poodle determine his fate. Johnny watches from behind a wire fence as the money, like the gold dust in Huston's *The Treasure of the Sierra Madre* (1948), blows away from the grasp of human aspiration. Kubrick has the film end with Johnny turning to face his captors, a man now stripped of plan and purpose, and admitting to a defeat ("What's the use?") that the film suggests is far more

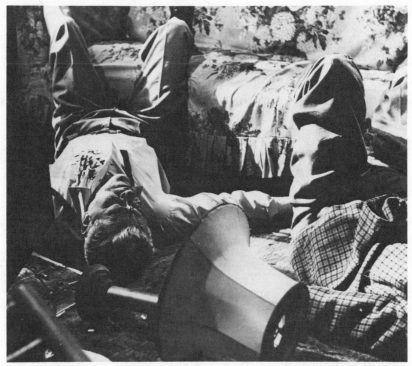

A Kubrickian image of disorder, the second "killing" in *The Killing*.

profound than merely the result of a jealous husband's intervention.

While Kubrick's treatment of the story and characters displays a thematic clarity absent in his first two feature films, his overall manipulation of narrative and cinematic point of view shows early signs of a mastery present in later works like *A Clockwork Orange* and *Barry Lyndon*. The narrator of *The Killing*, who sounds like the voice from the *Highway Patrol* television series which played during this time (1955–59), allows Kubrick to cut directly through tiresome exposition and convey essential information; while, at the same time, it strikes what Alexander Walker correctly perceives as an "aural note . . . to which he tunes the rest of the film." The "tune" it plays, in fact, recalls the kind of newsreel authenticity Welles so effectively parodied in the "News on the March" sequence (de Rochemont began *The March of Time* in 1935) of *Citizen Kane* (1941), but in *The Killing* this authenticity becomes a near-symphony of reflexive irony. Kubrick's narrator has an omniscience limited to the external and temporal movements of character and event. His voice is flat and neutral, although he hints at unfolding "puzzles" and "designs," which remain ambiguous for purposes of plot suspense. His dispassionate objectivity functions as an aural timepiece forever ticking off bits of data that have value only within the mechanical order of Johnny Clay's plan. More successfully than the film's characters, the narrator suppresses the contours of an individualized identity so that he may execute efficiently the temporal plan of the film. His voice is all surface and no depth, time-bound and blind to spatial nuances, at once a device for narrative coherence and a foil to Kubrick's irony. His role in the central action of the film parallels that of the announcer at the racetrack, another disembodied voice we hear in repeated cadences, who also puts his faith in the logic of a mathematically conceived form. As we watch Johnny in a dehumanized mask (one of the few surrealistic touches in *The Killing*) realize the success of his intricately timed and spaced design, we hear the racetrack announcer's confusion over the shooting of the horse and his conviction that "exact information" will be forthcoming. Just as Johnny's plan undermines the authority of the race, so does the narrator of the film command an omniscience far more Olympian than that of the track announcer; but, just as Johnny's cool and mechanical control turns to frenzy and then despair once it is exposed to a world outside the gameboard of his plan, the narrator plays second fiddle to the subtler themes of Kubrick's visual narration.

How Kubrick moves to defeat the authority of his "objective," or overt, film rhetoric is a first exercise in a temporal/spatial aesthetics whose subsequent development will produce a number of intricate and brilliant films. The film combines a series of horizontal tracking shots with repeated vertical compositions to create a spatial grid that suggests both a chessboard and a cage. As the narration impresses us with its temporal dexterity, the film's visual exposition shows that in the beginning the characters are more synchronized in space than time: The camera moves from *left to right* with Marv across the racetrack betting area to Mike O'Reilly's bar, with Randy in the cocktail lounge for a meeting with a loan shark, with Johnny Clay as he walks through the rooms of Marv's apartment to Fay sitting on the bed, with Mike as he goes to the sickbed of his invalid wife, with George Peatty as he walks through his apartment to his wife lounging on their bed. From the above account, it's not difficult to understand why the original working title for the film was *Bed of Fear*. Kubrick, as in *Killer's Kiss*, continues to use the repetitions of camera and mise-en-scène to deepen the emotive and conceptual content of his film. The bed motif slyly circumvents the Legion of Decency and, ironically, develops a far more pervasive sexual implication than is found in the novel. The movements of the camera, with far more subtlety than the narration, outline a world that allows the audience to see the bars of a black and white prison long before the characters admit defeat. As the narrator defines the various human pieces which make up Johnny's plan, and then as that plan is executed, the horizontal camera movements stay on a steady *left-to-right* course; the film's characters enjoy, with the audience, a greater sense of spatial than temporal continuity. Once the robbery is over, the camera movements indicate that escape out of the closed structure of the plan and its inevitable consequences will take a *right to left* course. Naturally, Johnny's escape from the track moves in that direction, imitating as it does a concept of film continuity as venerable as Muybridge's experiments with animal locomotion. Interestingly, when Johnny arrives at the airport and moves through the terminal, the camera continues to track with him from *right to left*; but when he flees from the one thing which might lift him out of his spatial trap, namely the airplane, he and the camera once again traverse a horizontal course from *left to right*. But this time Johnny retreats into a maze rather than a controlled plan, where far too many factors, interior as well as exterior, interact for a man with his limitations of vision to succeed. Johnny Clay, Kubrick tells us, is not quite a master criminal and not nearly an artist, even though in a conversation with Maurice at the Chess Academy Johnny contends that the best criminal is a kind of artist. In the end, both his success with the plan and his failure with contingency become Kubrick's sympathetic portrayal of an unsentimental and unheroic human tragedy.

At key junctures, Kubrick employs a vertical camera movement that helps to complete the chessboard/cage metaphor. In three places, the camera moves back in an identical manner as it records Johnny's movement outside a line of motel cabins. (Undoubtedly, these three scenes were combined in the film's shooting schedule.) In the first two scenes, Johnny moves with his usual steady resolution to the correct cabin, while in his haste to pick up the money on the third occasion he becomes spatially disoriented (he is fifteen minutes behind schedule) and almost goes into the wrong cabin. The vertical camera movement, however, remains the same—it continues to draw the lines of a cage—

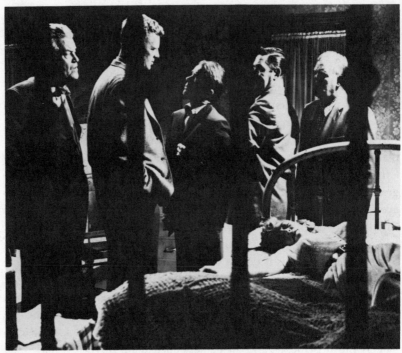

The conspirators of *The Killing* and the outline of
fate (Jay C. Flippen, Sterling Hayden, Elisha Cook,
Ted de Corsia, Marie Windsor, Joe Sawyer).

as the temporal scheme of Johnny's plan starts to unravel. The only
subjective shot in the film moves vertically with George Peatty across
a grotesquely disordered room of carnage as his fate comes to resemble
the bars of his bettor's cage and the cage of a parrot that will mock
him in death. And in three strategic places, Kubrick creates a composition of three human figures lined up and facing the camera: the card-
board G-men targets pointing guns on Nikki's firing range; the three
gang members (Marv, Mike, and Randy) looking expectantly toward
the door through which Val and another man will come and turn the
apartment into a shooting gallery with live targets; and finally, the
three figures (two plainclothesmen and, to complete the symmetry, an
airline employee) who move toward Johnny in the final shot of the film.

From the visual design of *The Killing*, in the way it totally encloses
the world of the film, we can infer that Kubrick decided to experiment
with a temporal definition of space. Besides the moving camera shots
and vertical compositions, he also uses source lighting to accent a claus-

trophobic darkness and an array of objects to suggest psycho/sexual entrapment. Kubrick, however, transcends the novel's emphasis on the contrary workings of design and disruption by creating a cinematic equivalent for his avowed fondness for games of deception and enigmatic works of literature; he extends the novel's *donnée* to include not only the opposition of intellect and passion, design and disorder, but of art and life as well. And yet, the style of *The Killing* remains deceptively clean and bare, one in which the geometric lines of movement and space are far more evocative than images of density and mass. The tight narrative focus of the novel, with its subordination of psychological depth to complex intersections of plot, offered Kubrick an opportunity to work out a firmer command of film time. And because *Clean Break* clearly defines its interior world, Kubrick, with the help of a competent cast, was able to move away from the internal probings of *Fear and Desire* and *Killer's Kiss* and develop objective correlatives for a psychological and emotional content. Adaptation, for the first time, provided him with an explicit verbal rhetoric from which he could create a more implicit cinematic one. In the final analysis, *The Killing* may be nothing more than just that: a cleverly executed exercise, Kubrick's "plan," both entertaining, in its action and pace, and revealing in the secrets it tells about a film maker whose conjurations far too often elude our grasp.

Humphrey Cobb's *Paths of Glory* would seem to be an ideal source for the film maker of *Fear and Desire, Killer's Kiss,* and *The Killing.* Its style and narration develop an ironic contrast between public and private worlds, the fictions of officialese and the fluctuations of an indeterminate truth; the novel is gorged with passages of hallucinatory intensity depicting the actual and imagined horrors of war and others showing an empty and formal masking of that truth by characters who are ambitious. Throughout, Cobb's third-person narration remains all-knowing, ironic, and moralistic; in one scene with an obvious appeal to Kubrick's demonstrated interests, the narrator tells us that General Assolant (Mireau, in the film), who is obsessed with viewing war as merely a "question of percentages," does not take into account that "a battle is a thing of flux, and that you cannot measure flux by the debris that it leaves behind." Elsewhere, Cobb has a scene between Assolant and Colonel Dax that contains very cinematic and Kubrickian overtones. Dax feels that the general's problem is one of "seeing," that he is "always looking through lenses, lenses which are made of the insignia of rank"; consequently, Dax tricks Assolant into confronting the human reality of war through a periscope in the trench:

> The telescopic lenses seemed to spring the mass of bodies right into his face. The bodies were so tangled that most of them could not be distinguished one from the other. Hideous, distorted, and putrescent, they lay tumbled upon each other or hung in the wire in obscene attitudes, a shocking mound of human flesh, swollen and discoloured.

Cobb concludes his strong indictment of the politics of war with a "note" at the end of the novel that forces the reader to extend its lessons to life itself and to see the historical truth behind the fictional lie.*

It is interesting that Kubrick's *Paths of Glory* duplicates neither the nightmare landscapes of the novel nor those found in his earlier films. The film contains only two sequences where subjective tracking shots are used, and neither travels over a field of carnage; in places where the novel calls for an expressionistic film treatment, Kubrick's style remains objective and realistic, and when he extends scenes for which there is little descriptive authority in the novel, such as the attack on the Ant Hill, the court-martial, and the execution, his camera and mise-en-scène become truly impressive. And although he follows the novel's three-part division (before the attack; the attack and after; the court-martial and execution), Kubrick does not choose to work out its ironic patterns of fate. Cobb, for instance, begins and ends by focusing on two soldiers named Langlois and Duval, the first a veteran and survivor who is convinced that "no German shell or bullet has my number on it" and the other a recruit who dreams of glory and especially admires Langlois's medals, even though they were won in a lottery. At

---

* Cobb's NOTE (p. 265) to *Paths* reads as follows:

All the characters, units, and places mentioned in this book are fictitious.

However, if the reader ask, "Did such things really happen?" the author answers, "Yes," and refers him to the following sources which suggested the story: *Les crimes des conseils de guerre*, by R.G. Réau; *Les fusilles pour l'exemple*, by J. Galtier-Boissiere and Daniel de Ferdon: *Les dessous de la guerre révélés par les comites secrets* and *Images secretes de la guerre*, by Paul Allard; a special dispatch to the *The New York Times* of July 2, 1934, which appeared under this headline: "FRENCH ACQUIT 5 SHOT FOR MUTINY IN 1915; WIDOWS OF TWO WIN AWARD OF 7 CENTS EACH"; and *Le fusillé*, by Blanche Maupas, one of the widows who obtained exoneration of her husband's memory and who was awarded damages of one franc.

the end of the novel, Langlois (Corporal Paris, in the film), as the result of another lottery, is tied to a stake, with his medals on the ground at his feet, and Duval (who is not in the film) is a member of the firing squad that executes him. The novel abounds in such devices, most of which are anticipated far ahead of time, and which reveal a temporal and psychological straitjacket no less confining than the one in *The Killing*. Kubrick's film likewise downplays the conventional appeal of the novel's manipulation of time—which is very cinematic in its parallel "editing" and the "high noon" suspense countdown that precedes the attack and execution—and instead chooses to develop spatial complexities through a more deliberate handling of scene exposition. If *The Killing* represents Kubrick's first real success with a temporal film rhetoric, what Pudovkin might have called the "filmic representation" through action (story) and images of a theme (time), then *Paths of Glory* could be considered his early masterpiece of spatial film communication, one that extends the philosophic implications of the novel far beyond the logic of its liberal/moral preachments. Kubrick, in other words, uses the temporal and psychological framework of Cobb's novel to develop more fully and more satisfactorily than before an aesthetics of contingency, one which by its very nature requires that the exigencies of any given moment in filmic time (whether psychic or "real") be measured against the larger spatial and ambiguous dimensions of a disparate cinematic universe.*

In *Paths of Glory* Kubrick combines, for the first time, a "sound" thematics—language, noise, music—with a visual complexity that illustrates his belief that film must achieve the ambiguity and "subconscious designating effect of a work of art" through images and music rather than words. It is evidence of Kubrick's early maturity as a film artist

---

* *Paths* poses difficulties in assigning credit for its verbal ideas. Undoubtedly, both Calder Willingham and Jim Thompson helped Kubrick with the ironic and literate nuances of the dialogue, although *Barry Lyndon*, scripted by Kubrick with help only from William Makepeace Thackeray, plays with language in much the same way. And the use of narration stands as one of Kubrick's most distinctive film signatures. Kubrick freely admits that the collaborative experience of putting a film script together is essential to its success, as the significant contributions of Vladimir Nabokov to *Lolita*, Terry Southern and Peter George to *Dr. Strangelove*, Arthur C. Clarke to *2001*, and Diane Johnson to *The Shining* will testify. However, Kubrick's career illustrates his stated belief that the writer-director who masters both crafts produces consistently the finest work.

The first pathway in *Paths of Glory*: The arrival of
General Broulard (Adolphe Menjou) outside the
chateau.

that he uses an offscreen narrator only at the beginning and yet maintains a documentarylike realism of style that develops a complexity of
ideas. Following the credits and the playing of the French national
anthem, and a title that identifies place and time ("France 1916"), the
narrator—his tone anticipates the computer voices of *Dr. Strangelove's*
narration and HAL of *2001*—briefly summarizes the beginning years
of World War I as first a series of attacks and counterattacks and then
a stalemate of "zigzagging" trenches and unchanging "battlelines." At
the same time, the camera from a distance shows the arrival of General
Broulard (Adolphe Menjou) outside a grand eighteenth-century chateau, which looks out onto a spacious but formal garden of walkways
more appropriate for a ceremonial promenade than a casual stroll. Two
lines of soldiers form a pathway for Broulard's entrance into a setting
of splendor, which, ironically, houses the headquarters of the French
regiment commanded by General Mireau (George Macready). In this
first shot, the narrator's unemotional voice undercuts the patriotic im-

plications of the *Marseillaise*, while visually the lines and paths anticipate later developments that will show a far more elaborate drama of
zigzagging political forces, of psychological attack and counterattack,
than the ones mentioned in the narration: the execution scene near the
end of the film, for instance, will traverse this very setting and bring together the contrary but complementary worlds of the chateau and the
trench; and the film will conclude on an ironic note as a frightened girl
(Susanne Christian, since married to Kubrick) in the bistro sings a sentimental *German* song.

The first half of *Paths* (the end of this half can be marked by the
film's initial fade-out, after the failed attack on the Ant Hill) further
develops this ironic structure of oppositions and parallels between the
chateau and the trenches, through which Kubrick will turn a system of
clearly defined conflicts into a maze of paradoxical associations. A comparison of the aural and visual treatments of the first two sequences
effectively illustrates this point. As the first scene begins, Broulard
walks between the lines of soldiers and along the pathway into the
chateau for a meeting with Mireau in the spacious and ornate room
commandeered for his office and apartment; he compliments Mireau
on the "pleasant atmosphere" of the room and on his taste in "carpets
and pictures." Mireau, obviously pleased, confesses that the room is the
"same as when I moved in" and that "I didn't have to do much." Broulard, with no visible indication that he appreciates the art of the setting
or the humor of this exchange, then goes to the "top-secret" reason for
his visit (it is not, after all, a social call, but Kubrick confuses the distinction between social formality and political manipulation). Mireau
interrupts, "reading" Broulard's mind and abbreviating these formalities with his reference to the Ant Hill; after some smiling cajolements
from Broulard, and an implied promise of promotion, Mireau slams a
fist into his hand and exclaims: "We might just do it!" Kubrick cuts
on this sound of fist and voice, first, to a bleak panorama of no-man's-
land through a horizontal viewer and then to Mireau, who like Broulard on his way to the chateau, walks down a pathway lined with
soldiers, but Mireau is in a trench where the lines are not as formal or
exact, and instead of the *Marseillaise* or the voice of the omniscient
narrator, we hear shells exploding and see dirt and debris falling from
above. Once again the film is showing us a general officer visiting a
subordinate, and at the same time implying a vertical line (i.e., chain
of command) both ascending (to Broulard and the gods above) and

descending (to Dax and the "insect" men below) outside the frame of
any given scene. Mireau must stoop slightly to enter Colonel Dax's
cramped bunker, but he does not neglect the verbal formalities of the
chateau: He compliments Dax on the "neatness" of his quarters. The
colonel (Kirk Douglas), unprepared for this visit, is naked from the
waist up and washing from a decorative porcelain bowl (a memento
from the chateau, expressive of his desire to stay clean in a dirty world).
He conforms outwardly to the rules of protocol by putting on his tunic
and addressing his superior officer as "sir," even though his bluntness
of language ridicules these formalities. He plays on Mireau's empty
rhetoric, turning "mice" into "mausers" and "pregnable" into a paradox
of birth and death; when Major Saint-Auban (Richard Anderson)
characterizes the fear felt by the huddled men as a herd instinct, an
"animal sort of thing," Dax objects, defining it instead as a "human
sort of thing." He completely asserts his verbal, as well as moral, superiority when he deflates Mireau's pomposity by citing Samuel Johnson's
dictum that "patriotism is the last refuge of a scoundrel." Yet, despite
Dax's fervor and his humane education, his final comment, "We'll take
the Ant Hill," echoes, ironically, Mireau's resolution at the conclusion
of the first sequence.

The film's deployment of camera and mise-en-scène, by contrast,
provides a larger and more philosophic perspective from which to view
and evaluate the psychological and verbal sparrings of these early sequences. When Broulard commits a *faux pas*, referring to the paintings
in Mireau's apartment as "pictures," Kubrick is revealing not just Broulard's artistic illiteracy but his historical and moral illiteracy as well.
(When Broulard returns to the chateau after the failed attack, Kubrick
shows him traveling on a course parallel to that of a huge painting being carried in the background, but in the opposite direction.) Kubrick's
use of the chateau as both primary setting and visual metaphor has
little or no precedent in Cobb's novel.[4] There, the chateau does not
become a factor until the court-martial and has little descriptive status,
except when the narrator alludes to its history by informing the reader
that Napoleon once slept there. In Kubrick's film, it visually represents
an architectural and philosophic embodiment of one period in human
civilization and a timeless passion for aesthetic expression, and at the
same time, it provides a commentary on the efforts of the characters to
duplicate in their activities its formal properties while ignoring the implications of its beauty and vertical reach. Throughout the film, char-

acters are shown walking down paths that lead either to a maze of personal ambition and delusion or to the endgame of death. In sequence one, as the generals circle an ornate round settee in the middle of the room, the camera moves with them to record the circular logic of both Mireau's thinking and Broulard's persuasion. We notice that Mireau, in his excitement over the prospect of personal glory, momentarily forgets formalities and pours himself a cognac without first offering one to his guest; and when he finally contrives a reason to believe in the likelihood of the attack's success, the camera stops its weaving motions and watches as the two men move into the background across a chessboard parquetry. While the vertical spaciousness of the chateau—as well as an implied scope of history and art—belies the horizontal and circular courses of its temporary inhabitants, the visual definition of the trenches leaves no doubt that their paths take a deadly straight and narrow course. Not only is no-man's-land visualized horizontally in that shot following sequence one, but literally it is part of a topography decorated by a series of horizontal trenches that look more like a surrealist graveyard than paths to glory. Above the trench line, instead of a suggestion of spatial expanses, Kubrick overexposes his film and clouds the air so much that the sky, which rains down shells of death, is also visually oppressing, like a ceiling or a coffin lid. Kubrick's first dolly/tracking shot—moving backward as it shows Mireau's progress through the trenches and past the three men who will later be scapegoats for his failure and vanity—captures a world dynamically in touch with the extremes of life and death but committed, along with the planners in the chateau, to a destructive and predetermined path.

Kubrick continues this ironic blending of explicit and implicit oppositions—of settings and action, words and images, a close-up versus distanced perspective—during the attack on the Ant Hill. Instead of prolonging the countdown to battle and extracting its full emotional and suspense value, as Cobb did, he cuts it short and stretches out the attack itself, perhaps to provide his "war" film with at least one traditional action sequence.[5] Typically, however, Kubrick does not give the audience an uncomplicated moment of human conflict without the intrusion of forces far more sinister than those German soldiers who, if not seen, at least are heard from in the deafening roar of battle. For one thing, the film never explains until after the fact the purpose of the attack or the value, strategically, of the Ant Hill (no such ambiguity exists in the novel). Later, in the last scene between Dax and Broulard, we learn that the attack was necessitated by political, not military, pressures. Only at the end, therefore, does the audience, along with Dax, fully appreciate the extent of Broulard's powers; that, in effect, he was a political and very corporeal *deus ex machina* who watched Mireau watching Dax watching after his men, only Broulard mistakenly assumed Dax's motives were as callous as his own. Kubrick indirectly prepares the audience for this possibility when he contrasts Mireau's activities during the attack with Dax's actual movement into battle. For the second time a binocular view of the Ant Hill is shown from Mireau's always distant perspective, in this instance as he absurdly anticipates a victory celebration with smiles, glasses of cognac, and formal toasts to "France." Kubrick then cuts to the film's first subjective shot, a bold movement with Dax through a trench lined with soldiers on both sides and the sounds of bombardment overhead; the shot ends by moving into a ghostly cloud of smoke and dust. For the attack, Kubrick employed six cameras; one he handheld to bring Dax and the battle into vivid, zoom-close-up. The cameras primarily move on a horizontal path with the attack and capture a remarkable three minutes of film. No doubt, it is as realistic and exciting a battle as any ever put on film: but its real power comes from the sheer magnitude of the disorder and death, the cacophony and volume of the noise, and that Kubrickian overview which lifts it from the immediate fictional context into a larger conceptual one. Kubrick now shows us nightmares taking place in broad daylight and in "real" moments of film time; and the faint but insistent sound of Dax's whistle exhorting his men, at the moment when Mireau fulminates against an artillery commander who "humbly" refuses to open fire on his own men, stands as a poignant mockery of both the destruction falling from a godless sky and the verbal and moral corruption descending from the echo chambers of the chateau.

Yet nothing in part one of *Paths of Glory*, not even this stunning attack sequence, necessarily prepares us for the aesthetic and conceptual brilliance of the last half of the film. The twists and turns of a psychological/political labyrinth bend in even more sinister directions as the action moves entirely into the chateau. The film's visual and philosophical emphasis on horizontal and vertical forms, paths and lines, becomes even more pronounced and intricate as the two worlds of the film begin to express the paradoxical outline of a single world.

Colonel Dax (Kirk Douglas) moving into the smoky nightmare of war and an overhead view of the reality of its disorder.

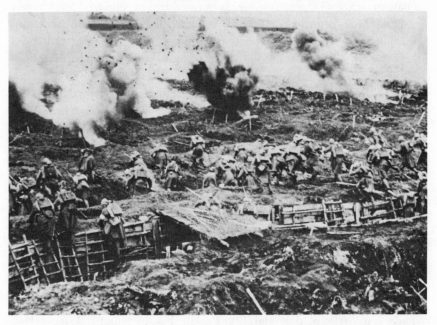

The early scenes of part two, for instance, show that the trench world has come to the chateau and, ironically, that it is not as out of place there as were the formalities of the chateau in the trenches. Dax now visits Mireau in his "quarters," with Broulard present, and brings his moral rectitude and candid tongue into the parlors of euphemism. They sit at the very table where earlier Broulard began to lead Mireau down that path to the ill-fated attack on the Ant Hill. Only now there are three men, and in the framing of the scene Kubrick implies an emerging alliance between Dax and Broulard: A series of two-shots showing Dax left and Broulard right, with a large classical painting between and over them in the background, oppose Mireau's isolation in one-shot. Here Kubrick is suggesting that there are not only deceptive political maneuvers at play but complex cinematic ones as well. Broulard, assuming that Dax's concern for the men is cynical, supports the colonel's request that he be appointed defense counsel, and thereby prepares the way for Mireau's downfall—Mireau will become the scapegoat for the general staff. And while Kubrick is framing this relationship—ironically, one that Dax, like Broulard, misinterprets—he implies another between them and the "higher" work of art in the background. Not unexpectedly, neither the politics of the trench nor those of the chateau acknowledge its value as an emblem of civilized expression and aesthetic beauty. For both, it remains, like the chateau itself, an uncomprehended and unappreciated decoration. For the audience, however, it will be a source for both comprehending and appreciating Kubrick's cinematic art.

The three prisoners and the animal stalls that serve as their cell make the presence of the trench felt. Even now, with their humanity so palpable, the soldiers of the trench are viewed by the officers in the chateau as a lower form of life occupying the bottom rung of an imaginary Chain of Being. (Although, ironically, their last meal is delivered on an ornate silver tray.) Politically, as the scene involving the killing of the cockroach implies, they have no more status than the ants that crawl over the ground. Here and elsewhere Kubrick shows their common humanity, their courage and their fears, while, as he did in *Killer's Kiss* and *The Killing*, intensifying a sense of tragic pathos through their ensnarement in a fate at once political and metaphysical: Lieutenant Roget (Wayne Morris) has a cowardly inability to deal with the stresses of war and its magnification of human mortality, and Corporal Paris is a victim of that inability; Private Ferol (Timothy Carey) is a misfit, someone who does not conform to socially acceptable conduct; and Private Arnaud (Joseph Turkel) has been selected by lottery, which epitomizes the trench concept of life as a metaphysical crapshoot. Significantly, Kubrick shows us that the same struggles exist, in disguised form, in the corridors and salons of the chateau. Mireau's fear of failure and his desire for an empty glory, Saint-Auban's smugness and sycophancy, Broulard's subservience to unseen forces offscreen, and, yes, even Dax's fervor and naïveté, may not result in their walking down that formal path to an undeserved execution, but they just as surely do not ascend to the more comprehensive understandings embodied in the lessons of history and art that surround them, radiant but unseen. The officers' paths, too, run a horizontal course, as the formal structures of the court-martial and execution make clear.

More than any other scene in *Paths*, or before it in his other films, Kubrick's handling of the court-martial achieves an impressive merger of concept and form.[6] From long shot, the camera shows a detachment of soldiers bringing the three accused men into a vast, elegant room. An enormously large landscape painting hangs high up on the wall, looming above their heads; light floods in from tall windows in the rear and to the right; while below, on the floor, are the ever-present chessboard squares of a marble floor. Again, the composition emphasizes the verticals of the chateau, but more strongly than before, while the painting overhead hints at an idealization of the trench landscape and, significantly, provides the one prominent horizontal presence in the shot. While space is enlarged, however, time is compressed. The court-martial proceedings begin at three o'clock in the afternoon and take up very little actual time, even though an elaborate consideration for the formalities of the occasion is evident. The Colonel Judge (Peter Capell) repeatedly chastises Dax for taking up too much of the court's "time" with technicalities that do not bear directly on the case (such as the reading of the indictment!). Formalities, not the "technicalities" of justice, are important here. And in the actual examination and cross-examination of the three men by prosecutor Saint-Auban and Dax, the court makes every effort to deny the reality of time: It will not allow Dax to offer as evidence the past histories of these men as soldiers, only what they did during the three minutes of the attack; and, of course, its primary purpose is to take from the prisoners a right to all future time. Yet this temporal evasion—an avoidance of the existential basis of life—takes on a spatial form as well. For the court to duplicate the

Three human pawns on an ornate gameboard/bat-
tlefield (Timothy Carey, Ralph Meeker, Joseph Turkel).

vertical grandeur of its surroundings would be tantamount to its recognizing its own folly; such duplication would entail an enlargement of
vision and perspective that would first lead to the court's acknowledging its own tragic absurdity. Kubrick's audience, however, does perceive
this disparity, especially when it realizes that the court-martial itself
assumes the formal properties of a battle on a gameboard. The camera
work and composition leave little doubt about Kubrick's intentions
here. On one side we have the battleline represented by the five judges,
symmetrically composed with the Colonel Judge in the middle, framed
by an archway in the background and the French flag overhead; on
the other, the three prisoners, sitting in chairs, enclosed from behind
like pawns by two lines of guards standing motionless in an attitude
of parade rest; on the flank to their left, and parallel to the windows,
is Major Saint-Auban's table and behind him General Mireau and a
line of spectators; and finally, to the prisoners' right is Colonel Dax,
opposite Saint-Auban and clearly outnumbered. This boxlike gameboard moves along horizontal paths, as the camera reveals when it pans

back and forth behind the line of judges during Saint-Auban's speech and tracks behind the line of prisoners during Dax's. The court-martial, Kubrick implies, formalizes the world of the trenches, not the reaches of the chateau. The scene ends in darkness as the screen fades to black following the Colonel Judge's final words: "The court will deliberate."

The implication that the politics of the chateau and the horrors of the trench differ only in form and not in substance crystallizes in Kubrick's handling of the execution scene. It begins with a high-angle shot looking across the garden to the massive chateau in the background and down a wide path formed by Mireau's regiment connecting chateau with execution. As the three men and the priest (Emile Meyer) move toward the camera down this ceremonial walkway, the film not only visually links the vertical chateau to the horizontal trench, but reminds us that each side of a chessboard mirrors (and so reverses) the other. The film began with an expansive but formal composition of the area where now stands the place of execution, while in reverse angle it returns to a shot that forms a path to the very entrance where Broulard first tread another path into the chateau; similarly, the second half of the film thematically mirrors the first by demonstrating that an existential struggle with mortality and paradox persists even after the internecine conflicts of state. Kubrick cuts from the prisoners and chateau to a subjective shot moving toward the stakes. In this, the audience's first view of the execution area, Kubrick's camera creates both a sympathetic identification with the three men about to die and recalls Dax's movements into the smoky nightmare of battle, except that now the shot is more generalized and leaves the impression that we, too, move down that same path. Only in this background we are confronted with the ultimate mockery of the chateau's vertical thrust. Three narrow stakes, like the three figures that close in on Johnny Clay at the end of *The Killing*, form a line and rise upward and above the sandbags; and while the camera shows in their balanced spacing and proportion that the stakes not only face but imitate the chateau, the time-worn splendor at the other end of the pathway continues to preside over this horizontal labyrinth in silent contempt.

But once its formal mask is defined, Kubrick penetrates the artifice of the execution and reveals a human content that the judges of the court-martial refused to admit as relevant evidence. Tied to the stakes, the prisoners form a line that resembles their position at the court-martial, only now they are upright and about to face a firing squad

A death sentence read (Richard Anderson) outside
the parlors of splendor.

rather than a kangaroo court. Major Saint-Auban stands before them
and reads the formal sentence of the court, only now, in his hesitations,
he expresses an uneasy awareness of death's presence; Sergeant Boulanger (Bert Freed) pinches the cheek of Arnaud, mercifully unconscious, who in the trenches had expressed his greater fear of pain than
of dying, while Ferol, no longer confident that he has an edge over a
cockroach, clings to the sacraments, and quite literally to the rosary,
of the priest; and Corporal Paris makes that final existential choice and
struggles to give his death some vestige of dignity; Lieutenant Roget
then walks down the line of prisoners offering them blindfolds, ironically asking Paris to forgive him. And all the while, the drums continue
to roll and off to one side a cart with three caskets waits. The last two
shots reverse perspective and draw the audience even more deeply into
the film's unresolved conflicts: the first offers a final look at the chateau
and the path that connects it to the stakes, only now the double lines
of a firing squad separate the prisoners from the spectators; the second
reverses this angle and looks over the executioners' shoulders as they

fire in unison at the three men. The audience, at once spectator and victim, watches death from afar and confronts it up close; and in the finality of that moment, it perceives that the same pathway that ends in death for Arnaud, Ferol, and Paris encloses the humanist Dax as well as the generals. It is a path beautiful in its symmetry and fearful in its meanings.

Alexander Walker calls *Paths of Glory* Kubrick's "graduation" piece, and no doubt it is a truly masterly film. It provides an early textbook of styles and preferences that will later be associated with a Kubrickian film signature. *Paths* shows the first signs of that passion for exact detail that establishes both the authenticity of a film and its expressiveness. Kubrick clearly wants to give each scene an interesting visual quality and at the same time to imply a latent coherence of emotion and idea. The imagery of the film blends grainy black-and-white realism and the documentary, handheld camera style of the attack (zooms and telephoto shots) with compositional effects achieved through deep focus and long camera takes. In every scene Kubrick is careful to provide an available-light look; when filming inside, he always identifies the "source" light, whether it is a naked bulb hanging in Dax's bunker, a candle on Roget's table, or the light-flooded windows of the chateau. He repeatedly gives value to unobtrusive objects in the background either through a brief compositional effect or as counterpoint. When Dax, for instance, meets privately with Broulard just before the execution, Kubrick slyly misleads the audience into thinking that the tables have been turned and that Dax's humanism yet may prevail over Mireau's vanity. The scene takes place in a library—walls lined with books, a warm fire burning in a fireplace, and carpets on the floor, all of which complement the intimate and liberal definition of Dax's character. Dax sips cognac and briefly plays Broulard's game before he plays his trump card—during the attack Mireau ordered artillery fire on his own positions. Broulard remains inscrutable and leaves Dax to wonder if, indeed, there is in the chateau even one spokesman for a humane politics. A china tea set in the background may provide the answer. The library is no different from any other room in the chateau; its books are decorative only, while the tea set at least has the virtue of contributing to the endless rounds of formal bartering which take place there.[7] Also, *Paths of Glory* is Kubrick's first film to use music for ironic counterpoint. A typical example, besides those already mentioned, would be the ballroom scene on the night before the execution, which shows a party of French officers and ladies dancing to the "Artist's Life Waltz" of Austrian composer Johann Strauss. One aspect of Kubrick's artistry that is seldom recognized is the superb editing in the best of his work. Because his films give an audience so much to look at and listen for, the artful transitions from one scene to the next often go unnoticed. *Paths*, for instance, shows Kubrick's fondness for merging his "sound" thematics with an editing style that strives for continuity and juxtaposition within a single cut. Besides the examples already cited, the most notable instance of such a cut in *Paths* is that from the explosions of the firing squad to the tinkle of silverware at Mireau's breakfast after the execution. (This cut has to do with what will be a leitmotif in later Kubrick films. Like Buñuel, Kubrick has a surrealist's appreciation for both the primal and ritualistic significance of eating and food, which finds its fullest expression in the futuristic mise-en-scène of *2001*.)*

Paths of Glory marks the full emergence of a distinct film intelligence and, to a greater degree than in his earlier work, Kubrick makes his presence known and felt in the complex worlds of the film. Kubrick uses his spatial definition of conflict to integrate a series of disparate perspectives through which the audience can respond to the emotional or psychological directions of character and, simultaneously, understand the film's paradoxical blending of irony and affirmation. The conflicting characterizations of Dax and Broulard illustrate this merger of a receptive and generative aesthetics. After their final meeting, when Broulard has used Dax's evidence not to save three innocent men but to bring down one foolish general, Dax and the audience experience a catharsis of sorts in the scene where the German girl's song turns leers into tears. But by that time, through the library scene and that final confrontation in Mireau's apartment, the film has clearly shown that Dax and Broulard are victims of equally confining moralities. They, in fact, embody the polarities of the film itself: Dax's character represents that "close-up" and personal view of the trenches found in Cobb's novel, the one which believes in the importance of moral

---

* In the breakfast scene, the tables are turned on Mireau, literally as well as figuratively. He and Broulard each sit where the other sat in the two previous scenes in the apartment, while Dax sits between them. Mireau's downfall is initiated by Broulard: as he spreads jelly on a croissant, he says casually, "By the way, Paul," and goes on to reveal Colonel Dax's information about the artillery fire. In the library scene Dax uses a similar verbal tactic ("By the way, General Broulard, did you know that General Mireau . . .").

victories in a world without moral order; Broulard's is the impersonal and distant view of the chateau, one which mocks in its vertical politics a defunct belief in an ordered and purposeful cosmos. The first expresses all the right sentiments and glimpses life's contingencies, but lacks an appropriately expressive and objective form, while the second shows an appreciation of form without an understanding of life's existential substance. Each travels in ignorance through the splendor of the chateau, a setting that gives the film and its audience an historical perspective on the tragic and absurd meaning of life in time and, in addition, an aesthetic perspective on the endurance of that meaning in the forms of filmic space.

3 LOLITA

Kubrick in Nabokovland

If there was a crossroads in the early part of Kubrick's career, it came between the completion of *Paths of Glory* in 1957 and his move to England in 1960 to film *Lolita*. During those years, the Hollywood studios were still adjusting to the economic consequences of the growth of television, and they were beginning to turn to foreign countries, where there were less expensive shooting locations and more lucrative distribution markets. It was a period when Hollywood recycled silent film spectacle into wide-screen puffery, from 20th Century Fox's *The Robe* (1953) to Paramount's *The Ten Commandments* (1956) and MGM's *Ben-Hur* (1959). The appeal of the so-called "small" film, with its social content and intimate treatment, was dwindling, partly because of the competition from television, then in its Golden Age, with an impressive number of dramatic series (*Studio One, Playhouse 90,*

and others). New York Studio actors like Marlon Brando and Paul Newman were drifting away from human interest films like *The Men* (1950), *On the Waterfront* (1954), and *Somebody Up There Likes Me* (1956) to the literary *kitsch* of *Sayonara* (1957), *The Young Lions* (1958), *The Young Philadelphians* (1959), and *On the Terrace* (1960). It was a period when independent production companies proliferated on the film landscape faster than bug-eyed monsters in 3-D, forcing the majors to flex their only remaining muscle, namely their control of the marketplace through distribution.[1] Harris-Kubrick was one of these independent companies, but one not as well-heeled as those associated with established stars like John Wayne (Batjac) and Kirk Douglas (Bryna). After *Paths*, Kubrick and Calder Willingham collaborated for six months on a script with Marlon Brando, an actor whose name alone could guarantee the money for a big film; Kubrick, by contrast, was only a pre-*auteur* director and not even thirty years old, at that. The Brando project fell through, and neither Kubrick's script nor his directorial services were accepted. He was paid off (handsomely, by all accounts), and Brando became the director as well as the star of *One-Eyed Jacks* (1960).

With the money from *Paths* and the *Jacks* work, Harris-Kubrick in 1958 purchased the film rights to Vladimir Nabokov's *Lolita* (1955), showing that even during the lengthy *Spartacus* work (1959–60), Kubrick was determined to continue an independent course. In 1959 Kirk Douglas's Bryna company hired Kubrick to replace Anthony Mann as director of *Spartacus* (Universal), which put Kubrick, then thirty, in charge of a $12 million Hollywood film production. Kubrick, however, was not quite "in charge." As the firing of Mann suggests, *Spartacus* was Douglas's picture, and that included the trendy leftist sentiments in Dalton Trumbo's script of the Howard Fast novel (Trumbo, in 1962, scripted another Douglas-Bryna film, *Lonely Are the Brave*). Expressing more regret than rancor, Kubrick's description of his role during the 167 days of shooting and months of post-production shows that he did what was typical for a Hollywood studio director: He directed the cast, composed the shots, and supervised the editing. What is missing from the list is that script control which was crucial to the artistry of *The Killing* and *Paths of Glory*, and which has lent distinction to all his films since *Paths* with the lone exception of *Spartacus* (1960).[2]

Spartacus, however, does exhibit several Kubrickian trademarks, and no doubt the experience taught him a great deal about handling the many thousands of details in a large film production. And, as several reviewers noted, compared with other wide-screen spectacles of the period, *Spartacus* is not a bad film at all. Its major weaknesses stem from the trite, simplistic, and sentimental morality of the script. The scenes between Spartacus (Kirk Douglas) and Varinia (Jean Simmons), for instance, are too insistent about the honesty and intuitive vision of a proletarian hero; and many of these scenes were not enhanced by being filmed in the studio—they have the look of later television products from Universal City. The epic panorama of battles and armies is well done and reflects Kubrick's skill at showing what he has referred to as the "weird disparity" between the aesthetics of warfare and its human consequences. As the Roman legions commanded by Crassus (Laurence Olivier) move across the plain toward Spartacus' slave army, a visual dance between Rome's formal grandeur and a solid (and stolid) rock of humanity changes into a disordered field of death.[3] The political conflicts of *Spartacus* have clear parallels with those in *Paths of Glory*, but unfortunately they, too, drown in a swamp of ideology. The struggle between Crassus and Gracchus (Charles Laughton) degenerates into a war between a sexually insecure militarist (Hollywood liberals have the illusion that all fascists are impotent proto-McCarthys) and a cunning but sympathetic republican (who, despite his old age, has several loving women in his service); the film glosses over the fact that Gracchus shows no real understanding of the slave rebellion and that he plays ruthless political games with a young and ambitious Caesar (John Gavin). In a few places, the film does suggest the kinds of irony present in the conflict between the trenches and the chateau in *Paths*. During a fight to the death between Spartacus and a black gladiator, provided as an entertainment for a Roman wedding party, Kubrick's composition shows in foreground an exchange between Crassus and one of his political protégés; and later, Kubrick parallels Spartacus' address to his army with Crassus' before his legions. But mostly these oppositions reinforce the didactic polarities of the script rather than meld into the complexity of a paradoxical unity.

Likewise, certain psychological and sexual implications in the story are sidestepped and confused. A scene that showed Crassus' homosexual desire for the slave Antoninus (Tony Curtis) was deleted, and in the process, the film indulges in reverse censorship by overprotesting the slave brotherhood theme, perhaps from fear that the friendship between Spartacus and Antoninus might be viewed as a Freudian joke. Indeed, the psychology of the film squeezes itself into a shell of Biblical/liberal allegory. Because the script wants to maintain Spartacus' purity, his character never achieves a convincing sexual identity, which means that the pregnancy of Varinia borders on an immaculate conception; and the overly hearty depiction of brotherhood without coitus contrasts with didactic precision to the sexual sneers of Peter Ustinov's Batiatus (whose thoroughly despicable character softens into the lovable rogue), the decadent voyeurism of Roman ladies (Nina Foch and Joanna Barnes), and the slightly effeminate manhood of Crassus. Overall, the film becomes a leftist fairy tale and fails to give either character or concept a scope equal to its epic pretensions. These flaws become especially apparent whenever Olivier is on the screen. His performance confers upon Crassus subtleties that are never fully realized in the film as a whole, and they command such attention that the scenes of slave brotherhood appear insubstantial in comparison.

Because he strives for perfection as a film artist, Kubrick must have felt disappointment and resentment over *Spartacus*. Later films like *2001* and *Barry Lyndon* clearly demonstrate his talent for matching epic form to an appropriately speculative and philosophic subject matter. A reflexive critique of *Spartacus*, in fact, may be present in its final scene. There, Varinia holds up her child before the cross on which Spartacus is dying and in a brief moment of film time communicates more poignancy and meaning than is present in all the fine speeches about freedom or the addlepated Christ symbolism of the ending.[4] Ironically, it is Douglas's best scene, and one where he asserts the more profound humanity of silence. Kubrick concludes the film with a composition that recalls the tragic irony of *Paths*. Varinia's cart moves away from the camera down a path lined on both sides with crucified slaves. In Trumbo's version, of course, the audience would assume that she and Spartacus' child travel into a democratic future which gives value to his sacrifice; in Kubrick's, one barely visible to this film's audience, they move into an indeterminate world where there exists only the certainty of death. Two years later, in *Lolita*, Kubrick seems to express even more strongly his attitude toward the missed opportunities of *Spartacus* when he has Quilty, adorned in a bedsheet Roman toga, utter a parodic response to Humbert's question about his identity: "No, I'm Spartacus, have you come to free the slaves or something?" And in the last scene, Lolita describes to a despairing Humbert her relationship with the perverse Quilty and how he had promised to take her to Hollywood where he was to write "one of those spectaculars." Lolita never gets to Hollywood, although Kubrick's *coup de grâce* implies that her trip to Quilty's ranch to make a pornographic movie ("art movie") may have been an equivalent experience.

The *Lolita* project began in earnest during the early months of 1960. In the previous summer, Harris and Kubrick had asked Nabokov to come to Hollywood and write the script. Nabokov refused, but after a "small nocturnal illumination" later that year and another request from Harris-Kubrick, he accepted the job.[5] On March 1, 1960, Nabokov met with Kubrick for the first time at Universal City (where he still was working on *Spartacus*), and under the jacarandas of Hollywood, he worked for six months on the *Lolita* script. By midsummer, Nabokov handed Kubrick a 400-page screenplay that included unused material from the manuscript of the original novel. Kubrick asked for a shorter version; in September Nabokov submitted a script half as long as his first one. Two years later (June 1962), Nabokov saw the film at the New York City premiere, and afterwards in a *Playboy* interview (January 1964), he expressed his admiration for it, while taking no credit for the excellence of its acting or production. One bit of confusion arises, however, when Nabokov's comments in 1964 are compared with those in the 1973 foreword to his published screenplay of *Lolita*.[6] In the earlier interview, he says that his only involvement with the film was the script, a "preponderating portion of which was used by Kubrick," while later he recalls that his first response to the film was "that Kubrick was a great director, that his *Lolita* was a first-rate film with magnificent actors, and that only ragged odds and ends of my script had been used." In the *Playboy* interview, Nabokov very graciously concludes that Kubrick's cinematic approach to the novel was merely different from his own, while recognizing the unique demands, both artistic and those from the Production Code, put on Kubrick by his medium. Regrettably, later critics have been less understanding about Kubrick's considerable achievement in adapting to film one of the most difficult and brilliant novels of this century. Alfred Appel, Jr., for one, incorrectly claims that Kubrick only used twenty percent of Nabokov's submitted screenplay and, through innuendo more than argument, deprecates the film. Rather than considering the film as an adaptation and transformation of both the novel and the screenplay—

and seeing them as sources of stimulation to Kubrick's creative interests—Appel (as do others) looks at the film through his vision of the
novel and proposes scenarios for what it should have done.[7] Nabokov's
comments, on the other hand, indicate that he clearly perceived Kubrick's talent (and the talents of the cast) and his rightful assumption
of artistic license.

An examination of Nabokov's published screenplay (1974) reveals
three very important factors: the screenplay includes scenes from the
400-page version that were deleted from the shorter version Kubrick
accepted; in its overall structure, the film uses considerably more than
twenty percent of the final 1960 script; and Kubrick creates several
visual and verbal translations of effects suggested in the Nabokov script,
which is more theatrical and poetic than cinematic. For Nabokov,
adapting *Lolita* to the "speaking screen," as he calls it, involved the
staging of a complex network of verbal revelation punctuated by an
occasionally obtrusive camera. Nabokov's cinematic ideas—some of
which obviously interested Kubrick—would, if strictly followed, have
announced an authorial film presence in tones louder than Kubrick
prefers. The screenplay's description of camera movements in the first
scene illustrates this point: Nabokov has the camera gliding around
and through Quilty's mansion like a theatrical invader (it "locates the
drug addict's implementa on a bedside chair, and with a shudder with-
draws"), which he probably visualized as an equivalent for the assertion in the novel of his parodic omniscience to the distortions of a first-
person unreliable narration. If Kubrick had adopted such a course, his
Lolita would have pleased those critics who feel that the baroque extremes of an Orson Welles provide the best model for a cinematic
translation of Nabokov's prose style; but, if my consideration of his
earlier films has revealed anything, it is that Kubrick manipulates cinematic point of view in ways that are far more covert (but not necessarily any more complex) than Nabokov's. Ironically, in the hands of
an expressionist like Welles or even Sternberg, the subtle and intricate style of the novel might have been transformed in the film to the
kind of cloying and pretentious seriousness that Nabokov disparaged
throughout his life. Kubrick's version, instead, strives to find its own
expression for both the subtlety and the playfulness of the novel. And
it should not be forgotten that *Lolita* is Kubrick's first effort at adapting
to film the novelistic convention of the unreliable first-person narrator,
an understanding of which will illuminate the narrational ironies of

two other films based on novels that confuse point of view in much the same way *Lolita* does, namely, *A Clockwork Orange* and *Barry Lyndon*.

For Kubrick, *Lolita* represents an important advance in the development of a psychological film style. Nabokov's *Lolita* gives Kubrick, for the first time, a novelistic source that constructs its world from inside the mind of a single fictional intelligence. And even though Humbert's imagination can mesmerize the reader with its richness of invention and distortion, Nabokov uses the parodic intrusions of his third-person "voice" to undermine and transcend his narrator's clever special pleadings. No such rhetorical strategy exists in either White's *Clean Break* or Cobb's *Paths of Glory*; there, the potentials of psychological conflict are either harnessed or suppressed within the impersonal order of an external activity (robbery plan or war), one in which a degree of anonymity is not only a virtue but a necessity. Consequently, Kubrick was able to develop a dramatic tension, in one film, between repressed psychological forces and the demands of a temporal mechanism (*The Killing*) and, in the other, between the human reality of war and the antiquated structures of a military politics (*Paths of Glory*). In each film, exterior contingencies combine to create a fate that ultimately overwhelms and frustrates the aims of a very elemental psychology. Nabokov's novel, by contrast, generates its narrative conflict from within Humbert's solipsistic universe, which is at odds not only with itself but also with the larger ironies of the novel. For the psychological world of his *Lolita*, Kubrick squeezes his style down to a more pinpoint, less expansive focus than the one conceived for *Paths of Glory*, where the puny ambitions of character are measured against grandeur, both historical and spatial in scope; he moves from the openness of location shooting to the interiority of performance and the studio where, as he mentioned while making *Lolita*,

> everything is inky darkness and the lights are coming from an expected place and it is quiet and you can achieve concentration. . . . I think that too much has been made of making films on location. . . . For a psychological story, where the characters and their inner emotions and feelings are the key thing, I think that the studio is the best place.[8]

Kubrick's avowed admiration for Chaplin's films, which also depend to a great extent on the studio for their psychological effect, reflects the importance Kubrick attaches to the actor; despite a lack of cinematic sophistication Chaplin developed a subtlety and complexity of performance that became a creative alternative to Eisenstein's greater range of film styles. *Lolita* shows that, for Kubrick, performance can be as important to the expressive substance of a film as camera and mise-en-scène.

In Pudovkin's *Film Technique*, Kubrick would not have found a very far-reaching critique of the film actor's role.[9] For Pudovkin, the actor was subordinated to the director, and performance, to filmic construction; he did stress, however, how the actor could focus a film's emotional manipulation of the spectator, while the director, through editing and images, worked on his mind. With the possible exception of *Spartacus*, Kubrick's films do not contain highly emotive performances of that kind, although, beginning with *Lolita*, they increasingly exhibit a variety of subtly expressive and emotional acting styles. Kubrick has mentioned that early in his career he found Stanislavsky's ideas about working with actors to be helpful and, even today, continues to recommend Nikolai Gorchakov's *Stanislavsky Directs*.[10] During the formative years of Kubrick's career, Stanislavsky's theories already had influenced and helped shape the so-called school of method acting brought to the Broadway stage by Elia Kazan and Lee Strasberg of the New York Actors Studio (founded 1947); and the Stanislavsky method was especially important for the expression of psychoanalytical themes found in the plays of Arthur Miller and Tennessee Williams. Interestingly, this theatrical movement coincided with American film neorealism (1945–55) and its treatment of "controversial" social issues; at times, however, the intimate, interiorized performing techniques of "method" actors would conflict with a less stylized visual realism (e.g., Brando's performance in *The Wild One*, 1953, or James Dean's in *Rebel Without a Cause*, 1955). Not until *Lolita* did Kubrick work with a cast capable of the kind of intuitive approach to performance recommended by Stanislavsky, which specializes in oblique psychological revelation through a manipulation of gesture, mannerism, and voice. In *Killer's Kiss*, he had the right kind of script for such a treatment, but not the right kind of actors; as a result, he experimented with a highly expressive visual style in order to suggest psychological complexities beyond the abilities of his actors, while *The Killing* and *Paths of Glory* only required their professional performers (except for Kirk Douglas, veteran Hollywood character actors dominate both films) to give functional life to roles that rarely stray from convention or stereotype.

Perhaps one reason why *Lolita* remains Kubrick's most unappreciated and misunderstood early film—why so many critics have failed to notice that, like Buñuel's *Viridiana* (1961), for example, it develops a surrealist mise-en-scène through a deceptively sparse naturalism—is the strength of its performances.[11] The cast of the film develops and improvises so many revealing details of character that its subtle repetition of images, objects, and decor can go unnoticed. Peter Sellers's spellbinding transformations, as well as the performances of James Mason, Shelley Winters, and Sue Lyon, command such attention that filmic complexities may travel through a receptive consciousness like so much visual muzak. And besides its almost perfect expression of a Nabokovian verbal playfulness, Sellers's conception of Clare Quilty parallels an attitude toward the unreality of conventional social poses that Kubrick described in an interview as early as 1958:

> The criminal and the soldier at least have the virtue of being against something or for something in a world where many people have learned to accept a kind of grey nothingness, to strike an unreal series of poses in order to be considered normal. . . . It's difficult to say who is engaged in the greater conspiracy—the criminal, the soldier, or us.[12]

The other principal performers strengthen not only the film's satiric assault on the "normal" but, more important, its strong emotional subtext. Shelley Winters plays a perfect foil to the parodic exaggerations of Sellers's Quilty and the vulgarity of Sue Lyon's Lolita: In that delightful tour of the Haze home early in the film, through a mannered control of hands (which wave a long cigarette holder around in assertive flourishes) and voice, she comically expresses Charlotte's social and sexual aspirations; later, she shows the child in Charlotte's character, the "lotte" Lolita, as she sits in the midst of a Kubrickian soft-textured close-up, smiling like a plump fairy princess and delicately ringing a bell for her maid to serve dinner. And even while we laugh at her vulgarity, Winters suggests a sadness in Charlotte's character, one that glimpses but does not understand its own pathetic desperation. (As she cries and embraces the urn, she yells at "Harold," her dead husband: "Why did you leave me? . . . I didn't know anything about life.")

Mason and Lyon repeatedly play off each other and likewise communicate both the satiric and the poignant truth of Humbert's obsession with Lolita. Mason develops a series of facial and gestural mannerisms to express Humbert's European archness and his terrible vulnerability.

When Humbert experiences moments of emotional exposure, Mason's face twitches uncontrollably as his hands move frantically to restore order to his facial landscape; finally, by the film's end, his formal mask collapses from the pressure of an inner despair. Especially moving is the scene in the hospital where Humbert, his entire physical being shattered by an incalculable emotional and psychological loss, discovers Lolita gone and himself surrounded on a dark corridor floor by four figures in white who interrogate him as if he were a candidate for an insane asylum. In a car with Humbert, just after they make love at the Enchanted Hunters Hotel, Lolita displays that harmonious relationship with the objects of her teenage environment which eludes Humbert, as she erotically sucks a straw in a coke bottle and wraps her tongue around potato chips in a bag; meanwhile, Humbert, the ever-present voyeur, drives the car and slyly glances at his nymphet now sitting next to him like a "date" prepared for an evening of heavy necking and petting. Significantly, the very next scene shows Lolita, childlike, curled up in Humbert's arms on a motel bed and crying over Charlotte's death and the loss of her "normal" existence. At Beardsley, in an argument with Humbert over her lies and deceptions, and dressed as an elfin princess, she chews gum and blows bubbles as Humbert's entreaties grow more manic; he pathetically rubs his hand on a pant leg and kneels in a gesture of total submission before his now frigid princess, while Lyon maintains Lolita's teenage imperviousness to his suffering. Not until the performances within the elegiac mise-en-scène of *Barry Lyndon* and the nightmarish mazes of *The Shining* will Kubrick's actors again lend such a tragic pathos to his larger and more ironic look at the disparities between the forms of social normality and the truths of an unarticulated but real psychological disorder.

Kubrick does fault his *Lolita* on one important count: because of pressures from the Production Code and the Catholic Legion of Decency, he could not sufficiently dramatize the erotic aspect of Humbert's obsession with the nymphet.[13] And even though Sue Lyon was thirteen when shooting began, she plays Lolita closer to 15 than 12. (In the novel, we are told, the nymphet exists on an "enchanted island" between the ages of 9–14.) Kubrick, however, does provide in the film a definition of the nymphet (it is different from the one in Nabokov's screenplay) and of Humbert's attraction that indicates the film's altered sexual and psychological focus. In voiceover while writing in his diary, Humbert defines the "twofold nature" of this nymphet as a mixture of "dreamy childishness" and "eerie vulgarity," thus suggesting that his obsession for Lolita has nothing to do with the unsuccessful retreat of Nabokov's Humbert into that timelessness lost in the "princedom by the sea" of his childhood; instead, Mason's Humbert starts as a whimsical satyr who, as he flees from the omnivorous clutchings of predatory American matrons, becomes enslaved to a tragic fascination for the iridescence and triviality of a child-woman. And in this movement from satire to poignancy, Kubrick weaves a pattern of sexual innuendo and implication that imitates the playfulness and pathos of the novel more than its eroticism. Brandon French, in an essay on the film, points out a few examples of Kubrick's attempt to give his *Lolita* a dense sexual subtext: in the first scene, Humbert's phallic gun (called "Chum" in the novel, forever eager to discharge its bullets, which Humbert fears will go "stale" from disuse) opposes Quilty's impotent ping pong balls, while later we see Charlotte fondling the same gun as she reminisces about the "late Mr. Haze." Humbert's introduction to Charlotte and Lolita initiates his early entanglement in a relationship where double *entendres* fly back and forth in a vulgar American mating ritual. Charlotte's falsetto laugh trumpets her first advance on Humbert's dark European handsomeness when she tells him that he couldn't get more "peace" (sic) anywhere than in her home. She then takes him into her bedroom to show off *her* collection of "reproductions" (Dufy, Monet, Van Gogh) after mentioning how "stimulating" Clare Quilty, a TV playwright, had been in his lecture on Dr. Schweitzer and Dr. Zhivago. (She, of course, had a pre-Humbert affair with Quilty, who also uses Charlotte to capture the nymphet.) In the hallway, Charlotte apologizes for the presence of a "soiled" sock, which, it is assumed, belongs to Lolita and prepares for Humbert's discovery, post-Camp Climax, of his nymphet's sexual precocity. Nabokov especially must have delighted in the ending of this scene, where Humbert has his first vision of Lolita in the garden and instantly decides to stay and enjoy Charlotte's promise of "late snacks" and "cherry pies."

The film develops the ultimate sexual irony when it shows Humbert's involvement in an American *ménage à trois* that subtly disguises Quilty's presence and the more sinister outlines of a *ménage à quatre*. In an early montage, Kubrick shows the comic drama of Humbert's naïveté as his advances toward the nymphet are checked by the moves

against him by Charlotte and Lolita. As Humbert peeks over a book at Lolita's hula-hooping in the garden, Charlotte's blowsy sexuality and flash camera break the spell; as Charlotte ponders a move in a game of chess with Humbert (a favored Nabokovian device, as well), Lolita slides in and gives him something more than a goodnight peck on the cheek ("You're going to take my Queen," moans Charlotte); while at a drive-in theater watching a Hammer horror film that shows the monster turning on his creator (*The Curse of Frankenstein*, 1957) Humbert is trapped between the clutches of mother and daughter; and finally, Charlotte moves against Lolita in a conspiracy with the Farlows (Jerry Stovin and Diana Decker), which puts Charlotte in the house alone with Humbert. Ironically, Kubrick casts Humbert in these early scenes as a sort of Daisy Miller in reverse: the European who is more innocent than decadent becomes the chessboard Queen to Charlotte and Lolita's Knights. This sardonic look at the American Peyton Place reaches a climax in the scene where Charlotte, dressed in a leopard-skin pants suit, mixes the rumba and pink champagne in a primal assault on Humbert's European reserve. Lolita unexpectedly returns (her "move" against Charlotte) because, she says, "salty fish eggs" were being served at the Farlow slumber party; and the audience is treated to a marvelous scene of Humbert, nervously cracking walnuts, caught between Charlotte's pink champagne and Lolita's turkey and mayonnaise sandwich. He gives Charlotte the cracked shells rather than his gonads, which anticipates his later implication during their brief conjugality that she leaves him as "limp as a noodle."

This bourgeois bacchanal within the pastoral simplicity of New England America turns darker whenever the film reasserts the surrealist humor of Quilty. Kubrick said that he and Nabokov agreed to have the film begin with Humbert killing Quilty without explanation, so that a narrative interest could be sustained after Humbert and Lolita are coupled at the Enchanted Hunters Hotel. What it also does is lend an atmosphere of impending menace to the lightly satiric quality of the early scenes. During the school dance, for example, Charlotte anticipates Humbert's walnut shells when she hands him her hot dog to dance with John Farlow; and later she skitters across the dance floor to say "hello" to Quilty, who, in a tuxedo and wearing horn-rimmed glasses, looks more cherubic than decadently spent. She whispers in his ear (as Lolita will in Humbert's just before she seduces him) and only

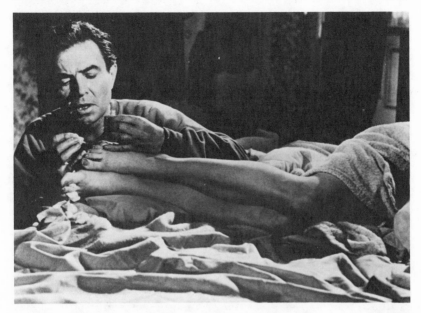

then does he associate Charlotte with the beautiful lilting name of Lolita. Quilty joins the film's game of playful innuendo when he knowingly smirks over Lolita's having a "cavity filled" by his Uncle Ivor, the local dentist. In this context, Quilty seems harmless enough, although the constant companionship of the darkly exotic and slightly lesbian Vivian Darkbloom (in the novel, an anagram for Vladimir Nabokov) hints at something kinkier than suburban exercises in playing post-office (Lolita will later extoll Quilty's "beautiful Oriental philosophy of life" and in her bedroom at Ramsdale a "Tokyo" poster is prominent). But in another scene, just after Humbert, sitting on Lolita's bed, reads Charlotte's "confession" of love and turns from the despair of losing Lolita forever to a gleeful and tearful appreciation of fortune's unexpected rewards (his laughter begins when Charlotte asks him to "link up" his life with hers and "be a father to my little girl"), the camera ominously pans to Quilty's picture on a cigarette poster. Now, Quilty-like, Humbert will add incest to his sins and so begin a journey into a nightmare where Quilty's presence, alternately spectral and corporeal, will provide a mirror image for both his own sexual degradation and Lolita's triviality.

While in *The Killing* and *Paths of Glory* Kubrick sacrifices complexities of character to the rigors of temporal and spatial structures,

his *Lolita* examines interior worlds with a delicacy of tone and distance that eluded him in *Killer's Kiss*. The imagery and decors of *Lolita* merge an ethereal softness of texture with a surreal dissonance in deep focus to create a style of presentation that, overall, develops a deceptive naturalism. The film starts with a girlish foot descending into an unfocused blur and the melodic piano music of Bob Douglas's romantic "Lolita" theme; a pair of masculine hands come into the frame and delicately administer a pedicure behind the film's credits. Completely removed from context, this initial shot creates an imagery that both gives form to Humbert's dreamy obsession with Lolita (including, perhaps, the wedding ring on the left hand) and satirizes his demeaning subjugation. Later, the first sequence at Beardsley will put this image in a dramatic context and reveal Humbert's sexual enslavement as he comically vacillates between the roles of whining lover and nagging father. Throughout the early part of the film, Kubrick tends to define Humbert's interiority through images and space, while Quilty, his alterego, is associated with objects and temporality. After the credits, the camera floats toward Quilty's medieval castle; once inside, the imagery sharpens into deep focus and delineates a mise-en-scène that, in its surreal merger of Classical and Camp, parodies Humbert's loving embrace of the illusory. This Humbert/Quilty doubling overshadows, in the film, the novel's focus on Humbert's desire to "fix once and for all the perilous magic of nymphets." Nabokov begins and ends Humbert's narrative with the word "Lolita" ("Lolita, light of my life" and "this is the only immortality you and I may share, my Lolita"), while Kubrick verbally frames his film with Humbert's call for "Quilty," a name that assumes, for Humbert as well as the audience, both an exclamatory ("Quilty!") and interrogative ("Quilty?") meaning. Who or what is Quilty? and what do his various appearances tell us about the psychological and conceptual assertions of Kubrick's film?

When Humbert first enters this Xanadu, we hear the ghostly ripplings of a harpsichord, which later will signal all of Quilty's menacing reappearances. Humbert moves through a bizarre clutter, unaware that it defines not only Quilty's physical domain but an inner sanctum: a three-dimensional surrealist canvas in which an ornate harp mixes with a ping pong table, Shakespeare's bust with boxing gloves, Venus de Milo with Victorian *bric-a-brac*, a tiger's head with an eighteenth-century portrait. Quilty, swathed in a sheet, rises from his chair and plays a parodic Spartacus and resurrected spook to Humbert's indignant civility. His invitation to play Roman ping pong, "like two civilized senators," mocks Humbert's urbane and scholarly mask, that pose of normality that conceals a mind as disordered as Quilty's. He mistakes Humbert for one "Jack Brewster," who, we find out backstage at Beardsley, is one of Quilty's flunkies ("Brewster, go buy me some Type A Kodachrome film"). This highly stylized encounter continues as Sellers improvises, in masterly fashion, a series of perverse impersonations that anticipate and parody the movement of the film into the "normal" social and psychological landscape of Ramsdale. He sprinkles his language with clichés like the Boy Scout motto, as he pulls from a robe pocket beneath his toga an endless supply of ping pong balls; he playfully prepares us for games to come when he responds to Humbert's brandished pistol with "it's not who wins but how you play"; he goes through an assortment of B-movie character parts (first an old Western codger who reads Humbert's painfully precious poem as if it were the "deed to the ranch" and then a boxing champion who wants to settle differences "like two civilized people"), which indirectly comments on Humbert's fatuous assumption of moral outrage. Even when he realizes that he cannot playact his way out of this situation, Quilty still mocks

the formal and civilized exterior of Humbert's Europeanism and, indirectly, later examples of suburban cultural pretense. He tells him to
"stop trifling with life and death" and that, being a playwright, he
knows all about this sort of "tragedy and comedy and fantasy." Yet
Humbert does not see his face in the reflexive mirror of Quilty's impersonations; in effect, his romantic infatuation with an image rather than
the reality of Lolita finds its demonic incarnation in Quilty and the
obscure objects of his desire.

Instead of expressing this important scene through the flourishes of
a Wellesian chiaroscuro, as Nabokov's screenplay invites, Kubrick
chooses to materialize the dreamy evasions of Humbert's character
through a realistic depiction of Quilty's nightmare world. He gives the
surreal a palpable shape and sound, thereby preparing the audience
for a flip-flop in scenes to come, one where a surreality shines through
the transparent façade of middle class normality and cinematic naturalism. In this remarkable scene, Sellers transforms the Evil One—
Quilty's Hyde to Humbert's Jekyll—into a pathetic creature trapped in
a black comedy he did not compose, futilely striving to find in Humbert a wit and humanity that could save Quilty's life. But to no avail.

His comic rendering of both Chopin's *polonaise* ("do you think it will make the Hit Parade?") and his own death ("you really hurt me . . . my leg will be black and blue tomorrow," he says after the first bullet strikes) does not dissuade the solemn avenger. He tries to bribe Humbert by appealing to his voyeurism—"I could fix it for you to attend executions, just you, do you like watching, Captain?"—but, instead, the executioner chooses to watch Quilty die. Kubrick concludes this prologue to his *Lolita* (Nabokov's novel begins with a parodic foreword by psychologist "John Ray, Jr., Ph.D.") with Quilty seeking cover behind a portrait of a child-woman who resembles one of Gainsborough's eighteenth-century "ladies" and whose beauty is violated by the bullets that extinguish the life of the hidden monster. The portrait introduces a metaphor of Humbert's tragic obsession with Lolita—a neoclassical serenity masking the grin of death—one that will serve as a backdrop to the film's titled epilogue: "Humbert Humbert died in prison of coronary thrombosis while awaiting trial for the murder of Clare Quilty." This demure image twice seen, and the repetition of that call for "Quilty" that immediately precedes it, provide the film with an aural and visual Rosebud which, like a recurring dream-nightmare, frames Humbert's loss of vision in the dark obstacle course of the self.

Within this prologue and its ritualization of both Humbert's enslavement to Lolita (pedicure) and his execution-killing of Quilty, Kubrick establishes a third-person detachment from the subjective (first-person) narration that begins just afterwards in a flashback to "four years earlier." By materializing the surreality of Quilty's character and linking it, through the eighteenth-century portrait, to Humbert's romantic fondness for images rather than objects, Kubrick is able to wrest the film from Humbert's subjective perspective and imply that, from the moment he steps into Charlotte's garden, his course inexorably leads to Quilty's mansion. Throughout the film, Humbert's attachment to the illusory is juxtaposed with various objects and characters that, in a different way, illustrate Quilty's view that people are interchangeable with furniture (he knows a man "who looks just like a bookcase"). In his first tour of the Haze domain, Humbert runs a gauntlet through the obscure objects of Charlotte's desire as he crosses a chessboard foyer into an interior that shows signs of a mental landscape almost as disordered as Quilty's: In every room, decorative wallpaper—vertical lines of a cage downstairs, flowers in the bedrooms, sailboats in the bathroom, fish on the shower curtain, and a clutter of table settings in

the kitchen—clashes with a rococo collection of objects. Charlotte takes
him into her bedroom and shows off a shrine to her late husband,
which includes an urn holding his ashes (on which Humbert inadver-
tently rests his hand), the gun that will kill Quilty (a "sacred" treasure
wrapped in silk), and Mr. Haze's picture voyeuristically gazing down
from the wall onto the bed where the future Mr. and Mrs. Humbert
will play at marital bliss. The upstairs hallway is cluttered with ghastly Mexican art and a porcelain cat, and downstairs various objets d'art
fill out a world of cultural poverty and sexual desperation. (Lolita later
will play with a bronzed hand holding a phallic arrow as she traces
the sculptured outlines of an African head in the scene where she undermines Charlotte's rumba lesson in leopard skin.) Kubrick concludes
this sequence, and its doubling of Charlotte's home with Quilty's Pavor
Manor, by giving cinematic form to Humbert's dreamy idealization of
Lolita. We first see Lolita in the garden, from Humbert's point of view:
She is wearing a bikini, a sun-hat, and heart-shaped sunglasses, and she
is bathed in soft light and an aura of sensuality, mysteriously abstracted
from time and linked to the imagery behind the credits and the portrait
in Quilty's mansion. And, once again, Kubrick immerses his audience
in Humbert's imagination and simultaneously inserts an ironic compli-
cation: first a pedicure, then a bullet hole through the face of the portrait, and now the sounds of a vapid teenage song ("yah-yah") playing
on Lolita's radio, which firmly locate her in time and objectify an existence on the other side of the mind's eye.

Throughout, Humbert has trouble dealing with the material and
mechanical substance of a world that frustrates his every move. Characters close in on him as he fumbles with a plate of cake and cup of
punch during the dance; he investigates the gun in Charlotte's bedroom
and the bullets fall out; and at the Enchanted Hunters he is as intimi-
dated by the mechanics of a folding cot as by Quilty's impersonation
of a policeman. Humbert prefers, instead, the private sanctuary of
words in his diary and the elusive sounds of "Ulalume," written by
"the divine Edgar." He fails to deduce Quilty's identity partly because
it exists in a dark and very corporeal part of the imagination, the one
that emanates from the loins rather than the cerebral cortex. Kubrick's
Humbert, given a more sympathetic form by James Mason's performance than in the dense forest of Nabokov's prose style, wants to glide
through space rather than tread the ground of primal instinct. In one
of the film's most inventive and original scenes, Kubrick shows that

Humbert, balancing a drink on his chest and listening to the faint sounds of Lolita's "yah-yah" garden music playing in his mind, is more at home in the dreamy and masturbatory delights of a hot bathtub than in the clutches of Charlotte's voracious libido.* Humbert relaxes in the very bath water that Charlotte had been drawing for herself just before reading his diary and fleeing to her rain-soaked death; and in a devilish joke at the expense of his protagonist, Kubrick has Humbert's position in the bathtub duplicate Charlotte's in the street, including the supplicatory presence of one Mr. Beale (James Dyrenfoth), whose son's car ran over Mrs. Humbert, and who moves from sitting on the curb next to her covered body to sitting on the toilet seat next to Humbert's submerged one.

Scenes in bedrooms and bathrooms abound in *Lolita*, as they do in Nabokov's novel, and indicate the film's highly developed use of studio-bound settings to express the comic and tragic modalities of a psychological/sexual content. Within these private chambers of an otherwise public domesticity, where the guilty and repressed secrets of suburbia find both release and purgation, Kubrick develops a visual and musical coherence that binds setting to both character fate and film concept. Throughout much of the film, bedrooms and bathrooms come together in an expression of primal irony. Charlotte, just before she escorts Humbert into her bedroom, makes a point of illustrating her home's old-fashioned plumbing by pulling the toilet chain and synchronizing her vulgar laughter to its flushing. Later, on the morning Lolita leaves for camp, Humbert crawls from his bed, and with the bathroom visible in the background as counterpoint and the theme music rising in pitch, receives Lolita's embrace as she winks and tells him not to forget her. He then goes into Lolita's room to sit on her bed, flanked by innocence on one side (a teddy bear) and vulgarity on the other (Quilty's picture on the cigarette poster), as he reads Charlotte's confession of love. In marriage, Humbert escapes from Charlotte's bed

---

*Humbert in the bathtub might be an ironic allusion to Jean Paul Marat, the eighteenth-century French revolutionary who was stabbed in his bath by a Charlotte, Charlotte Corday. In Nabokov's novel, Humbert refers to Marat's tub when he recounts his unfortunate marriage to Valeria, an ur-Charlotte. Nabokov especially associates Quilty with bathrooms and Humbert with beds: Quilty flushes the toilet ("waterfalls") all night long from the room next to Humbert's at the Enchanted Hunters Hotel; Humbert finds Quilty at Pavor Manor coming out of the bathroom and finally kills him in bed where "a pink bubble with juvenile connotations formed on his lips," which is another of the many signs linking Quilty and Humbert as fellow nympholepts.

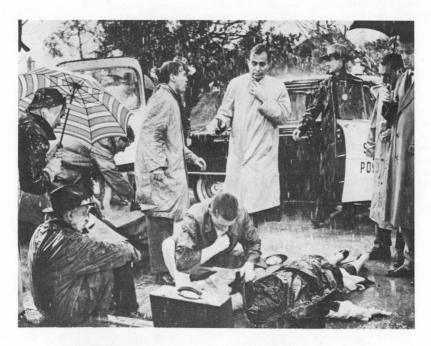

into the bathroom where he scribbles his secrets in the diary and is pursued by her pouty snoopings into his private life. And in that same bed, Charlotte starts to tell him about her "most ambitious fantasy" as he simultaneously makes love to her body and *his* fantasy embodied in Lolita's picture on an end-table. When he discovers that Charlotte's fantasy also involves Lolita, namely sending her off to boarding school so that she can have him all to herself, Humbert rolls over and contemplates the gun lying opposite Lolita's picture. At the Enchanted Hunters, Kubrick creates a sense of *déjà vu* as he delivers Humbert and Lolita into a room that mirrors the decor of Ramsdale, with flowered wallpaper in the bedroom and a bathroom in the background with a chessboard floor. Humbert comes out of that bathroom and hovers in a state of cleansed readiness over the sleeping beauty, but, alas, she wakes up and sends him scurrying to the cot. The next morning, Lolita bends over a tired and unshaven Humbert lying in his "collapsible" bed and whispers *her* dirty secret into *his* ear.

In later scenes, this comic movement within a maze of private passions takes darker and more poignant courses; and more successfully than in any of his previous films Kubrick demonstrates in *Lolita* a remarkable talent for directing his actors and developing a profound emotional content within the larger structures of an ironic distance. In a motel, he shows a tearful Lolita walking through another bathroom, this one separating her room from Humbert's, to seek comfort (Humbert told her of Charlotte's death) on a bed in semi-darkness, illuminated from behind by the light from the bathroom. Humbert consoles her with promises to restore her life to normality and never to leave her ("cross my heart and hope to die") as we see the child in Lolita break through the mask of teenage precocity. In a moment that is both touching and satiric, Lolita clings to her middle-class belief that normality can be measured in the continuity of such objects as records and record players, while we fully appreciate the tragicomic nature of Humbert's obsession. Despite his failure to find Dante's Beatrice in Ramsdale's Eve, he eventually must comfort and love the real Lolita, who later will double back and become another Charlotte. Lolita, even at the end, with Quilty gone ("the only man who I was ever really crazy about") and Humbert wasted and herself facing the tawdry prospect of her existence as Mrs. Richard T. Schiller (in Nabokov, the middle initial is "F"), still takes refuge in the enduring value of things and resists both Humbert's vision and his love. In their last scene together,

Lolita's final descent into normality (Sue Lyon and
Gary Cockrell).

Humbert faces a new Lolita—no longer dreamy or magical, but bloated
by pregnancy and wearing horn-rimmed glasses like Quilty—and sits
with her on another bed (on which, ironically, there is a copy of *Seventeen*), this time in a living room cluttered with domestic junk and
the ubiquitous decorative wallpaper. He tearfully begs her to come
away with him, "to live and die" with him, only to be rejected by her
in her new-found morality and her tragic triviality. She only accepts
from Humbert a last gift in the form of money and property settle-
ments. He flees in despair to confront Quilty, as we hear the last chords
from the theme music, which now express pathos rather than satire.
And Lolita sends him on his way with a cascade of clichés ("what's
past is past" and "keep in touch," as she waves hand and money in a
gesture of farewell) and documents the ultimate shallowness of her
character and the futility of Humbert's dream.

But as the film sympathetically records Humbert's loss, it visually
develops his entrapment on a gameboard far more deadly than he ever

imagines. Kubrick creates a cinematic chess game, reminiscent of both his earlier films and Nabokov's novel, that opposes Humbert's White to Quilty's Black. Chess, of course, superbly objectifies a state of paranoia and the themes of deception and entrapment; it demands from each player a constant vigilance lest he become the butt of an opponent's malicious joke. In *Lolita*, Kubrick allows his audience to watch the game from his vantage point by providing both privileged glimpses of Quilty's moves and, long before it dawns on Humbert, the knowledge that Lolita longs to be Quilty's Black Queen rather than Humbert's White. Not only is Humbert's first view of Lolita cast in soft light, but throughout the early part of the film all their encounters are brightly and realistically lit. Thus, Humbert has the illusion that his dream of Lolita might take shape in the daylight of a "normal" world. Quilty, at first, disguises his true role, although Kubrick brings him into the high school dance where Humbert's white dinner jacket opposes his black tuxedo; and, of course, Quilty travels with his Dark Queen, Vivian Darkbloom (Marianne Stone). And, on the soundtrack, blasts from Humbert's romantic piano oppose the subtle but sinister sounds of Quilty's harpsichord. Kubrick initiates a visual shift in the film at the Enchanted Hunters, even though the mood remains lightly satiric as the lighting becomes darker. On the hotel veranda, the camera is positioned so that the audience watches Quilty's face while Humbert, sitting in the background, remains ignorant of his identity (which, incidentally, parallels the camera's independent pan away from Humbert to the picture of Quilty in Lolita's bedroom). Quilty dominates the frame while Humbert tries to maintain his composure despite a latent paranoia about policemen and his anticipation of incest with his "daughter," Lolita. Quilty fidgets with his glasses and speaks in nervous, broken phrases about how he wishes he had a "lovely, pretty little girl" and indirectly mocks Humbert's pretense of familial normality (one "normal guy" to another) by expressing a concern that their "accommodations" (read "bed") might not be comfortable enough; at one point, he ironically says that Humbert should have the "bridal suite." He surrealistically objectifies for the audience Humbert's internal disorders, and when he asks to have a look at the room so that he might use his influence with the hotel desk clerk, Humbert beats a hasty retreat to a sleeping Lolita and a battle with an intractable cot.

Humbert next confronts his sinister incubus in the form of Dr. Zempf, sitting in the dark of Beardsley ("to save you electricity," he tells Humbert). By now, Humbert's cultured and cool exterior shows signs of breaking up as he imagines sexual competition from nonexistent forces (the "Rexs" and "Roys" of Lolita's adolescence) and misperceives the true nature of Quilty's game. And while the audience could appreciate Quilty's earlier pranks as forms of poetic justice, it surely must feel an uneasiness about his Zempf impersonation. The game now takes on sinister and cruel tones, as Sellers twists his conception of Quilty toward that neo-Nazi monster who will roll out of the cavernous shadows of *Dr. Strangelove*. First as Zempf, and then as a voice on the telephone, Quilty cuts to a darkness within Humbert and forces him to experience the nightmare that lurks beneath his dream, the one facing him on the other side of the gameboard. Zempf's psychological profile of Lolita ("a sweet little child" who suffers from an "acute repression of the libido") denies Humbert's love for Lolita and ridicules his debasement. Zempf exaggerates Humbert's European pomposity through his psycho-babble and Germanic anality, his thick glasses and efficient row of pens protruding from a breast pocket. And Kubrick, as before, has Quilty performing for our benefit; there is an inside joke at "Dr. Hombart's" expense when Zempf offers Humbert a Drome cigarette (the poster in Lolita's bedroom) and maliciously tells him to "keep the pack." Humbert's final contacts with Quilty, before Lolita's escape from the hospital, are nightmarishly disembodied ones. Quilty's car follows him across the barren Southwest ("the designation of doom"), and as he contemplates a rear projection image through the window of his car, Humbert's daylight world begins to match his nocturnal one. Sick and obviously dying, Humbert drags himself out of bed in a darkly lit and ominous motel room to answer the call of a telephonic nightmare: Quilty refuses to identify this impersonation by name ("my name is really obscure and unremarkable") and more successfully than before exposes Humbert's comic fear that policemen and faceless civil authorities have formed a legion of decency (Kubrick's gibe at the Catholic Legion of Decency?) against his quest for the dream of Lolita. Tragically, Humbert never sees the twofold truth Kubrick shows us: Quilty mirrors the perverse underside of that dream, and Lolita never embodies its romantic substance.

4 DR. STRANGELOVE

Kubrick had been preparing for a number of years to make a film like *Dr. Strangelove, or How I Learned to Stop Worrying and Love the Bomb* (1964). As part of his fascination with the aesthetic and moral implications of forms and plans, he began to read books during the 1950s on the subject of nuclear warfare and strategy, subscribed to *Aviation Week* and the *Bulletin of the Atomic Scientists*, and finally was struck by "people's virtually listless acquiescence in the possibility—in fact, the increasing probability—of nuclear war."[1] And in his films of the 1950s, he indirectly expressed this interest through film structures that thrived on the tensions between a human world of design and the unexpected intrusions of contingency. In many ways, *Dr. Strangelove* merely exaggerates and externalizes the satiric irony of *Paths of Glory* and expands the temporal complexities of *The Killing* toward more profound philosophic conclusions. As he had once decided

to move from the interiority of *Killer's Kiss* to the disparities of plan
and accident in *The Killing,* so Kubrick in the early 1960s moved from
the psychological focus of *Lolita* to the more generalized and mythopoeic expression of *Strangelove,* but not without incorporating the
comic lessons learned in adapting Nabokov's novel to film. Despite its
temporal and spatial limits (the film has a running time of 94 minutes
that closely approximates the fictional time it covers, and almost all the
action takes place in three confined settings), *Strangelove* is a much
more expansive and ambitious film than *Lolita.* It clearly advances beyond *Paths of Glory* in its development of complex ideas within a film
rhetoric that mixes a realism of detail with a surrealist visual and verbal
stylization; and, more than any of his previous films, it gave Kubrick
an opportunity to refine a film aesthetic that would, in the years to
come, increasingly blend satiric irony with cosmic speculation.

In Peter George's *Red Alert* (published in 1958 as a novel by "Peter
Bryant"), Kubrick found a novelistic source for his belief in the possibility of an accidental nuclear war. Moreover, *Red Alert* is written in
an explicit prose style reminiscent of the dramatic and thematic clarity
of White's *Clean Break* and Cobb's *Paths of Glory.*[2] Its tightly organized plot structure recalls White's manipulation of time, although it
moves along a more straightforward but equally relentless course;
George, like White, captures a sense of temporal urgency as his characters grapple with contingencies and barely avert an impending doom
(the novel was published in England as *Two Hours to Doom*). His use
of parallel and isolated settings—Sonora Air Force Base (Texas), the
B-52 bomber ("Alabama Angel"), and the War Room in the Pentagon—
is structurally comparable to Cobb's development of the conflicts between the intimate world of the trenches and a more distant military
hierarchy. And like both these novels, George's adopts a third-person
omniscience which intensifies the apocalyptic content through a docu-
mentary-like style of reportage. George makes every effort to impress
his reader with the very real possibility of nuclear war by accident
rather than design. He carefully delineates the technology of nuclear
politics and its complex tangle of procedures, communication, and security safeguards, as well as the presence of basic human elements that
turn this "fail-safe" system into a weapon of global destruction. He
carefully motivates General Quinten's decision to launch an unpro-
voked attack against Russia (General Quinten [Ripper in the film] is
dying of a terminal disease and sincerely believes in the Red menace).

The book, more than the film, shows how Quinten's nuclear paranoia has a rational basis in fact; Quinten, for instance, persuasively counters the objections of his rational and humane executive officer, Major Howard (Mandrake, in the film). George's novel is not particularly descriptive, except in its elaborate and convincing network of technical detail; he allows events in the novel to assert an empirical authority which confronts the reader with the promise of nuclear war. In the end, however, George backs off from this seemingly implacable logic and ends on a note of liberal/moral fortuity: The bomb the "Alabama Angel" drops does not fully detonate, and a very forceful and competent American President (an idealized Adlai Stevenson type) effects a rapid and hopeful detente with the Russian ambassador.

After working on a screenplay of *Red Alert* for about six weeks, with every intention of developing it into a serious film treatment, Kubrick found that comic ideas repeatedly intruded and altered his thinking on how to make a "truthful" film about this subject, a subject, he says, in which "the things you laugh at most are really the heart of the paradoxical postures that make a nuclear war possible." The most acclaimed "serious" nuclear war film before this time was Stanley Kramer's *On the Beach* (1959), which, in its Cold War liberal positions, thematically resembles George's *Red Alert* in ways that Kubrick's film never does. And, coincidentally, in the same year *Dr. Strangelove* came out, Sidney Lumet released *Fail Safe* (1964), a realistic but hopelessly ponderous depiction of the same thesis (with Henry Fonda as the President who is faced, like the President in *Red Alert*, with deciding whether to allow the Russians to retaliate in kind and without interference after an American bomber accidentally drops an H-bomb on a Soviet target). Both these films are highly dramatic and appropriately sober, but from Kubrick's perspective they would not necessarily be "truthful" or even "serious" renderings of the nuclear theme. Kubrick's comments about how he eventually gravitated toward the comic style of *Strangelove* not only support this point, but reveal a film imagination that strives for the widest possible scope:

> But after a month or so I began to realize that all the things I was throwing out were the things which were the most truthful. After all, what could be more absurd than the very idea of two mega-powers willing to wipe out all human life because of an accident, spiced up by political differences that will seem as meaningless to people in a hundred years from now as the theological conflicts of the Middle Ages appear to us today?[3]

Kubrick lining up a shot for *Dr. Strangelove*.

For Kubrick, the filmic expression of something "truthful" about a given subject requires, first, an aesthetic and philosophic detachment, and then an appropriate dramatic context and perspective to direct an audience toward new or unexpected discoveries. From what point of view, for instance, should nuclear destruction be considered? How can a film embody both its immediate (political and moral) and theoretical (historical and philosophic) implications? Kramer's and Lumet's films adopt approaches as limited as they are predictable: Nuclear war is a serious business, their films say, one that demands a naturalistic film treatment, with primary characters who impress the audience with their humanity and sense of responsibility; for, after all, it is a problem we all must share and for which we all must be held accountable. Like Dax amid the madness of *Paths of Glory*, films like *On the Beach* and

Fail Safe play it both earnest and safe: They would rather be on the "right" side of a morally complex issue than transform or unsettle an audience's perception by showing how such a problem, more often than not, originates from deep inside the structures of a social mythology and the paradoxes of human nature.

That Kubrick brought in comic novelist Terry Southern to help with the development of satiric ideas for *Strangelove* is not surprising.[4] Beginning with *Killer's Kiss*, Kubrick's films increasingly show signs of a satiric distance that, in part, opposes the humanity of their characters. Before *Lolita*, his interests were focused on temporal and spatial structures that enveloped the characters in a blanket of speculation and irony, even though he always gave them internal dimension. But in *Lolita*, his first "comic" film, Kubrick complicates a sympathetic identification with Humbert, Lolita, and Charlotte through satiric performances and a control of point of view which force the audience to see conspiratorial ironies at work which expose either a perverse or trivial underside to character. In Peter George's *Red Alert*, Kubrick works with a novel oriented toward plot and issue, where two primary questions dominate, one immediate and the other implied: Will the B-52 be stopped? How can a nuclear accident like the one depicted be prevented? George's characters, as a result, are not very interesting, except when they or their psychology become factors in either the main plot device or the thematic single-mindedness. What Kubrick does, in collaboration with George, Southern, and a fine cast, is redirect and expand the psychological/thematic emphasis. *Strangelove* is not only a highly satiric and exaggerated treatment of a madness that far too many people accept as "normal," but, unlike *Red Alert* or the other nuclear films of the period, it matches every plot suspense device with a set of ideas and speculations that reveal Kubrick's mythopoeic intentions. The film not only shows how a nuclear accident could happen (something which George's novel does just as well), but deals with its less visible causes and implications. Kubrick shows a more profound interest in origins, both psychological and philosophical, than does George's novel, which indicates that *Dr. Strangelove* more properly should be seen as a halfway point between *Paths of Glory* and *2001*.

By characterizing the subtext of *Strangelove* as "mythopoeic" and cosmic, I mean to separate its satiric ambitions from those conventionally associated with normative satire.[5] Kubrick's films never outline a model of individual or social behavior against which an audience can

measure and evaluate psychological aberrations. Like most traditional
satire, however, they do throw light into the spaces and cracks that
exist between illusion and reality, between the splendor of the chateau
and the chaos of the trenches; but for Kubrick, that area where design
and disorder intersect inhabits a large and inexplicable universe which
any definition of the "truthful" must also ponder. Kubrick's satire has
no immediate corrective or utilitarian purpose, unless its exploration
(both ironic and sympathetic) of a human tendency to create myths
and reinvent the universe through form and structure constitutes an
"arm against fantasy." Instead of resolving the opposition between
illusion and reality, Kubrick's films before *Strangelove* suggest an ever-
present paradox that involves three primary factors: namely, the existential but dynamic terrors of life experienced in time and in the self
(i.e., Johnny Clay's "what's the use?," the trenches of *Paths*, and Humbert's despair); the attraction of aesthetic form, which embodies a contrary progress away from time toward both an expressive release and
a deadly enclosure (i.e., Johnny's plan, the chateau, and Humbert's
dream of Lolita); and finally, the presence of a contingent universe
that quietly and almost invisibly presides over this cinematic world in
conflict and that in its vastness and duration both diminishes the efforts
of its fictional inhabitants and inspires the achievement of its actual
creator. If *Strangelove* continues Kubrick's indictment against humanity for preferring fantasy to reality, especially fantasy that may result
in the ultimate evil of self-genocide, then it also indicts itself, for the
film, too, is a fictional construct and, whether or not we succeed in
destroying our planet, who, in the twenty-first century or on some distant world, will care that one film or one book tried to signal an alarm?
All that a film aesthetic based on a recognition of contingency can do
is speculate and entertain both disparities and possibilities, and, in the
absence of a total belief system, be true to itself in the act of creation.

As in *Lolita,* Kubrick depends on both performance and dialogue
to carry, at least overtly, most of the satiric weight of *Dr. Strangelove.*
Almost without exception, his actors use exaggerated postures, facial
contortions, and idioms that externalize their respective characters into
recognizable comic types.[6] Slim Pickens (as Major "King" Kong), cast
against type as a B-52 bomber pilot, is enough in himself to inspire
laughter and incredulity, but after his first words when told about Wing
Attack Plan R ("I've been to one World's Fair, a picnic, and a rodeo,
and that's the stupidest thing I've ever heard over a pair of earphones"),

the film, along with his cowboy hat, redneck mentality, and the sounds of "When Johnny Comes Marching Home," accelerates a satiric style that grows more absurd and surrealistic as Kong's plane nears doomsday. George C. Scott develops an array of facial and postural gestures that define Turgidson as the blockheaded jingoist; he chomps down on his chewing gum like a cud, prowls around the War Room with the same grunting intensity he employs in the bedroom, and obscures nuclear war through a mixture of military euphemism and homespun verbosity (destroying the Russians becomes "catching them with their pants down" and causing the deaths of 20 million Americans "getting our hair mussed"). Sterling Hayden portrays the mad Ripper as the prototypical 1950s right-wing general eager to bomb the world back to the Stone Age in order to preserve the American Way of Life ("Better Dead than Red"); his absurd phallic cigar and machine-gun in a golf bag give comic tangibility to his babble about Communist infiltration and "precious bodily fluids." And Peter Sellers, in three brilliant impersonations, gives us a gamut of character types who collectively express humanity in the grip of an hilarious and deadly madness: President Merkin Muffley, the bald-headed and ineffectual man of reason in a world of madness, a Stevensonian egghead satirized, who worries as much about decorum as he does annihilation ("I have never heard of such behavior in the War Room"); Group Captain Lionel Mandrake, whose civilized English reserve provides a foil to Ripper's impenetrable American obsessiveness; and Dr. Strangelove, the archetypal mad scientist with a mechanical arm that assumes an independent life in its repeated salutes of "sieg heil," whose madness becomes animated only when the prospect of death and darkness looms near.

And Kubrick gives his audience a great deal to consider, more than in any of his earlier films, while it is being assaulted with the ambiguities of a visual style that lends an unfamiliarity to the real and an empirical life to the surreal. During the early 1960s, by his own admission, he wanted to develop such a style, one barely glimpsed in the films before *Lolita*:

> The real image doesn't cut the mustard, doesn't transcend. I'm now interested in taking a story, fantastic and improbable, and trying to get to the bottom of it, to make it seem not only real, but inevitable.[7]

In the three settings of *Strangelove*, inner and outer worlds mingle so that each not only distorts but comments on the other. In the B-52,

The machine in space, traveling toward Doomsday.

once the "go" code is received, fantasy should take a backseat to both the hard reality of the machine and Kubrick's *cinéma-vérité* camera, which, in a cramped atmosphere illuminated only by source lighting, works close-in through quick zooms and jerky motions to expose the intricacy of instrument panels and attack profiles. Yet the satiric exaggeration of Kong's character turns realism toward the fantastic, as Kong acts out a private drama in an Old West showdown with civilization, while his crew, drawn in more naturalistic terms, suppress forces from within as they work in harmony with the plane. Without Kong, the scenes inside the B-52 would assert the kind of technical and mechanical authenticity found in *The Killing* and, incidentally, Peter George's *Red Alert* (characters in both join to execute a plan); but in *Dr. Strangelove*, Kubrick externalizes the inner/outer conflicts of the earlier film and shows how a plan or machine can be an extension of an instinct or obsession rather than an agent that directs such dissonance underground. The earlier film stresses the dramatic ironies between, for instance, the presence of George Peatty's sexual jealousy and the rigors of Johnny Clay's plan, while *Dr. Strangelove* develops the mythopoeic paradoxes of a Ripper/Kong pathology finding expression through the orderliness of Plan R.

In Ripper's office, Kubrick allows the audience to see and consider everything within the frame through long camera takes and a depth of field. From a distance, the wide-angle lens pulls this enclosure into sharp focus and exaggerates its low ceiling and horizontal geometry. It reveals all the details that make up Ripper's world and, as a parallel to Mandrake's role within this setting, challenges the audience to decode its meaning. While almost everything we see has a vivid but surreal clarity, what we hear transforms that imagery into the logic of a nightmare. In the early scenes, Kubrick alternates between medium shots that place Ripper within the symmetry of balanced compositions and low-angle close-ups that blur out surrounding space and visually reinforce the madman's verbal muddle. Later, spatial order is demolished by both the machine-gun fire from outside and Ripper's rapid mental distintegration from inside. In each case, Kubrick uses the arrangements of setting and object in both literal and expressive ways. He constantly reminds us of the existence of a material world, that it is concrete and real, and that when its inanimate substance becomes confined or organized, and in the process removed from a place in contingent space, it can assume the properties of a dream or nightmare. All the things that envelop and define Ripper—i.e., the "Peace Is Our Profession" slogan behind his desk, a tool/weapon for clipping cigars, his guns and model airplanes—in another film might play only a functional role in a credible visual landscape. But here and elsewhere, Kubrick reaffirms his talent for taking everyday minutiae and, through context, charging it with a conceptual and surrealist energy; he leaves the audience no choice but to explore the imagery of *Dr. Strangelove* by undermining their faith in the inviolability of surface reality. As a result, the viewer's position in relation to this film is like that of those soldiers who are defending Burpleson and Ripper's madness from an advancing "enemy" (American troops). The defenders, who are themselves part of the film's most documentarylike sequence (shot in the grainy telephoto realism of Orthochrome), like the viewer, temporarily question the evidence of their senses: "You sure gotta hand it to those Commies, those trucks sure look like the real thing."

Throughout the film, Kubrick characterizes the War Room as a

place where civilization appears to make a last stand against an en-
croaching barbarism, only to reveal that the attention given in the War
Room to verbal and formal aesthetics springs from a source not far
from the deadly logic of Plan R and Dr. Strangelove's devotion to the
perfection of the Doomsday Machine. Everywhere one looks there is a
visual geometry: The room itself is triangular (designed by Ken Adam,
who has worked on several James Bond films), with the Big Board and
its square displays tilting above a world of circles (the large conference
table with its ring of lights overhead) on a metallic black floor. Kubrick brings the visual style of Burpleson into this more formal realm
when he blends incredibly sharp and deep wide-angle imagery with
close-ups in which the edges of the frame lose resolution and adum-
brate an ever-present mental disorder. From a high angle, the camera
reveals a world encircled by darkness but internally organized, suggesting from the beginning that it already inhabits a mine shaft.
Strangelove, in particular, is isolated in close-up and medium shots,
enveloped by darkness and patterns of light from the Big Board; at
first, he is separated from the rational processes of the table, only to be
sought out like an alter ego once madness breaks through the illusions
of formal order. When he cuts to shots around the table, Kubrick shows
another kind of paradox, both in the collapse of language as tool and
in the tangible objects that exist within the formal patterns admired
from a distance. We see the lettering on Turgidson's top-secret note-
books, which coexist with his gum wrappers: one says "World Targets
in Megadeaths" and the other "War Alert Actions Book." We notice
the careful place settings on the table (pitchers of water, recessed
phones) which are duplicated in a circle like reflections in a trick
mirror; and, finally, we notice how ordinary human distinctions become
blurred through either a sense of uniformity (the characters wear suits
or military uniforms, and with few exceptions maintain placid expressions) or the exaggerated and dehumanized postures of a Turgidson or
Strangelove. In such ways does Kubrick visually link the surrealism of
the War Room with both the B-52's steady course toward death and
Ripper's mad asylum.

   Strangelove, more than anything else, demonstrates Kubrick's genius
for translating ideas into temporal and visual film structures. And because the film defines character satirically, thereby subordinating psychology to concept, Kubrick is free to play with the forms of his me-

dium in ways that earlier scripts made impossible. Even the humor relies almost as much upon the use of narrative and visual contexts as it does language, contexts that, according to Kubrick, place everyday human behavior within nightmarish situations:

> like the Russian premier on the hot line who forgets the telephone number of the general staff headquarters and suggests the American President try Omsk information, or the reluctance of a U.S. officer to let a British officer smash open a Coca-Cola machine for change to phone the President about a crisis on the SAC base because of his conditioning about the sanctity of private property.[8]

Such a strategy recalls the way *Lolita* reveals a surreality and absurdity beneath the bland surfaces of normality, only here the stakes are higher (the ultimate endgame) and the cinematic contexts more expressive. In one reflexive moment, for instance, Kubrick seemingly parodies the sexual fantasies and bathrooms of *Lolita*: Buck Turgidson is introduced through his "private" secretary and aging nymphet Miss Scott (Tracy Reed), wearing a bikini and sunglasses, whom we first see sunbathing, not in a garden, but under a heat lamp on a hotel bed in her best centerfold pose; Buck, in the bathroom off-camera, grunts and complains as she simultaneously talks to him and another general on the telephone. Besides being an indication that the film's libido, as well as Buck's, has escaped from the closet of *Lolita*, this scene illustrates Kubrick's definition of *Dr. Strangelove*'s comic method:

> Confront a man in his office with a nuclear alarm, and you have a documentary. If the news reaches him in his living room, you have a drama. If it catches him in the lavatory, the result is comedy.[9]

The sexual content of *Dr. Strangelove*, what Anthony Macklin labels a "sex allegory" and George Linden calls an example of "erotic displacement," represents the most discernible and widely discussed mythopoeic element in the film.[10] The progress of the film from "foreplay to explosion," to quote Macklin, is clearly and almost too patly connected with the satiric characterizations. Consider the following:

1. General Jack D. Ripper is named after history's most notorious sex offender. He disguises his loss of potency by raving about fluoridation as a Communist plot to poison our vital bodily fluids; he launches a phallic retaliation against the Russians (in the shapes of B-52 bombers, a jutting cigar, which, before his death, has burned down to a stub,

and the machine-gun that he fires at his own countrymen); and finally, defeated and spent, he takes a pearl-handled pistol into the bathroom and kills himself rather than endure the "torture" his madness envisions as his fate. Later, Colonel "Bat" Guano (Keenan Wynn) will look at Mandrake's "suit" and peg him as a "prevert" (suggesting that he confuses transvestism with foreign military service) rather than a man trying to save the world.

2. Aboard the B-52 bomber, Major "King" Kong is introduced reading *Playboy* and admiring the film's parodic Fay Wray, namely Miss Scott, who is Playmate of the Month. Her pose in the centerfold photo is identical to her pose in Buck's hotel suite, only here a magazine (*Foreign Affairs*) rather than a bikini covers her backside. Inside the door of the safe where packets outlining the procedures of Plan R are stored, we see girlie pictures; we then discover that the name of the primary bombing target is "Laputa" (Spanish for "whore") and hear Kong detail over the intercom the contents of a survival kit, which includes silk stockings, lipsticks, and prophylactics ("shoot, a fellah could have a pretty good weekend in Vegas with all that stuff"). Later, Kong goes into the bomb bay, where sexually suggestive salutations adorn the tail-end of two H-bombs—"Hi There" and "Dear John" (Peter George's novelization of the screenplay names the second bomb "Lolita"). He straddles one as he would a bronco, becoming an extension

of a gargantuan phallus moving toward the ultimate score, a doomsday orgasm.

3. When we first meet General "Buck" Turgidson, whose name decodes as "swollen male animal who is the son of a swollen male animal," he is on the toilet and in the company of his playmate of the month, and as he goes off to either save or help destroy the world, he tells her in the language of the occasion to start her "countdown" and be ready to "blast-off" when he returns (in George's novelization, Buck instead talks about "reentry"); and in the War Room, just before the final explosions, Turgidson's jaw hangs open in stupefaction as he envisions the demise of monogyny in Strangelove's brave new world of mine-shaft cohabitation.

4. In the War Room, the presiding figure is President Merkin Muffley (whose name Anthony Macklin has identified as a reference to the vulva, and even though both "merkin" and "muffley" suggest a "covering," he is bald, which makes his head look like a phallus.) His prissy and effeminate manner stands between Turgidson's overly erect postures and Strangelove's crippled impotence. Muffley talks on the hotline to the Russian Premier, named "Kissoff," who is both drunk and with his mistress.

5. Finally, through the title character, Dr. Strangelove, whose real name is "Merkwuerdigichliebe" (which decodes as "cherished fate"), the film directs this sexual satire into thematic implications that go beyond the lighter antics of Turgidson and Kong; Dr. Strangelove brings Ripper's madness into the deliberations of the War Room and links it to man's intercourse with the machine and a sinister love affair with death.

But while the narrative logic of *Dr. Strangelove* may indicate that the world goes up in mushroom clouds because of one general's madness or as a result of sexual malfunctions and transference, its aesthetic and thematic texture says that there is more, that, in fact, its "sex allegory" is only one of several conceptual levels that are interconnected and hold this fictional world together. Everywhere you look in the film, for instance, there are hints of primal and infantile regression, of a symbolic descent in time, from Kong's Neanderthal Man to Turgidson's primitivism (he slaps his hairy belly while standing over his mistress, and in the War Room he repeatedly assumes apelike stances) and Ripper's crawling on all fours as his mind degenerates to the same level as those juvenile scrawls on the notepad that contains the recall code. The opening images of the film, a B-52 bomber being refueled in midair,

suggest both copulation and a mother giving suck, while on the soundtrack we hear "Try a Little Tenderness" and on the screen read pencil-
line credits that resemble a child's graffiti. Kong's bomber assumes the
characteristics of a womb (once he tries to sleep and let the plane fly
itself) from which he is dropped screaming and bellowing into a cata-
clysmic world. Ripper's base is called *Burp*leson and houses a character
who yearns for a world of neoplatonic "purity" and "essence" where
ice cream cannot be contaminated and who is humored by a nervously
smiling Mandrake. In the War Room, Turgidson, who is forever chewing gum like a masturbatory adolescent, clutches his top-secret note-
books to his chest and whines about security when informed that
Russian Ambassador de Sadesky (the name alludes to the Marquis de
Sade; the character is played by Peter Bull) will be allowed to see the
"Big Board." In every setting, language breaks down and characters
revert to either the antiquated clichés of a primitive value system (Ripper's "the Redcoats are coming," Kong's "*nuculur* combat, toe to toe
with the Rooskies," and Turgidson's "prayer" of deliverance before the
Big Board) or the conversation of children (Muffley's baby talk with
Kissoff and Turgidson's with Miss Scott). And in the end, Dr. Strangelove becomes both sexually erect and child-like as he learns to walk in
preparation for a descent into the mine shafts.

Kubrick gives food and eating a primal importance almost equal to
sex. The first scene in the B-52 shows several members of the crew
eating, and when Lieutenant Goldberg (Paul Tamarin), the radio operator, reports to Kong that he received the code for Wing Attack Plan
R, his words mingle with a sandwich he is stuffing into his mouth. At
Burpleson, Ripper never eats, no doubt so as to maintain a purity of
bodily fluids, and he drinks only branch water and grain alcohol; but
when Mandrake is collecting a transistor radio from inside a computer
printout machine, we see that someone has left behind an uneaten sandwich and two pieces of fruit (an apple for the Garden, a banana for
the Jungle, and the Machine). In Turgidson's hotel suite, through a
mirror reflection behind Miss Scott, a table of dirty dishes is prominent,
as this long camera take visually decodes as the recurring cycle of
food, sex, a lavatory purgation, and sleep. And in the War Room there
is a large buffet of gourmet food and pastries displaying the ritualization of a primal function and an absurd attention to pre-apocalypse
formality. (Kubrick shot a custard-pie fight, which originally was to
conclude the film, but he deleted it before final release.) At the very

end, when all is lost, the President sits next to the buffet, drink in hand, and calmly considers Strangelove's mine-shaft computations, which include, among other things, greenhouses for plant life (food and oxygen) and breeding places for animals to be *slaughtered* (with particular emphasis on that last word). As civilization descends into a new Dark Age, another survival kit provides for the nourishment of the body as well as the libido.

Dr. Strangelove recalls *The Killing* in the way its plot and settings are geared to the clock. The narrator's soothing, documentary voice in a prologue alerts us to the possibility of time's end in his comment that "ominous rumors" continue to circulate about the "ultimate weapon, a Doomsday device"; a few minutes later (in his final intrusion), he tells us that the SAC bombers are "two hours from their targets deep inside Russia"; the "fail-safe" system itself—defined by manuals, decoding books, and attack profiles—represents the human obsession with the mechanics of time and the hope of anticipating both the designs of a known enemy and the unseen courses of fate; once triggered, the causal logic of the fail-safe system meshes with the doomsday machine to complete a timetable as inexorable as a mathematical formula. In the War Room, attempts are made to cancel out this clockwork doom through the improvisation of counterplans that, ironically, try to circle back and frustrate what was originally envisioned as the ultimate contingency plan (Plan R was invented in case all other nuclear safeguards failed). While Muffley conspires with the Russian premier to foil both the Doomsday Machine and a plan devised to destroy Russia, Mandrake decodes Ripper's mad doodles; however, a third factor, chance, intervenes and not only knocks out Kong's receiver, but, even worse, causes a fuel loss that directs the B-52 to the "nearest target opportunity," where there are no Soviet missiles waiting to intercept and destroy (chance is not nearly so inventive in George's novel). Meanwhile, in the War Room, where the comic inertia of "rational" deliberation makes a contrast with the B-52's mechanical and efficient pace, Kubrick shows a world that has reduced the vastness of space to the smaller dimensions of human time: A huge circular table and halo of fluorescent light visually embody the processes of reason, while overhead the Big Board arranges space into finite expressions of time (its lights and geometric shapes outline the "fail-safe" system on a "map" of the world); and below, in patterns of circularity, we see a human world moving toward the temporal mockery in the final scene, in which we hear Vera Lynn singing "We'll Meet Again" while the doomsday shroud forms a halo around the film's last image: the billowing cloud of the hydrogen bomb and the extinction of life.

Within the involutions of this temporal/spatial paradox—of plans and counterplans, a cinematic world circling back on itself in both time and space—Kubrick employs straight cuts to go back and forth between settings and to intensify a narrative pace that confers an omnipotence on the rule of time. The film shows that once the exercise of free will and choice becomes overly formalized in the machinery of "fail-safe" systems and "human reliability" tests, options and possibilities shrink as characters fall victim to the ceaselessly creative and unpredictable intervention of either psychology or chance. Ripper's telephonic communication to the War Room, the one read aloud by Turgidson, not only captures his comic madness ("This man is obviously a psychotic," says the President) but verbalizes a temporal condition that leaves little room for human choice. Ripper dictates a doomsday morality when he institutes Plan R and tells them that "my boys will give you the best kind of start, 1400 megatons worth, and you sure as hell won't stop them now." Turgidson then talks about the "moment of truth" and the necessity of choosing "between two admittedly regrettable but nevertheless distinguishable post-war environments; one, where you got twenty million people killed and, the other, where you got one hundred fifty million people killed." The President, who always believes "there are still alternatives," eventually faces both the logic of Buck's argument and a world caught between a Doomsday Auschwitz and Mine Shaft Dachau.

Consider, finally, these examples of simultaneity and juxtaposition, which link the film's temporal rhetoric to the ethics of endgame:

1. While Kong is reassuring his men that he shares their "strong personal feelings about *nuculur* combat" and promising them "promotions and citations" once their mission is over, Turgidson is likewise assuming the existence of a future of "normal" human activity when he tells Miss Scott to keep her sexual clock ticking until he returns.

2. As Kong is reading the lock-step procedures for Plan R aloud to his men, Mandrake becomes a prisoner in Ripper's office and listens to a recitation of how that plan will determine life and death on a global scale ("while we are chatting so enjoyably," says Ripper).

3. As de Sadesky and Strangelove explain the purpose of the Doomsday Machine as ultimate deterrent, one designed as an "irrevocable decision-making process that rules out human meddling," Ripper details for Mandrake his paranoid delusion that fluoridation represents an insidious and invisible evil ("on no account will a Commie drink water").

4. Once Kong's CRM 114 is destroyed, he and his crew have no choice but to drop the bomb, which they do at the same moment that Dr. Strangelove is reassuring the President that computers are better equipped than mere mortals to make the difficult decision of who goes into the mine shafts and who stays behind to breathe the deadly Cobalt Thorium G.

Paradoxically, in a film that carefully details a twentieth-century descent of man, the machine, for the first time, plays a prominent role in Kubrick's work. *Strangelove* predates *2001* and remains his darkest vision of what an emerging "machinarchy" could mean to humanity and human civilization. The presence of machine technology dominates the visual landscape in each of the film's three settings and ironically complements a human world which symbolically moves back in time almost as fast as Kong's B-52 flies through space. In some respects, this machine environment compares with the merger of World War I barbarity and eighteenth-century neoclassicism in *Paths of Glory*: It provides both a context for evaluating the human madness within the

film and a perspective on where that madness comes from and where
it may be going. Each setting becomes a dark cave or womb, where
characters are surrounded by machines that once served as tools of
communication and progress, but now function as weapons of destruction and descent. Ripper cuts off all telephonic communication with the
outside world and, closing the venetian blinds in his office, wraps himself in the artificial illumination of fluorescent lights and the psychic
darkness of a primitive mentality. The antique guns mounted on the
wall, the model airplanes on his desk, an aerial photo of Burpleson,
and photographs of bombers frozen in space define his alignment with
the technology of death. One of his last contacts with the outside is
the cryptic FGB code, which mechanically clicks into the B-52's CRM
114 and turns an instrument for receiving messages into one that cuts
off all communication (except with Ripper's mad OPE code prefix),
directing the plane on a predetermined course toward death. Our first
sight of Mandrake is as a figure obscured by a large printout sheet, in
a computer room where machines outnumber people; he then sits down
at a console and talks with Ripper on the phone (it is the only phone
at Burpleson that is still working, except for the pay phone that he
will use in the Coca-Cola machine scene), as computer tapes move
back and forth in circles behind him. Kong's B-52 becomes a machine
that not only seems capable of flying itself, but in the intricacy and
fineness of its craftsmanship (a set based on a photograph from a British aviation magazine) lends a grossness to the human beings who give
it direction. This machine which moves forward through space (horizontally, not vertically) and propels its inhabitants backward in time
cannot be recalled because a Russian missile, characterized as a blip
on a circular radar scanner, destroys the CRM 114 at almost the same
moment that Guano reluctantly shoots off the lock of the Coca-Cola
machine so Mandrake can get the change to use the pay phone to communicate the recall code to the President. Kubrick had a huge triangular set especially built for the War Room. It is both realistic (it resembles a similar complex in NORAD's Cheyenne Mountain at Colorado
Springs) and highly expressive. In it the Big Board with its sophisticated machine language and brightly lit, complex displays towers over
the increasingly trivial and primitive verbal intercourse below. Here,
too, Kubrick shows a world cut off from reason and outside contacts,
both actual and imaginative, cut off, indeed, from everything that
might enable it to see the ironic truth of machine logic, which is that

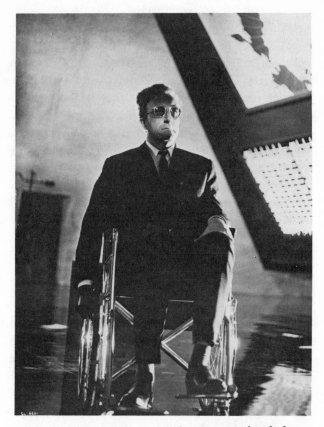

The Monster patiently waits in the darkness.

the very technology which assists the human dream of order and duration—nuclear deterrents, "fail-safe" systems, and a "contingency" plan like Plan R—is based on a principle of mechanical predictability that must, if it is to have purpose, work itself out: Once committed to their course, and no longer subject to rational intervention, Kong and his plane find a target and not only fulfill their mission but the Doomsday Machine's as well.

But Kubrick implies that this merger of madness and machine originates as much in a human passion for beauty as it does in the primal darkness of the Id. The first image of the film, from high above the clouds over the Zhokhov Islands, shows us the pure beauty of space from the machine's (or God's) vantage point, even though, paradoxically, it is linked to the "ultimate weapon" and the regressions of time both here and in its resemblance to the doomsday imagery of the ending. Throughout, Kubrick uses the machine to embody not only an efficiency (a temporal value) lacking in the psychological and political worlds of the film but a sense of harmony (a spatial value) as well: the imagery behind the credits of planes mating in midair may prepare for sexual themes to come, but it also literalizes a principle of conjunction that repeatedly eludes the timebound characters. In those opening images, Kubrick reminds us that in space harmony and conjunction are functional requirements, not merely formal adornments of civilization or abstract goals of artistic expression. In *Dr. Strangelove*, however, the machine assists a descent into time rather than an ascent into space, one where the perfection of its logic and beauty of its form paradoxically objectify a human retreat into fantasy and death. It stimulates Ripper's desire to play God and turn the clock back to a world of purity and the stasis of death. It creates the illusion in the War Room that mini-universes can be created and insulated from existential truths (i.e., death no longer is even real) outside computerized gameboards. And finally, Sellers's performance as Strangelove provides Kubrick with both a human form and marvellous conceit for the futuristic tool-as-primitive weapon: in his love of the Doomsday Machine's invulnerability to human interference and his perversion of scientific discourse (he refers to future survivors as a "nucleus of human specimens"), in his means of locomotion (wheelchair) and mode of animation (a mechanical arm that turns against him), and in his doomsday "rebirth" as the New Man who will lead the chosen people into darkness.

5 2001 A SPACE ODYSSEY

None of the available evidence regarding the conceptual and technical beginnings of Kubrick's next film indicates that he fully anticipated the enormity of its scope and impact. Now, almost two decades after its initial inception, *2001: A Space Odyssey* (1968) stands not only as one of his most important and controversial films, but as a landmark work in the history of cinema. Yet it was not suddenly born full-grown like Athena from Zeus' skull: what started in 1964 as a harmless and intriguing speculation about what might happen if contact was made between human beings and an extraterrestrial intelligence evolved into a creative and logistical leviathan that eventually took years to complete, involved hundreds of people and an incalculable number of details, consumed hundreds of thousands of man-hours and millions of dollars, and succeeded primarily because of the indelible stamp of one man's creative film sense.[1] Like *Dr. Strangelove*, this film began as an embryonic idea, which in the process of creation grew and expanded itself well beyond the explanatory boundaries outlined by Kubrick himself:

> Man must strive to gain mastery over himself as well as over his machines. Somebody has said that man is the missing link between primi-

tive apes and civilized human beings. You might say that that idea is
inherent in *2001*. We are semicivilized, capable of cooperation and
affection, but needing some sort of transfiguration into a higher form
of life. Since the means to obliterate life on Earth exists, it will take
more than just careful planning and reasonable cooperation to avoid
some eventual catastrophe. The problem exists, and the problem is
essentially a moral and spiritual one.[2]

Whether one reads Jerome Agel's *The Making of 2001* (1970) or Arthur C. Clarke's account of how the script developed from short story
to novelized screenplay (in *The Lost Worlds of 2001*, 1972), or considers the technical exposition of experts like Douglas Trumbull (a
supervisor of special effects) and Kubrick's own elaborate commentary
in countless interviews, one cannot help but be awed by the incredible
achievement of *2001*.[3] But awe should not be confused with understanding, and for that one must turn, first, to Kubrick's cinematic past
and consider how it is as much a part of *2001*'s evolution as any of the
published accounts detailing the various stages of its production.

As early as *Paths of Glory*, Kubrick had tried to give visual coherence to a philosophic conflict between a closed world of time and intimations of an open world of space. He used the ambiance of the chateau to embody a "higher" perspective from which to view the circular
and horizontal courses of a world moving toward political and moral
extinction. He suggested to his audience that outside the closed systems
and formal compositions of *Paths* there exists a world so vast and mysterious that even the film maker must acknowledge it as a creation
greater than his own. In such ways does Kubrick imply rather than
fully dramatize a belief in the possibility of an expansion and even
transformation of human consciousness. While *Paths* places its audience
in the middle of a paradox between irony (execution) and hope (the
German girl's song), *Strangelove* forces it to contemplate the *reductio
ad absurdum* of man's infatuation with mechanical perfection at the
expense of life itself. Within such a context, *2001* could be considered
as the philosophic double of *Dr. Strangelove*, as a Kubrickian mirror
that reflects a positive harmony of form and substance rather than a
madness in the disguise of beauty. During the twenty-one months
(April 1964–January 1966) in which they worked on the script, Kubrick
repeatedly channeled his and Clarke's thinking toward an overall conception that transforms irony into wonder and magic. Originally,
Clarke conceived of the project as an extension of Kubrick's previous

film (jokingly titled "Son of Strangelove") and intended to emphasize terrestrial themes in which nuclear bombs orbited the Earth only to be detonated by the Star-Child in an act of cosmic purification (a conclusion which remains intact in Clarke's novel), but Kubrick steered the film version away from the Swiftian satire of *Dr. Strangelove* toward an emphasis on mythic journeys and transformations (the Homeric title was Kubrick's idea and replaced the original one of *Journey to the Stars*); and just before final release, he removed both a ten-minute prologue of scientific "background" material and the explanatory narration in "The Dawn of Man" sequence, thereby completing his ultimate goal of turning *2001* into a "mythological documentary" rather than a more conventional blend of science-fact and film-fiction in which the fantastic is explained and rationalized.*

Before creating the evocative visual structures of *2001*, however, Kubrick again turned to what he considers the objectifying powers of the word. By this point in his career, Kubrick's success in developing a cinematic organization of images and sounds can be measured in part by how well a fully novelized and explicit script fills out the essential temporal outlines of story and character. Beginning with *2001*, his output diminished to an average of one film for every four years, while he increased the time allotted for working out the organization and conception of the script as well as the usual pre-production details. Two reasons why *2001* took so long to complete are its epic scope and the necessity of creating from a ten-page short story (Clarke's "The Sentinel") a full novelistic treatment. Significantly, Kubrick and Clarke spent as much time on the screenplay as Kubrick and a battery of technical advisors took to create the 205 special-effect process shots required by the futuristic landscapes of *2001*. The shooting schedule began in December 1965, even as Clarke continued to struggle with alternative endings for the screenplay. More than two years later, in April of 1968, Kubrick released the film; Clarke's novel, published in the summer of 1968, is an extremely lucid version of the film's story

---

* Here is how Kubrick compares the film and novel versions of *2001*: "The novel, for example, attempts to explain things much more explicitly than the film does, which is inevitable in a verbal medium. The novel came about after we did a 130-page prose treatment of the film at the very out-set. This initial treatment was subsequently changed in the screenplay, and the screenplay in turn was altered during the making of the film. But Arthur took all the existing material, plus an impression of some of the rushes, and wrote the novel. As a result, there's a difference between the novel and the film" (Gelmis, *The Film Director as Superstar*, p. 308).

and an exposition of some of its more overt themes.[4] But what is more important for our purposes is its great value as a source for understanding some of the cinematic intentions that took shape in Kubrick's mind between 1965 and 1968, long after Clarke had completed his task and gone home to Ceylon.

Between them, Clarke's "The Sentinel" (1950) and his novel (*2001: A Space Odyssey*) provide further evidence of how Kubrick works as a film maker; they especially illuminate an aesthetic that develops a conceptual complexity through a masterly manipulation of the inherent conflict between the temporal rhetoric of a film (i.e., plot, character, narration) and its spatial/musical rhetoric. Basically, it is a conflict between the causal logic of linear conventions (where the world is organized into straight lines and rationalized forms) and the associative logic of a creative interiority (where the world is assembled into parallel planes and imaginative shapes): The first is scientific and external, like Johnny Clay's robbery plan and *Strangelove*'s "fail-safe" systems; the other is dreamy and internal, like Humbert's vision of Lolita or the nightmare surrealism of the War Room. As we have seen, Kubrick likes to turn his audience's expectations upside down by challenging the authority of the "real" and elevating in importance intimations of less visible worlds more resistant to easy categorization. He especially must have been struck by two passages in "The Sentinel" that describe the meaning of the alien moon-machine (a pyramid, not a rectangular monolith) and speculate about its ancient creators:

> The mystery haunts us all the more now that the other planets have been reached and we know that only Earth has ever been the home of intelligent life in our Universe. . . . It was set there upon its mountain before life had emerged from the seas of Earth.

> Think of such civilizations, far back in time against the fading afterglow of Creation, masters of a universe so young that life as yet had come only to a handful of worlds. Theirs would have been a loneliness of gods looking across infinity and finding none to share their thoughts.

Throughout the novel, Clarke combines these evocations of exploration and wandering amid the lonely expanses of space with an elaborate substructure of explanatory material, which subordinates the idea of "mystery" to the speculations of science. The film, by contrast, is more open-ended than Clarke's novel, perhaps because Kubrick realized that mystery, whether futuristic or local, becomes trivialized on the screen once it assumes a clear and definable shape; as a result, his *2001* relies less on narrative background than does the novel and more on the free play of images and ideas.

While Clarke builds a series of clear connections between the six parts of his novel, Kubrick takes a more audacious course. The film compresses the action of the novel, omitting expository scenes and narration, and creating, in effect, a series of ellipses. The audience must fill in the gaps through a combination of visual attentiveness and subliminal penetration. An obvious example of this method is the famous match cut between bone and satellite, which spans four million years of film time. Clarke concludes his first section ("Primeval Night") with a chapter that briefly outlines the "ascent of man" and his tools following the alien visitation, and only then does he move on to the year 2001 and Dr. Heywood Floyd's trip to the Moon (titled "TMA-1," for Tycho Magnetic Anomaly-1, identifying the monolith and the moon crater where it is found). Kubrick does not title this part of his film, and through the visual association of Pleistocene bone and twenty-first century space hardware, he initiates an important doubling pattern in *2001* that has no source in Clarke. The novel maintains its linear and connective structure when it moves from the moon excavation scene to the Jupiter mission. In a chapter called "The Listeners" at the end of part two, Clarke explains how signals from the monolith are picked up by space monitors on the dark side of Mars; then he goes to part three ("Between Planets") and the journey of the spaceship *Discovery* on a line toward Saturn and the receiving end of those signals.[5] Kubrick, by contrast, cuts from the piercing sounds coming from the monolith and a conjunctive image of monolith, Earth, and Sun to a title on a black screen that identifies part three of his *2001* as "Jupiter Mission: 18 Months Later." As before, he leaps over time into space (the darkness behind the titles, into which *Discovery* moves from screen left) and, in an image of conjunction reminiscent of "The Dawn of Man," continues to build an associative rather than strictly logical visual structure. The film does not "explain" the purpose of the monolith or the mission to Jupiter until the end of part three, just after Bowman performs a lobotomy on HAL's Logic Memory Center; in this way, Kubrick enlarges the role of the monolith and its value as object and symbol far beyond the role it plays in the novel, where it is a teaching device and a cosmic burglar alarm. When he goes to the fourth and last part of the film ("Jupiter and Beyond the Infinite"), Kubrick uses the same kind of abrupt transition that he used between parts two and three: He shows Bowman suspended in the space inside HAL's brain room, watching a small screen and listening to Floyd's "explanation" for the mission and TMA-1, which, Floyd ultimately admits, remains a a "total mystery"; the film then cuts to the blackness of space both behind the titles and in a shot that precedes the camera's downward tilt to reveal yet another conjunction, this one between Jupiter, its moons, and a huge monolith in orbit; while, as before, we hear the sounds of György Ligeti's unearthly music. Finally, when Kubrick moves Bowman out of an eighteenth-century enclosure (what he calls a "hospital room") at the end of the film, he repeats the music from Richard Strauss's *Thus Spoke Zarathustra*—associated earlier with planetary conjunction, the monolith, and an important evolutionary moment— and pushes the camera through the blackness of the monolith and back into space as we witness the Star-Child's journey toward Earth. In ways that remind us of both *Paths of Glory* and *Dr. Strangelove*, the film turns the familiar (in this case, the room) into the surreal and transports the viewer into a world where the ordered memories of time oppose the mysteries of contingent space.

Kubrick internally organizes *2001* in ways which likewise combine a minimum of explanatory clarity with a maximum of visual ambiguity. Clarke's third-person narration, for example, clearly defines the life cycle of a near extinct tribe of ape-men on an African savannah and how Moon-Watcher, the one hominid with a spark of humanized intelligence, senses the significance of the monolith's lessons. Clarke tells the reader what this moment means and provides a cosmic perspective from which to evaluate its importance to following chapters. Kubrick, on the other hand, both plays a malicious joke on his audience and challenges it to develop more perceptive film viewing habits. On one level, he makes the monolith as much a mystery for us as it is for the ape-men, unless we perceive an almost subliminal connection, that of the film's opening image of conjunction (Moon, Earth, Sun), significantly accompanied by the Strauss, and seen from the Moon, with the longest-distanced reverse angle in the history of cinema, the one that looks from the base of the monolith up to show the Sun and a partially eclipsed Moon seen from the Earth. While Kubrick directs his audience toward a visual rather than verbal definition of the film's complex structure, Clarke works in a medium that requires that even the notion of mystery be circumscribed within a system of temporal and verbal logic.

In the novel, for instance, the monolith "means" several things (otherworldly machine, teaching device, cosmic alarm, and gateway to a universe of "pure energy"), while in Kubrick's film its value is defined by its shape (rectangular), its color (black), and the sound of Ligeti's monolith music, all of which associatively blend with other shapes, colors, and sounds to make a visual and aural symphony in space. As an element in Kubrick's overt narrative, the monolith has the same "meanings" it does in Clarke's novel, while in the context of alternating and expanding visual structures, it becomes an otherworldly version of such artifacts and extensions as bone, fountain pen, satellite, spaceship, computer, eighteenth-century room, and crystal glass.

These narrative and visual ambiguities in *2001* would seem to have even less precedent in Kubrick's earlier work than in Clarke's novel, although certain revealing comparisons can be made. With the exception of *Lolita*, the films before *2001* are restricted in both time and place. *Fear and Desire* develops a single action of about twenty-four hours in one setting (forest); *Killer's Kiss* takes place in New York City, covers no more than a few days, and focuses on Davy's rescue of Gloria and escape from an alter ego (Rapallo); *The Killing* isolates a handful of settings and characters within the mechanics of a single plan in a time span of one week; *Paths of Glory* telescopes three highly dramatic events (battle, court-martial, execution) within two settings and a time period of about four days; and *Dr. Strangelove* deals with the ultimate drama within three enclosed settings during a two-hour countdown to doom. Each of these subjects provided Kubrick with a dramatic situation in which he could compress a great deal of psychological and thematic material without sacrificing the continuity or logic of film narrative. With few exceptions, the films depend for their aesthetic and conceptual effect on a structure of juxtapositions and repetitions from one setting and scene to another, while avoiding a more deliberate method of exposition or development that would confer an autonomy on individual narrative segments. Kubrick's film universe before *2001* thrives on associations and connections, no matter how paradoxical or surreal, and the workings of separate elements within larger and more ambiguous wholes. Johnny's plan and the racetrack become inseparable parts in a larger thematic and aesthetic game; the trenches and chateau project different forms of the same paradoxical truth; and the three worlds of *Dr. Strangelove* are variations on a single global madness. *Lolita*, even though its story spans four years, develops the same kinds of involution through settings that mirror one another (Quilty's mansion and Charlotte's home; bedrooms and bathrooms) and patterns of psychological doubling (Humbert and Quilty; Lolita and Charlotte). In significant respects, Kubrick's films always put the "cinematic" (images, sounds) in opposition to the "novelistic" (story, language, character), even though at times such a conflict functions on a level of implication rather than assertion. What particularly distinguishes 2001 from these earlier films is its frontal assault on the traditional conventions of narrative film making. The temporal range of 2001 is infinity instead of days or years, yet the film omits explanatory background and transitional connectives; and spatially, it embodies a kind of ultimate cinematic universe, where all the assurances of "normal" perspective are literally turned upside down and "settings" project either an eerie remoteness despite their authenticity or a disturbing lack of localized definition.

Unlike the novel, where thematic elements merge with both the intricacies of a good story and the psychology of the characters, 2001 stages its emotional and intellectual drama within a visual and musical framework. Clarke, for instance, not only goes inside the mind of Moon-Watcher but in moments of narrative drag, such as Floyd's trip to the Moon or Bowman and Poole's trip to Saturn, he does the expected thing by fleshing out the psychological subtext of the novel. Although the film has been faulted for what some see as a "dehumanized" or minimal treatment of character, it could be argued that its space psychology is entirely plausible. Once in space, away from the familiar reality of Earth, Kubrick's ironic point that a highly intelligent computer, programmed both to operate a spaceship and provide "companionship" for astronauts on journeys covering great expanses of space and time, could assume a more expressive humanity than that of isolated, sentient travelers seems probable enough. What may be lacking in 2001—and may explain this critical stir—is that abundance of earthbound "human drama" we are conditioned to expect from most films.[6] More important than this debate between "dehumanization" and authenticity, however, is how Kubrick departs from the novel's illusion of psychological depth and aligns character to the film's symbolism and mythology. In each of the four parts, Kubrick places his characters in psychological situations that alternate between wakefulness, sleep, and awakening. Moon-Watcher (Dan Richter) huddles in a darkness illuminated by the Moon (an appropriate presence in a film about suprarational consciousness and transformation) and a leopard's glowing eyes while watching for the terrors of a primeval night, and only after he has touched the monolith does he show an awakening of consciousness, over the pile of bones.[7] Dr. Heywood Floyd (William Sylvester), a twenty-first century man with his primitive instincts well in hand, sleeps while his "bone" (fountain pen) floats in the weightless air of a shuttle carrying him to the space station; and when he is awake on the Moon, we discover that, like Moon-Watcher, his childlike reaction to the presence of the monolith seems almost preconscious. Aboard *Discovery*, David Bowman (Keir Dullea) and Frank Poole (Gary Lockwood) take turns sleeping, and even in their wakefulness, they seem lethargic and remote; their only companions are three figures in coffin-shaped hibernacula and a computer whose red and yellow eyes seem to never sleep. Only after HAL reasserts the primitive's instinct for survival by killing Poole and the three hibernators does Bowman begin to show indications of an internal "awakening." And finally, in a journey through the Star-Gate's slit-scan corridors and a scene on the bed of an eighteenth-century room, the film makes its last evolutionary leap and shows us, in Bowman's rebirth as Star-Child, a symbolic awakening.

Again, some significant comparisons can be made between the psychological rhetoric of *2001* and Kubrick's earlier films. Since *Fear and Desire* and *Killer's Kiss*, his first two features, he has shown a greater interest in states of mind and emotion than in character itself. Although the second film outlines a "background" of guilt and frustration for the characters of Davy and Gloria, its best psychological moments—visualized in dreamlike and nightmarish imagery—suggest forces at work on the other side of consciousness. *The Killing* traffics in the very basic emotions of sex, greed, and a pathetic desperation, all of which endanger a "rational" plan, while *Paths* defines character within a more abstract conflict of politics and morality. In each of these four films, psychology defers to Kubrick's development of ideas and perspectives beyond the comprehension or expression of any single character. And, it is to his credit that these films contain several moving and poignant scenes, even as they force the audience to perceive the workings of larger cinematic worlds rather than encouraging a strict identification with any one of their fictional inhabitants. Only *Lolita* confers on character a function equal to more inclusive thematic and aesthetic concerns, mainly because its primary subject is psychological rather than philosophic. Even there, however, Kubrick offers his audience the means to escape Humbert's subjectivity and perceive both its self-deception and pathos. And *Dr. Strangelove*, in a more exaggerated fashion than *2001*, totally subordinates "character" to satire and mythopoeic speculation. Perhaps, therefore, it is not so much that Kubrick's conception of Floyd, Bowman, and Poole is "dehumanized" or represents a radical departure from the humane sensibilities of *Paths* and *Lolita*, but that his conception of them, in its realistic particularity, as opposed to the dominating mythic generality, seems inappropriately small compared to the gargantuan dimensions of *2001*'s technological and spatial mise-en-scène. But, of course, that is one of the film's more obvious points.

While the concept of character assumes an almost nascent definition in *2001*, language becomes a tool as obsolete as Moon-Watcher's bone would be to a scientist of the future like Dr. Heywood Floyd. In order to make the film as complete a visual and musical experience as possible, Kubrick not only deletes narration and an introductory prologue but assigns dialogue a minimal expository function.[8] The film is 141 minutes long, but only about 40 minutes of it involve scenes where language has any importance; for the most part, the formal and laconic emptiness develops subtle thematic ironies as much as it illuminates the workings of plot or character. About thirty minutes into the film, during which four million years have passed, *2001* picks up language in a state of decline; Floyd is moving through space toward a meeting with the monolith and carrying with him an archaic and earthbound verbal baggage. At Hilton Space Station 5, in the Howard Johnson Earthlight Room (printed language makes similar statements, but with less circumlocution), Floyd's empty ritual of sounds in the company of Soviet scientists hardly has any more value as communication than Moon-Watcher's grunts of bewilderment or screams of triumph. At this second waterhole, Kubrick shows that battles for territory and tribal dominance persist even in the rarefied air of space; we learn that the Moon, a dead and arid world, has been divided into American and Soviet sectors and that language, at least in its political and social functions, has evolved into a polite and banal mask (e.g., the "cover story" of a Clavius epidemic) for Pleistocene struggles.* Suggestions of other worlds and other universes elude these travelers as the evolutionary and

---

*At Space Station 5, just after the Picturephone scene, Smyslov tells Floyd that the telephones at Clavius have not worked for ten days, which later can be

linguistic gravity of Earth pulls them back towards moral and spiritual extinction. Ironically, as Floyd goes "up" to Clavius, Smyslov (Leonard Rossiter) and Elena (Margaret Tyzack) go "down" to Earth, where, she tells him, her husband works on ocean floors ("underwater research in the Baltic") while she travels in space; at no time do they comment on the wonder of their spatial environment, or imply that it has stimulated an exploration and expansion of inner or outer worlds. It is significant that the first spoken words in the film reveal that the one tool that could assist such an endeavor has not kept pace with a technological entry into a universe far beyond the boundaries of Earth: The flight stewardess's "Here you are, sir" and Floyd's "See you on the way back" illustrate the kind of timebound and linear vocabulary repeatedly used by the characters of *2001*; they ignore the fact that in space directional terms like "forward" and "backward" or "up and down" no longer have the same meaning as they do within Earth's gravity, just as positional definitions of place and time seem primitive in their insistence that concepts like "here" and "there" or "now" and "then" continue to have a Newtonian authority. Throughout the two middle sections of the film, where all the spoken utterances are con-

---

explained as part of the "cover-up." Paradoxically, communications are broken off at the same time that an extraterrestrial machine (the monolith) makes contact with an earthbound intelligence. The telephones of Burpleson AFB (*Strangelove*) are still dead.

centrated, characters persist in the illusion that the verbal contours of Earth can chart a journey through the infinitude of space.

One scene in particular illustrates how language in *2001* works in opposition to a visual communication that constantly rearranges spatial perspective and spatial relationships. At Clavius, the American Moon base, Floyd tries to "beef up morale" during a briefing that takes place in a small room, around a horseshoe-shaped table, and illuminated by fluorescent, rectangular wall-panels. In this boxlike enclosure, one where geometry seems more important than understanding, Floyd reenacts Moon-Watcher's role as bone-carrier and tribal leader in his polite but authoritative enforcement of an ancient pecking order.* As before, language conspires with politics and a primitive social hierarchy to mask and conceal the discovery of the monolith, a discovery so immense that it could allow mankind to escape the bondage of those very instincts that now threaten rather than guarantee survival. For this scene, Kubrick not only used a small and sparsely decorated room to complement a sense of verbal and moral regression, but employed his camera in a textbook manner to outline visually the stasis and circularity of this world's thinking: He filmed the scene by making, first, a "master" shot, used to introduce and conclude the action, and then a series of angle shots to be either inserted into the finished film or discarded in the editing room. In a long take (the "master" shot) we look over the conference table from Floyd's empty chair (which he occupies only in the beginning) toward the podium where he is introduced by Halverson (Robert Beatty) to the applause of an audience, and then we listen to his words about the scientific importance of the "discovery" and necessity for both a "cover story" and "secrecy oaths" (to preclude culture shock on Earth); while the scene verbally unfolds, the camera cuts to a series of setups that, in a back and forth pattern, unfold different perspectives on an action that inevitably returns to the original "master" shot; significantly, unlike the scenes in space that precede and follow, where shifts of camera angle signal possible changes of perception and apprehension, these remain as conventional in their failure to communicate any "new" visual information as do Floyd's verbal responses to the mystery of the monolith. Later, aboard *Discovery*, Ku-

---

* The rectangular geometry of the conference room (fluorescent wall panels in the form of horizontal rectangles; a horseshoe table; a white podium resembling a small monolith) is complemented by the circular movements of the characters: Halverson moves to the left around the table and introduces Floyd and then circles right when he returns to his seat as Floyd walks left.

brick will punctuate this scene when he links the death of machine intelligence with the last words in the film, appropriately spoken by Floyd in another "briefing," this time on a tiny screen in the narrow confines of HAL's defunct brain before Bowman's speechless gaze:

> Good day, gentlemen. This is a prerecorded briefing made prior to your departure and which for security reasons of the highest importance has been known on board during the mission only by your HAL 9000 computer. Now that you are in Jupiter space and the entire crew is revived it can be told to you. Eighteen months ago, the first evidence of intelligent life off the Earth was discovered. It was buried forty feet below the lunar surface, near the crater Tycho. Except for a single, very powerful radio emission aimed at Jupiter, the four-million-year-old black monolith has remained completely inert, its origin and purpose still a total mystery.[9]

Only when Bowman leaves the spaceship, and the almost irresistible tugs of Mission Control and HAL's 9000 twin on Earth, does he move through interior space into outer space and escape the tyranny of words.

Beginning with *The Killing*, his first novelistic adaptation, Kubrick's films repeatedly express an ambivalence toward language. We know how much his success as a film artist depends on written sources to provide a framework of action and character that is prior to the creation of ambiguous visual structures; yet he constantly undermines and even ridicules the authority of these verbal "objective correlatives."[10] Excluding *Fear and Desire* and *Killer's Kiss*, which are based on original scripts, the films before *2001* devalue words at the same time they rely on their temporal assertiveness. Lest we forget, *The Killing*, *Paths of Glory*, and *Strangelove* are full of "talk" and narration, even though it could be argued that much of it lacks a substance or quality equal to its formal expression. In *The Killing*, Kubrick gives language a deceptively authentic and "objective" ring, only to reveal its limitations: The narrator knows something about time, but nothing about space; and the racetrack announcer expresses confusion over the killing of a horse, while we know the hidden truth. Here and elsewhere, Kubrick's film worlds suggest that understanding and mystery are matters of visual context and perspective and not of words. A great deal of talk bounces off the interior walls of the chateau in *Paths*, but none of it reaches the ceiling; instead, characters clothe a smallness of vision in an inflated suit of euphemisms, moral axioms, and hypocritical platitudes, while the visual music of the chateau and the grim symmetry of

the execution, like the exploding shells over the trenches, metaphorically drown out these verbal encounters. In *2001*, several scenes of
dialogue inside spaceships are shot silent and then enhanced by such
musical selections as Herbert von Karajan's version of "The Blue Danube" (aboard the flights of *Orion* and *Aries* with Floyd) and the adagio
movement of Aram Khatchaturian's "Gayne Ballet Suite" (aboard *Discovery*). Very little, however, drowns out the complex verbal exchanges
of *Lolita*, although in an appropriately Nabokovian manner they tend
to nullify the authority of language as explainer or clarifier. Puns,
innuendo, and double *entendres* function as a perfect linguistic expression for Kubrick's earlier tendency to oppose words with images; they
embody aurally the kind of punch and counterpunch found in *Paths*'s
opposition between politics as conversation and the chateau's visual
splendor. *2001* imitates the word/image disparities of *Paths* more than
it does the verbal involutions of *Lolita*, probably because the second
is both too civilized and too decadent a mode for a psychological world
that vacillates between insentience and a birth into a post-linguistic
consciousness. While in *Dr. Strangelove*, Kubrick shows language's last
orgasm in an explosion of bombastic clichés, overwrought euphemisms,
and a strangulating jargon very much like the Mission Control "Technish" of *2001*, all of which accelerates the declinations of Eros and
Thanatos rather than the upward flights of Reason and Imagination.[11]
The Earth world of *2001* may have dodged the apocalyptic consequences of Ripper's madness, but it clearly inherited the banality of
his language.

What makes *2001* such a fascinating and enduring film is the sheer
emotional and conceptual appeal of its spatial aesthetics, which vi-
brates with a plurality of universes within universes. Throughout, Kubrick combines the linear demands of narrative with an associative and
repetitious system of images, activities, and sounds to unfold a cinematic world moving on parallel but opposing courses: one that not only
ascends into space and descends into time, but collapses from within
in gestures of reflexive mockery as it expands outward toward implied
dimensions beyond even its own 70 mm Cinerama frame. In parts one
and two, Kubrick links a prehistoric and eroded dwelling place with
excavations on the Moon, and intimates that while Floyd moves up in
space he descends in time; parts three and four parallel HAL's retro-
gression from machine logic to primitive instinct with Bowman's trip

to an eighteenth-century memory room, as we perceive that journeys through space also involve backward glances toward both "real" and psychic time. Patterns of psychological doubling reappear throughout the film—the metamorphosis of Moon-Watcher into Floyd, the pairing of Poole and Bowman, and their symbiotic relationship with HAL and his twin on Earth—as Kubrick explores inner worlds that shuttle between extinction and renewed vision. Repeatedly, characters engage in ritual activities and inhabit settings that double back on the past and point to a new future in space: namely, (1) in the celebration of birthdays on a primeval Earth, on screens and ships in space, and in a neoclassical room that magically appears and disappears; (2) in the evolution and regression of eating from, first, an act of survival (the primate as vegetarian) and relish (the ape-man as carnivore) on an African wasteland to one of synthetic functionalism in the spaceships of the future, and, lastly, to that ironic reversion embodied in the eighteenth-century formalism of Bowman's last meal; (3) in the development of those patterns of sleeping and awakening mentioned earlier, particularly the hominid's terrified gaze into a waking nightmare, the implied connection between Floyd's weightless sleep and Poole's description on a BBC newscast of the dreamless voids of hibernation, and between HAL's death and Bowman's "awakening" before his completing the monolith's ancient mission and becoming a luminous beacon moving toward Earth and a new generation of Moon-Watchers and sleepers. Shapes of the past merge with and comment on shapes of the future. In the first shot of the film, the camera tilts up from the Moon to reveal a partially eclipsed Earth, and in "The Dawn of Man," it shows the Moon in a similar waning phase as seen from the Earth, while one cannot help but notice that planets are enclosed circles within other circles, and that each occupies a place in a boundless darkness. Moon-Watcher's bone goes up in space only to descend, while a bone-shaped satellite orbits in circles; spaceships create the gravity of Earth within large centrifuges, which provide a treadmill for Poole's jogging and primitive shadow-boxing, as well as wombs for hibernators in the twenty-first century. Externally, these futuristic machines resemble the fossil remains of an ancient race's technological and psychic evolution. Everywhere one looks there are eyes and shapes of eyes, either framed within a larger geometry or themselves framing and reflecting what is seen, just as Kubrick and his special-effects crew repeatedly create within the wide-screen frame an impression of screens within screens,

of inner worlds within outer worlds. Overall, *2001* invites its audience
to "see" beyond the earthbound (and filmbound) limits of time and self
and to experience a cinematic imagination that gives form to its own
dreams of duration in the amorphous expanses of contingent space.

Within the four-part structure of *2001*, Kubrick creates a maze of
visual and narrative motions that develop this paradoxical tug of war
between centripetal (collapsing) and centrifugal (expanding) forces.
Consider, for instance, these examples of how the film associates planetary conjunction with narrative doubling in parts one and two: (1) In
a prologue behind the title of the film, the vertical alignment of planets
(Moon, Earth, and Sun) and Richard Strauss's *Zarathustra* not only
anticipate an evolutionary event but provide a cosmic perspective
that both looks "up" (the camera tilt) and descends to Earth ("The
Dawn of Man"); ironically, the "space odyssey" of *2001* begins in darkness and time (Earth), and in this film universe "up" sometimes means
"down," and backward movement in time precedes forward leaps in
space. (2) In "The Dawn of Man," Kubrick alludes to the first alignment in the vertical imagery of that low-angle shot showing monolith,
Moon, and Sun, only there an extraterrestrial artifact assumes a status
equal to a planet's and locates a cosmic intelligence within the film
which stimulates in both the minds of the hominids on the screen and
the audience in the theater a sense of impending revelation; from this
reverse angle, Earth is "down" and Moon is "up," just as the narrative
declines in time only to advance in space, and the monolith and its
blackness become part of a vertical symmetry that points toward the
darkness of space and opposes the horizontal and static contours of an
African landscape littered with bones and projected in a series of still
photographs, augmented only by the sounds of a desolate wind. (3)
Part two concludes with a repetition of both Ligeti's music, including
sounds of alien "voices," and a second vertical alignment of monolith,
Sun, and Earth, as the film comes full circle; it is significant—an indication that involution more than evolution is the theme of this scene—
that Strauss is not invoked either before or after six figures imitate their
primordial doubles by descending into an excavation to encircle, touch,
and photograph the Earth monolith's Moon twin, their humanity obscured by spacesuits rather than the hairy disguise of Pleistocene pri-
mates.[12] Some four million years in film time after that initial tilt-shot
on the Moon, Kubrick shows Floyd and his generation doubling back

on Moon-Watcher, weaving concave circles of time in the convexities of space.

Especially prevalent in part two, therefore, are the first signs of a cinematic *déjà vu* that prompts the audience to jog its memory and participate in both the film's dreamlike reflection on its own past and its vision of things to come. It is not only the match cut from bone to satellite that stimulates such a responsive process but an array of other associations as well. The camera, as before, initiates the second movement of this film symphony by tilting up and revealing a visual alignment of Sun, Earth, Moon, *and satellite*, while the silent grace and harmony of the camera's slow and deliberate motions are complemented by the sounds of "The Blue Danube." This shot not only recalls earlier conjunctions, particularly the one anticipating Moon-Watcher's slow-motion expression of evolutionary victory; it also introduces several intriguing complications: (1) The first monolith-conjunction of the film expressively announced the presence of an unseen but superior intelligence, while the satellite imitates the bone (another tool/weapon) and signals the existence in space of Moon-Watcher's legacy. (2) Ironically, its visual harmony represents a by-product of technology and space travel rather than a necessary enlargement of vision, as, perhaps, the nineteenth-century music (from Johann Strauss) in a twenty-first cen-

tury environment implies. (3) The bone and satellite are not only artifacts but extensions of man in time and in space, respectively, while
the monolith ultimately functions as a gateway to a realm of consciousness where such objects, like language, dissolve into the void once their
purpose has been served. (4) And finally, the monolith is a highly expressive film device that stands as an emblem, more than an artifact,
of the Mystery Beyond, while the space hardware of *2001* both asserts
an authentic science-fiction landscape and expresses Kubrick's concept
of Man as Tool-Maker.[13]

Floyd's trips to Hilton Space Station 5 aboard a Pan Am shuttle
(the *Orion*) and to Clavius Moon Base aboard a spherical spaceship
(the *Aries*) provide two additional sequences in part two where images
of conjunction reinforce the film's early emphasis on visual and narrative circularity. In the first, Moon-Watcher's bone assumes a more
streamlined and expressive shape in *Orion*'s arrowlike and phallic
movement toward a conjunctive rendezvous with another ancient tool
duplicated in space; from close-up, the rotating wheel of the space
station rivals in size a luminous Earth, while the diminutive *Orion*
completes another harmonic trinity of artifacts and celestial bodies.
More so than before, Kubrick's camera now travels in space on conjunctive paths and creates a *ballet mécanique* among itself, *Orion*,
and the wheel, while inside the shuttle it records parodic enclosures in
an alignment of the bone/phallus disguised as fountain pen, the sleeping Floyd's left arm floating in harmony with the pen, and a "movie"
screen that trivializes man's sexual instincts in its depiction of a banal
love scene in a futuristic car. Through this pairing of external beauty
and internal reflexivity, Kubrick, as he did in *Dr. Strangelove*, suggests
the disparities between a technological aesthetics in space and evolutionary factors that create a countermotion toward descent at the moment of ascent. But while Floyd sleeps like a baby before a screen,
dreaming the memories of his race, the pilots of *Orion* watch computer
readout screens that both visualize a complicated docking procedure
and record through a system of coordinates and grids the perfect conjunction of two human artifacts disguised as futuristic machines.* Fol-

---

* One particular shot and composition during the *Orion*/Wheel sequence recalls an earlier film; Kubrick's camera, from inside the Wheel's docking area,
moves back to frame outer space within the narrow confines of a horizontal mail-
slot, recalling the way in which no-man's-land is first visualized in *Paths of Glory*.
For Floyd, as well as the viewer, space in *2001* represents a different kind of
"no-man's-land."

lowing the second "waterhole" scene, namely the one inside the wheel between Floyd and the Soviets, Kubrick returns the film to space and conjunctive visions complicated by temporal and psychological disorders: initially, one notices how the spaceship *Aries* resembles a planet as it keeps company in a single shot with the Sun and Moon, while inside Floyd reenacts the ancient cycle of sleeping, eating (through straws from a tray that pictorially identifies what he's "eating"), and elimination ("Zero Gravity Toilet"), and flight stewardesses walk upside down and watch on screens the formalized aggression of judo wrestlers. Floyd's two-part journey concludes with another docking maneuver, this one between *Aries* and the Clavius Astrodome, which resembles the union of a descending seedpod and a flower/vulva opening its petals in a rite of outer-space pollination.

Particularly through the use of screens and windows in part two does Kubrick develop a conflict between, on the one hand, temporal inversion and a spatial reduction and, on the other, breathtaking 70 mm visions of harmony and expansion. The space travelers in the early scenes are confined in a series of enclosures that prevent direct access to space itself. They inhabit spaceships, space stations, Moon bases, and spacesuits that frame through window screens the infinity of space. By contrast, Kubrick's camera—through its "inside" and "outside" trips, its angles and reverse angles—records these enclosed perspectives as it contends with the boundaries of a Cinerama frame which both registers its aesthetic presence and, as if to acknowledge the Mystery Beyond, encircles itself in a rim of darkness. In the space station, Kubrick brings Floyd into a setting that at once suggests an antiseptic cage and resembles the interior of Moon-Watcher's bone: it is long and narrow, curved slightly at both ends, blindingly white, and decorated with ghastly pink chairs shaped like surrealist rock formations; and along each wall are windows containing small-screen, fragmentary images of an enormous Earth and a boundless space far more at home within the film's Cinerama frame. Inside the Picturephone booth, Floyd has a "screen" conversation with his daughter (Vivian Kubrick) which, in its banality (it recalls the love scene on an *Orion* screen), evokes not the mystery of the monolith, but a drama closer to man's dawn. It contains such revelations as a mother not home, a babysitter in the bathroom, and a daughter's birthday and request for a "bush baby" doll. At no time does Floyd turn away from these domestic trifles to look through the window on his left, which partly frames a brilliantly luminous image of Earth; instead of beauty and spatial expanses, his mind responds to the murky involutions that unfold on small screens, in polite conversation, and during top-secret briefings. Following the conference at Clavius, in an enclosed room with no windows or screens, Kubrick places Floyd inside a bone-shaped "bus" that transports him to the Tycho excavation and TMA-1. Again, exterior wonders conflict with interior comedy: Outside the moonbus and its horizontal movement over a ghostly but stunning lunar surface, we hear the faint sounds of the Ligeti monolith music and see a partially eclipsed Earth hovering in a dark sky; inside, Floyd and two men discuss the mystery of a four-million-year-old monolith and the difficulty of distinguishing a "real" ham sandwich from a synthetic one. As he has done so often before, Kubrick places the familiar within surreal or remote contexts and forces his audience to acknowledge worlds unaccounted for by those conventions that dominate psychological frames of reference as well as film screens.

Reminiscent of *Dr. Strangelove*, parts one and two assume the characteristics of an involuted surrealist comedy: (1) A series of four fades, from the *2001* title to the discovery of the first monolith, mark the different phases of "The Dawn of Man," which describes a cycle, beginning with signs of the ape-men's near extinction on an arid landscape of bones and sparse vegetation, to territorial struggles around a waterhole and the terrors of the night, and finally the sudden appearance of an alien artifact before a "magical" evolutionary event. (2) Part two begins by showing another silent landscape littered with "bones" (satellites) and illuminated by a dawn (the sun appears from behind a dark Earth), then goes into the wheel for a second "waterhole" encounter, follows with people eating food no more appetizing than those roots foraged earlier, and ends with the appearance of another monolith and lunar dawn. Significant differences, however, indicate the film's satiric attitude toward its futuristic tribe of civilized humanity. As mentioned before, at no time does Floyd gaze into his world in an expression of terror or awe, partly because his vision is framed and enclosed while Moon-Watcher's directly confronts his world. Technological man, the film tells us, exchanges vision for a self-satisfied security, and while he sleeps better than his primitive ancestors, he also loses the capacity to dream. When Floyd descends into the crater containing the monolith, he is not as well-prepared as is Kubrick's audience to deal with its mystery; he remains locked into his spacesuit and frames of ignorance, while the theater-viewers, with the help of some highly expressive film techniques, both transcend this reflexive content and detect promises of release from the film's circularity.[14] Earlier, for instance, Kubrick used the subjective powers of slow-motion to suggest Moon-Watcher's elation and escape from extinction, while here the handheld camera that follows the six figures introduces an element of mental disorder into an atmosphere previously dominated by slumber and stasis. Lights around the monolith and Ligeti's music combine with camera movement and composition to enhance the importance of this scene. Like a recurring but incomplete dream, six indistinguishable figures move in circles around a rectangular totem; then, in one striking shot, Kubrick blackens half the screen with a close-up of the monolith's impenetrable surface and shows Floyd emerging from behind its darkness on screen right; his gloved hand reaches out, like Moon-Watcher's tactile one, and ritualistically confirms its reality. Ironically, these men turn magic into farce when five of them line up in front of the monolith so that it can be framed and trivialized as a backdrop for a photographic memento. Kubrick, himself a former still photographer, completes this surreal moment by interrupting their efforts with the light of a lunar dawn, which not only triggers the monolith's piercing alarm but provides that necessary element (the Sun) for his camera's low-angle conjunction shot and a transition to unfinished journeys into the mysteries of space.

Khatchaturian's desolate and lonely music sets the tone for part three and the actual beginning of *2001*'s "space odyssey." In the first half of the film, Kubrick's primary emphasis was ironic and timebound, even to the point of linking technological evolution in outer space to a process of psychological regression. But in parts three and four, perspectives change as interior and exterior space finally come together to express the kind of harmony found only between machines or planets in earlier scenes. In part three the most complex psychological situation of the film takes place in an environment that recalls part two and internalizes the death-into-life paradox of "The Dawn of Man." Only now, a computer with human characteristics assumes control over a self-sufficient technological universe and threatens to reverse the parable of *Genesis* by destroying its creators. The fossil-like shape of Spaceship *Discovery* reasserts Pleistocene landscapes as it floats through dark, empty space like a prehistoric leviathan. Inside this colossus,

human consciousness inhabits a twilight world somewhere between insentience and a traumatic new life, one in which the involutions of part
two pull against the expansive journeys of part four. Bowman and
Poole become extensions of Moon-Watcher and Floyd, while HAL's
"death" climaxes the film's treatment of Man as Tool-Maker and provides a necessary step to the symbolism of an eighteenth-century room
and the birth of Star-Child. Visually, "inside" enclosures dominate "outside" worlds, and the use of subjective camera devices and disorienting
angles signifies the presence of an important internal struggle. Images
of circles and corridors convert the interior of *Discovery* into a well-lit
womb of death where hibernators are aborted, and one character, from
the darkness of space, gains reentry to destroy the tool-turned-Dooms-
day Machine and begin a new evolutionary cycle.

To fully appreciate the conceptual complexity of this section of
2001, one must recognize how it evokes shapes and images seen earlier.
Throughout, Kubrick has emphasized eyes and shapes of eyes to complement themes of visual blindness and perceptual awakening. "The
Dawn of Man" matches the leopard's inhuman yellow eyes against
both Moon-Watcher's look of terror and his dawn of awareness. Floyd
either sleeps too much or uses his eyes to express the rational man's
detachment rather than the space traveler's sense of wonder; he looks
at and touches the monolith's blackness, as Moon-Watcher does, but he
fails to explore its mystery.* In contrast, Kubrick assaults his audience's gaze with an array of shapes that convert aesthetic beauty into
evolutionary paradox. The hominid's bone is transformed from a primi-

---

* In "The Dawn of Man" the hominid's sentient eyes contrast with the yellow
glow of the leopard's eyes. In part two, the detached or cool expressions in human
eyes contrast with the glowing white "eyes" of Aries and the glowing red eyes of
the moonbus. In part three, HAL's single eye with its red iris and yellow pupil
seems more alive than the remote, even absent, expression Bowman and Poole
have. HAL has eyes throughout the spaceship; his eye is always flanked by the
screens of monitoring boards, four square screens on each side of the eye, which
reinforces the sense that he "sees" and controls everything on a technological
gameboard. In the birthday scene, orange goggles enlarge the significance of
Poole's eyes, even though his eyes continue to show only an eerie disengagement.
The pods have a cyclops eye with two white lights on each side that when acti-
vated make the machine look like an alien monster. During Bowman's conflict
with HAL, Bowman's eyes come alive and are framed in color and light. In part
four, Bowman's blinking eye fills the screen several times during the Star-Gate
sequence, and our first view of the eighteenth-century room is framed through the
pod's eye. When Bowman, as aging gentleman, looks toward the bed to acknowledge his dying twin, he noticeably *squints*. And the Star-Child's distinguishing
feature is his huge eyes which, in the last image of the film, look directly into the
camera.

tive tool/weapon into a graceful, bone-white satellite; together with *Orion*'s imitation of a phallus and *Aries*' of a head/planet (with glowing white eyes), it gives form to Kubrick's futuristic vision of technological man filling the lonely expanses of space with artifacts and rivaling both the duration and harmonics of planetary bodies. Initially, for instance, the film teases the audience into believing that HAL represents the ultimate tool for man's exploration of space. His manual dexterity (he opens and closes doors, operates pods, and keeps the spaceship on course) and the rational, mathematical precision of his electronic brain would seem to provide an ideal environment for human discovery. Instead, Bowman and Poole are HAL's tools, servants to his omniscience, and inevitably, like Moon-Watcher's bone, nothing more than artifacts to be contemplated or objects to be tossed into space once their function has been fulfilled. HAL climaxes the film's thesis that machines are physical and psychological extensions that merely sublimate rather than transcend Moon-Watcher's instincts, while aesthetically they express the rule of imitation over the struggles of vision. The outer space of *2001*, like the Big Board of *Dr. Strangelove*, represents a mirror universe in which mankind shrinks infinity to the measurements of mechanical form. Rather than toys, machines here become man's children, ones that inevitably grow to gargantuan proportions and turn on him in acts of self-sufficiency.[15] They perpetuate his instinct for survival even at the expense of inner growth; his love of beauty and passion for order; and, tragically, his secret longing for the immortality of the Inanimate. Only the monolith's shape and color deviate from this anthropomorphic geometry, for its mode is transcendent and futuristic rather than imitative and nostalgic. In part three, *Discovery*'s skeletal shape anticipates the demise of technological man, while HAL's distorted vision, which envelops everything inside but understands nothing outside, indicates that Reason, some four million years after its escape from primeval barbarity, has evolved into another defunct tool blinded by its own arrogance and mechanical certainty.

The psychological content of part three recalls the doublings of *Lolita,* but in *2001* Kubrick shows a character shedding his *doppelgänger* and opening his eyes to new perceptions. Poole's physical and earthbound activities balance Bowman's slightly more dreamy and spatial definition: Poole jogs and shadowboxes, wears gym shorts, sunbathes under a heat lamp (like Miss Scott of *Strangelove*), and watches his birthday celebration over a screen transmission from Earth while reclining between two coffin-shaped hibernacula; Bowman prefers to draw pictures of figures, like himself, who sleep time away in anticipation of an awakening in deep space. Overall, however, Poole and Bowman represent mirror twins more than true doubles, especially after it becomes apparent that a computer, not Poole, will play Quilty to Bowman's Humbert. Not only does Kubrick choose two actors with significant physical resemblances, but he repeatedly places them in visual or comparative contexts that create a mirroring effect: Bowman is left-handed and Poole right-handed, and both eat the same food while narcissistically watching, on separate newspad screens, a BBC telecast (ironically titled "The World Tonight") where their images, along with HAL's eye, are duplicated. Poole loses a game of chess to HAL (a foreshadowing of his death) while Bowman sleeps, and Bowman displays his simple drawings of the hibernators before one of HAL's appreciative fish-eyed lens while Poole sleeps. In most two-shots, Bowman occupies screen right and Poole screen left, while in one-shots an empty space or chair recalls the missing twin. Whenever the two astronauts are seen in two-shot through one of HAL's eyes, for instance, Bowman is screen right and Poole screen left. When Bowman shows HAL his drawings, Bowman is framed to the right and an empty chair is prominent on the left; at the end of this shot, Bowman brings the pictures closer to HAL's eye so that they fill the screen-left position. Later, when they talk in the pod just before the lipreading scene, Bowman (right) and Poole (left) are profiled as twins, while between them Kubrick has framed HAL's eye within the pod's oval eye; just above HAL we see the empty red helmet of Bowman's space suit, which, surrealistically, seems to stare into the pod as well. In this one shot, Kubrick both twins Bowman and Poole and doubles HAL and Bowman. Poole and Bowman each take an extravehicular trip outside the spaceship while the other watches on a screen from inside; and finally, after Poole is murdered by HAL's "bone" (the pod), Bowman uses another pod in an attempt to rescue his twin from the darkness of space. Both serve HAL in a janitorial capacity and depend on him for companionship, knowledge of their world's status, and the very air they breathe. In addition, HAL has a 9000 twin on Earth (the Jekyll to his Hyde), and his "character" is defined by shots of his eye, which recalls both the hominid's watchful look and the leopard's yellow stare,* and by the

---

* Herb A. Lightman (*American Cinematographer*) claims that the yellow glow in the leopard's eyes was an accidental effect caused by the front projection inno-

Bowman as a reflection in HAL's eye.

sound of his voice (Douglas Rain), which imitates Floyd's language of calm reason. Through visual and dramatic associations, Kubrick both doubles Bowman and HAL and recalls the pairing of Moon-Watcher and Floyd. Bowman is first seen as a revolving and distorted reflection in HAL's eye (as he "descends" and rotates from the ship's hublink) and each experiences a journey into memory at the moment of "death," one ends with a song called "Daisy" and the other on a green and gold bed in an eighteenth-century room. Symbolically, HAL reenacts Moon-Watcher's primitivism and Floyd's blindness when he becomes the first Cain in space and denies knowledge of the monolith. Bowman, by contrast, both reaffirms the humanity of that first struggle for life in a hostile environment and transcends the earthbound limitations of Floyd's vision.

Consider the following rearrangement of the narrative logic of part three and how it reveals the importance the film attaches to the HAL/Bowman doubling: (1) On numerous occasions, HAL expresses pride in his infallibility and that of his 9000 counterparts, even though he knows that in the event of a malfunction his Earth twin will take control of *Discovery*. (2) In the Logic Memory Center, Bowman learns that, from the outset, HAL and the three hibernators knew about the

---

vation. In Clarke's novel, the leopard is described as having "two gleaming golden eyes" (p. 31) that stare out from the night at Moon-Watcher. Clarke did see some of the early rushes before he finished the novel, but in his version HAL's pupil is not yellow, as it is in the film.

Discovery's twins (Gary Lockwood and Keir Dullea)
separated by the eye of madness.

monolith and the ultimate purpose of the Jupiter mission. (3) Earlier,
just after he has looked at the drawings of the hibernators, HAL expresses a latent insecurity about his "secret" knowledge when he asks
Bowman if he has any "second thoughts" about the mission. (4) Immediately thereafter, HAL detects a fault in the AE-35 communications
unit that connects the space travelers with Mission Control and himself
with a 9000 twin. (5) When the tests on the AE-35 prove negative,
HAL finds it "puzzling" and attributes it to "human error," while Mission Control tells Bowman and Poole that the 9000 twin confirms it as
computer error. (6) Bowman and Poole go into a pod, cut off all outside communication, and discuss HAL's "strange" behavior and how,
if the AE-35 does not fail as predicted, they will have to disconnect
(kill) him and let the Earth twin take over his mechanical functions;
ominously, another subjective shot then shows HAL reading their lips
through the window of the pod. (7) Finally, HAL murders Poole and
the three hibernators and denies Bowman access to the interior of the
spaceship, only to be violated by a forced reentry and disconnection.
Most critical responses would, quite correctly, cite this sequence of
events as evidence that HAL's hubris combines pride and guilt, but
then they would neglect to comment on its symbolic importance to
Bowman's eventual transformation into the Star-Child. Why, for in-

stance, does HAL make such a simple and uncharacteristic mistake about a well-functioning AE-35 unit?[16] Could it be an expression of insecurity about his role in the Jupiter mission and a desire to cut off communication with Earth? After all, only Mission Control, the 9000 twin, and the hibernators know the truth: that HAL's infallibility as a machine and benevolence as a deity are compromised by his part in one of Floyd's earth-inspired conspiracies. Once programmed to be "human," HAL loses the machine purity which, no doubt, his twin still possesses; he becomes imbued with a consciousness of his own autonomy and denies his function as a tool. Therefore, his unconscious mind —where, like a hibernator, the truth sleeps—associates Bowman's drawings with his own fallibility and initiates a plot to break contact with Earth and the threat of his "perfect" twin. Later, when Floyd's screen image and voice are brought into the Logic Memory Center, Kubrick not only "explains" the mission but HAL's behavior, as that play of light and sound represents the last flickerings of his unconscious mind and the secret that drove him to madness. Bowman, on the other hand, succeeds at the expense of HAL's failure: symbolically, once Poole, Bowman's Earth twin, is murdered by his "rational" and mechanical alter ego, Bowman undergoes a traumatic awakening even more dramatic than Moon-Watcher's discovery of the bone. He forces himself back into *Discovery's* fossilized womb, destroys HAL, and frees technological man from the tyranny of his own tools.

In this showdown between man and machine, Kubrick creates one of his most evocative cinematic encounters. While the distortions of angle and HAL's fish-eyed lens define interior scenes, and give visual shape to latent psychological disturbances, deep-focus clarity and symmetry outside *Discovery* reinforces the ambiguity of spatial darkness. More so than before, he characterizes space travel as a frightening and mysterious equivalent for the monolith itself. Rather than visions of planetary conjunction or luminous images of other worlds, he only shows a surreal spaceship or occasional meteor moving through this black universe. In the three extravehicular pod trips, the film takes its characters into this spatial context and, for the first time, creates a psychological syntax at war with the past tense. Each trip begins with a shot of the pod emerging from behind and rising over *Discovery's* enormous head, an image of "dawn" and conjunction involving two man-made machines but not the "magical" association seen earlier between planets and monolith; it does reenact, however, a pattern from

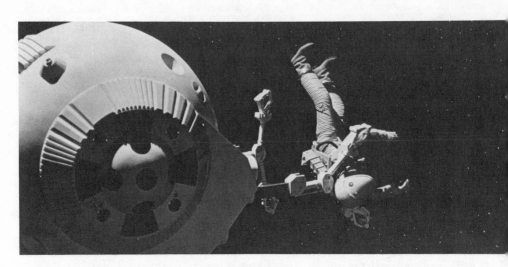

"The Dawn of Man" and anticipates the reappearance of the monolith. Later, *Discovery*'s head will assume the characteristics of a partially eclipsed planet (repeating an image of Earth in the film's credits) as it enters Jupiter's space and the alignment of planet, moons, and orbiting monolith. Inside the pod, Bowman and Poole's faces are animated by the distortions of red and blue lights from the control panels, and both look out through a window shaped like an eye; each emerges from the pod like a fetus from a womb, with helmet tops shaped like heads and decorated with two "eyes"; and each drifts upside down in space toward the hull of *Discovery* like a newborn child in search of its mother's body.[17] As Poole works to replace the AE-35 and the ship's link with Earth, the pod suddenly moves toward him with its mechanical arms extended like claws, its empty eye intercut with a zoom shot of HAL's eye inside the ship, and severs his umbilical cord, sending his body swirling into space. Inside the spaceship, as Bowman is confronted with the loss of his Earth twin, his placid mask begins to break up as Keir Dullea indicates the first signs of his awakening and transformation. In his anxiety to rescue his twin, Bowman figuratively loses his head (he leaves his red helmet behind), the one that protects him from an airless space but insulates him from perception. From inside the pod, his face changes color and his eyes are framed in light as he searches the darkness and becomes the first character in the film to look through a window/eye in an act of spatial exploration. Symbolically, Bowman searches for himself, that earthbound twin whom he

must shed before his eyes can open and experience the colors and shapes of the Star-Gate. He finds Poole—now an object more like *Discovery* than like Bowman, floating in space like the shell of an extinct species—and cradles Poole's body in the motherly arms of the pod, only to be denied entrance into a technological womb that aborts its children (hibernators), turns pods into weapons, and creates the sterile perfection of a reflexive universe. Bowman releases Poole's body into the darkness and uses the pod's explosive bolts to force his way through the red, uterine corridor of an emergency air lock. Not since Moon-Watcher has a character in *2001* taken such a life-affirming action, although paradoxically Bowman's involves an act of divestment rather than accumulation. Once he chooses to survive and battle his way back into *Discovery*, Bowman begins a process in which he will shed a sense of self-identity (Poole as twin), the extensions of Reason and technology (HAL as alter ego), and the temporal reservoir of memory (eighteenth-century room). His prenatal breathing on the soundtrack and the use of handheld camera to film the scene internalize Bowman's last struggle against HAL's verbal authority ("Look, Dave. I can see you're really upset about this. I honestly think you should sit down calmly, take a stress pill, and think things over"). Significantly, as he disconnects HAL amid the red and vertical enclosure of the Logic Memory Center, Bowman only speaks in reply to HAL's childish desire to sing

a song ("Yes, I'd like to hear it, HAL. Sing it for me"). He then gazes
in wonder before the innocence of creation ("Daisy, Daisy, give me
your answer true,/I'm half crazy all for the love of you") and the experience of time (Floyd's prerecorded briefing). It is a backward journey for the film as well, a return to Moon-Watcher's legacy, one that
not only reverses but nullifies time.[18]

Of all the sequences in *2001*, Bowman's journey through the Star-
Gate represents both the most "cinematic" (visual) and least enduring
part of the film. When first seen, it was as dazzling for the audience as
it was for Bowman, but I suspect it was not entirely unexpected.
Throughout the film, Kubrick indirectly promises such a development,
a pushing out into the world of the monolith and away from the languid, Newtonian movements of a clockwork universe. Science-fiction
films of *2001*'s scope normally require at least one pyrotechnic orgy and
an audience most assuredly demands it. Once *Discovery* enters Jupiter
space and is dwarfed by a conjunction of orbiting monolith, planet,
and moons—and the camera repeats the kind of upward tilt that began
the film—the audience expects something "magical" and momentous
to occur. And Kubrick delivers: the Star-Gate shows Bowman's escape
from earthbound forms through both a screen bombardment of shapes
and colors not seen before and the repetition of familiar images in new
visual contexts. Bones, satellites, spaceships, and the previous predom-
inance of black and white are superseded by slit-scan, multi-colored
corridors of light, crystal diamonds, explosions of worlds, fetal shapes,
intimations of new dawns, and the sensation of rapid movement. Time
and space acquire a plasticity not realized before, just as Bowman's
face, through a series of freeze frames, undergoes a radical transformation. His blinking eyes become a huge and repeated presence which
as they come to life in colors not seen before in the film, recall HAL's
multiple distortions of interior space, except that now, like Moon-
Watcher's, his look outward in an expression of wonder. Earth-like
landscapes pass below (Scotland's Hebrides and America's Monument
Valley), but are visualized as color-filtered negative images of a universe on the "other side" of reality. Like the surface of an oversized
camera lens where the refractions of inner and outer space intersect,
it is a world of unbridled perception and "seeing" in which anything
is possible and nothing is certain.[19]

But in part four ("Jupiter and Beyond the Infinite"), as Bowman
confronts new visions and new worlds, both Kubrick and his audience

grapple with an aesthetic problem that, in all probability, has no satisfactory solution. How does a film maker give form to something "beyond
the infinite" without a loss of thematic integrity or narrative clarity?
For a start, he can undermine the authority of "objective" temporal
structures—that is, the continuities of plot, character, dialogue, narration—and require, as Kubrick does, an audience to scan his images
and sounds for an associative or symbolic logic. He can refuse to "explain" in conventional film terms such things, for instance, as why
Dr. Heywood Floyd has less psychological dimension than either a
hominid or a computer. To a certain extent, Kubrick plays all these
cards, and sometimes he even does more. He turns a computer into the
calm, impassioned voice of reason for a journey into the unknown, and
then, in a flashback to the narrator of *The Killing*, uses him to parody
the very concept of omniscience and detachment. HAL "knows" everything aboard *Discovery*, but, for purposes of "morale," pretends (or is
programmed to pretend) ignorance so that an illusion of "democracy"
can remain intact. His role resembles Floyd's at Clavius and Kubrick's
in *2001*: All seemingly give direction to the events in their respective
worlds and assure an audience (at Clavius, aboard *Discovery*, in the
theatre) that the rule of reason functions even during moments of mystery. Eventually, HAL's omniscience breaks down in a fit of paranoid
uncertainty and then expires in the sounds of a slow-winding tape that
exposes this god as man-made creation. But Kubrick is no fiction, his
reality is palpable, and although his presence informs every scene and
image in *2001*, his omniscience is more imaginative than authoritative.
In a gesture of creative fallibility, he all but announces through the
film's conclusion that the Mystery Beyond eludes his grasp as well,
that, like Moon-Watcher and Floyd standing before the monolith, he
touches it without fully apprehending it. Just what are the aesthetic
implications of a film, or a work of literature, concluding on such a
note of ambiguity? Is it not an admission by the artist of his own in-
sufficiency? That, while he and God create worlds with beginnings and
endings, which by their very nature assert some form of cognitive
order, an indeterminate universe never ceases to create or unravel itself
in the silence of infinity.[20]

By his own admission, Kubrick did not settle on an ending for
2001 until just before he had to shoot it. In the original screenplay, he
and Clarke concluded Bowman's journey in an extraterrestrial cage or
observation tank resembling a hotel suite from the space traveler's

earthbound memory. Bowman was to wander around in a room tricked out with familiar artifacts (a Washington, D.C., telephone directory, modern furniture, a ceiling television screen) and then witness the monolith's final appearance. According to Clarke's account (in *The Lost Worlds of 2001*), the Star-Child transformation became a factor in the script about two months before shooting began. Evidently, Kubrick was enthusiastic about this ending but had not decided how to reconcile it with Bowman's entrapment in an alien zoo decked out as a "modern" hotel room. Clarke's novel partially clarifies the ending of the film, although it does not explain why Kubrick decided to give the room an eighteenth-century definition. In a ending that is similar to an idea in the novel *The Man Who Fell to Earth* (1963), Clarke's Bowman realizes that his mysterious hosts have duplicated a hotel room seen on a television transmission from Earth and goes so far as to characterize it as a "movie-set."[21] He eventually connects the room with the discovery of the TMA-1 and assumes that it has some purpose beyond his understanding. In a chapter called "Recapitulation," after Bowman goes to sleep on the "hotel" bed, Clarke describes the room "dissolving" back into the mind of its creators as the astronaut recalls his past and finally is drained of identity: "As one David Bowman ceased to exist, another became immortal." On the simplest narrative level, Kubrick's ending does not depart all that much from Clarke's: the orbiting monolith, Bowman's Star-Gate journey, the Ligeti "voices" within the room, the reappearance of the monolith, and Strauss's *Thus Spoke Zarathustra* continue visual and aural patterns developed throughout *2001*. They tell the film audience that something "magical" is happening and that Bowman as mankind is evolving toward some form of spatial/planetary consciousness. Here is how Kubrick explains it:

No, I don't mind discussing it, on the *lowest* level, that is, straightforward explanation of the plot . . . When the surviving astronaut, Bowman, ultimately reaches Jupiter, this artifact [monolith] sweeps him into a force field or star gate that hurls him on a journey through inner and outer space and finally transports him to another part of the galaxy, where he's placed in a human zoo approximating a hospital terrestrial environment drawn out of his dreams and imagination. In a timeless state, his life passes from middle age to senescence to death. He is reborn, an enhanced being, a star child, an angel, a superman, if you like, and returns to earth prepared for the next leap forward in man's evolutionary destiny.[22]

But why, for instance, does he use an eighteenth-century decor or have Bowman witness his aged counterpart breaking a crystal wineglass? What are the implications of this ambiguity? Does this mysterious scene have a legitimate conceptual function and complete the film's covert as well as overt intentions?

While the experience of seeing represents the meaning of the Star-Gate, understanding what is seen defines the ambiguity of the film's last sequence. Subjective/framing devices, associative reoccurrences, and a sense of spatial/temporal dislocation—that is, the initial shot of the room through the pod's window/eye, the return of breathing sounds, a mirror and doorway, the reappearance of the monolith and the disappearance of the pod, a hand-held camera in the bathroom, jump-cuts and temporal ellipsis, the Ligeti and Richard Strauss musical themes—merge the enclosures of memory and involutions of cinematic structure. As Bowman sheds his earthbound identity, as both astronaut and man in time, *2001* meditates on itself and, before its final odyssey into an undefined future in space, invites the audience to integrate the images and activities of the room with the film's "past." Bowman, minus his Earth twin and mechanical double, assumes an anthropological and historical generality before he "dies" and evolves into a mythic progenitor of a new race of man. Once again a setting resembles the inside of a bone or artifact, as Moon-Watcher's life cycle and Floyd's territorial regressions are formalized in the room's stark white fluorescent floor, complete with chessboard squares, and pale green and blue walls.[23] Pleistocene waterholes and twenty-first-century space stations become indistinguishable from a nostalgic eighteenth-century mise-en-scène which encloses the astronaut Bowman in the primal and ritualized processes of human time, from awakening and sleep (large bed) to eating (formal table setting), cleansing (ornate bathroom), and a solipsistic contemplation of self (Bowman's aging mirror twin). Only the slightest hint of green (the walls, a dressing gown, a headboard, bedsheets, and paintings) suggests the presence of "vegetation" on this landscape of death and the possibility of survival through rebirth. History and identity are merged and nullified as Bowman wanders through this surreal dream of innocence and experience—his "Daisy"—and divests himself of temporal and mechanical form. He escapes the artificial enclosures of technology (pod and spacesuit), the formal remains of premechanical man (an eighteenth-century gentleman eating dinner and breaking the crystal glass), that missing link between the hominid/bone and Floyd/machine, as well as Moon-Watcher's legacy of ignorance before the mysteries of infinite space (in death, he also reaches out toward the monolith). *2001* brings man to the limits of his growth, where, like the bone, he is converted into an artifact that turns to crystal and shatters from the weight of evolutionary gravity. Bowman's last form before death resembles that of a shrunken and fossilized chrysalis, one transformed into a luminous and transparent bubble containing the Star-Child who, with Kubrick's camera, penetrates the blackness of the monolith, escapes a room without windows or doors, and moves through space as a world unto himself. Earlier, Moon-Watcher's bone ascended in space only to descend, Floyd's machines moved forward in space while Floyd regressed in time, and Poole died in space where now the Star-Child lives. This enhanced being carries no tools, speaks no tongue, and contemplates space without the mediation of the primitive's instincts or the rationalist's machine logic. The mirror world has been broken and beyond its reflexivity stands the unknown and unexplored. In the final images of the film, the camera shows the Moon before it tilts down to reveal Earth on screen right— reversing the upward movement of the camera in the opening titles— and suggests the beginning of a new cycle, only now the Star-Child assumes its cosmic perspective. He enters the frame from the left to create the film's only conjunction between man (not machine) and planet. The Star-Child in his bubble rotates like a planet, and his huge eyes look not only toward Earth below, his home and destination, but directly into the camera, like a humanized monolith mutely imploring the audience to ponder its mystery.[24]

6 The Performing Artist
A CLOCKWORK ORANGE

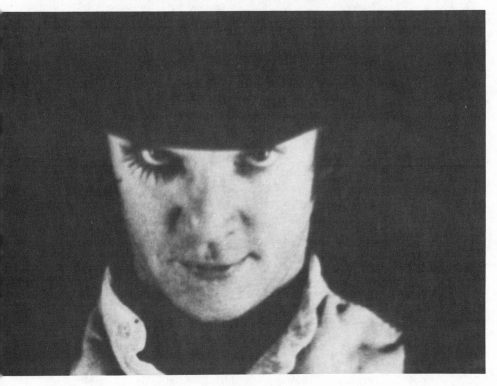

As it often does in the film business, economics in the late 1960s put the squeeze on artistic grandiosity and forced Stanley Kubrick, at the moment of a great achievement, to postpone his ambitious Napoleon film project. No doubt it would have been an impressive sequel to *2001*, dealing with the paradoxes of history as inventively as *2001* had dealt with the mysteries of space. But a financial rollback in film production dictated other choices and other directions. In the summer of 1969, Kubrick read Anthony Burgess's *A Clockwork Orange* (1962), a Swiftian fable and linguistic *tour de force*, set in the future, about the loss of ethical choice through psychological conditioning.[1] Not only was Kubrick excited by the novel—"the narrative invention was magical, the characters bizarre and exciting, the ideas brilliantly developed"—but for the first time in his career as an adapter of novels to film, he could start with a *finished* story:

> the story was of a size and density that could be adapted to film without oversimplifying it or stripping it to the bones. In fact, it proved possible to retain most of the narrative in the film. . . . Some of my films have started with the accumulating of facts, and from the facts narrative ideas seemed to develop, but of course A *Clockwork Orange* started with a finished story, and I was quite happy to skip the birth pangs of developing an original narrative.[2]

The language of the novel, a Slav-based invention called Nadsat (Russian for "teen-age"), is chiefly oriented toward sound (onomatopoeia) rather than concept, and the limited use of it in the film blends well with Kubrick's musical selections. Alex, the first-person narrator, prefers action and fantasy to the pontifications of abstract reasoning, and therefore inhabits an interior world accessible to the image-making powers of film. Burgess's plot structure emphasizes picaresque movement and fairy-tale coincidence, what Burgess characterizes as a "moral parable" and Kubrick as a "psychological myth," where the central thesis is stated by at least three characters in different contexts. Alex constantly repeats his call to action—"What's it going to be, then, eh?" —which, in the moral framework of the novel, suggests his intuitive exercise of free will, while the prison chaplain and F. Alexander (in the film, Mr. Alexander) extend this theme into theological and political areas. By January 1970, the script was completed (Kubrick's first solo as a screenwriter) and the real work just beginning. Here is how Kubrick defined his intentions in the film:

> I'd say that my intention with A *Clockwork Orange* was to be faithful to the novel and to try and see the violence from Alex's point of view, to show that it was great fun for him, the happiest part of his life, and that it was like some great action ballet. It was necessary to find a way of stylizing the violence, just as Burgess does by his writing style. The ironic counterpoint of the music was certainly one of the ways of achieving this. All the scenes of violence are very different without the music.[3]

Most discussions of the novel center on Alex's character and his Nadsat dialect and how they express Burgess's Christian belief in original sin, the importance of moral choice in a fallen world, and the dangers of behaviorist application. As a Catholic, Burgess accepts the reality of human evil—that man is more inclined to the bad than the good—while he believes in the redeeming grace of free will. If inherent evil is denied, as it is in the works of behavioral psychologist B. F. Skinner, and relocated in an external function like environment, Burgess argues, our definition of human nature becomes dangerously simplified and life morally empty: "one in which everything is made easy, in which you shall be wound up like a clockwork machine and be good all the time and not worry about making ethical choices."[4] Alex may be nasty and completely despicable as an ethical or social being, but in Burgess's ethos he is undeniably human: "He has the three human attributes—love of aggression, love of language, love of beauty." When the novel begins, he is young (fifteen years old) and does not understand the significance of his freedom; he exists in an imaginative Eden or Hobbesian state of nature, and only after he *falls* from a window in a suicide attempt does he show signs of moral awareness. In the original British ending (Heinemann, 1962), which is not included in the American version (Norton, 1963), Alex "chooses" this other course: At eighteen, burned out by teen-age amorality, he longs for the domestic orderliness of marriage and family. Although it has been much debated, and openly condemned by Kubrick himself, this conclusion does conform to Burgess's belief that human beings and societies are part of a cyclical process moving back and forth in time between goodness and evil, totalitarianism and freedom. In the novel, Alex eventually chooses (like a *man*) in response to an organic and natural instinct (like an *orange*), rather than lose that uniqueness through the mechanical (clockwork) imposition of goodness through aversive therapy (the Ludovico Technique). In the final analysis, he is neither a machine nor an orange, for in that last act of denial and choice he moves toward a more complete embodiment of Burgessian humanity.[5]

A Clockwork Orange could be read as Anthony Burgess's "modest proposal," except that in its original form (no longer available even in the British edition) Burgess breaks from the novel's satiric style and overtly asserts a cyclical affirmation. Like Swift's essay and its outrageous analogy between political oppression and cannibalism, however, Burgess's work masks its serious intent through metaphor, satiric exaggeration, and ironic misdirection. It employs an unreliable first-person narrator—an ironic "persona"—who both shocks the average reader's sensibilities and illustrates the novel's satiric thesis. Alex's love of "ultraviolence" and Beethoven, especially the "Glorious Ninth," come together to express Burgess's view that cultural or artistic sensitivities are no guarantee of moral elevation; instead, they spring from the same source as Alex's anti-social behavior—human nature—and one does not exclude the other. Alex's Nadsat casts a futuristic spell over the action of the novel and provides a linguistic alternative to the tiresome slogans articulated by the proponents of social and moral order, whether from the Right (prison chaplain and Minister of Interior) or Left (F. Alexander, author of another *Clockwork Orange*). The prison chaplain may believe in free will ("Goodness is something chosen. When a man cannot choose he ceases to be a man") but his hellfire and brimstone oratory is far too severe for either Alex's pleasure principle or Burgess's irony; and F. Alexander may deplore the clockwork tendencies of the State, but in both his radical zeal and his belief in human goodness ("a creature of growth and capable of sweetness, to ooze juicily at the last round the bearded lips of God"), he opposes his creator's more conservative and humane Catholicism.[6] In such a fictional world, understanding comes to the reader *covertly*, through the intricacies of style and rhetoric, rather than in the direct assertions of character or narrator. In fact, not everything in Alex's story is as clear as his "unmuddied lake or azure sky of deepest summer." As Nabokov does in *Lolita*, Burgess creates a system of literary/cultural allusion—the subtext as text—that frees the alert reader from Alex's perverse grip and allows him to appreciate the novel's merger of artifice and thesis, its "choice" of creative mode. Alex lacks not only conscience, like an innocent, but knowledge as well. His sense of history is personal and solipsistic, extending no further than the three-year period of his "memory" story, a story in which he converts English history and literature (for instance, Queen Victoria, Disraeli, Shelley, Joyce) into the idiom of private myth. But Burgess is no Alex, and ultimately his tale addresses those readers who love language and beauty more than physical or psychic violence, which ironically forces them into identifying with Alex and not with the behavioral engineers and political fanatics. He speaks to those who have struggled with their natures, made choices, and accepted, in the positive spirit of irony, the challenges of a fully expressive life.[7]

In discussing B. F. Skinner's *Beyond Freedom and Dignity*, Kubrick reveals how his thinking parallels and, in significant respects, departs from Burgess's rigidly dualistic philosophy.[8] He agrees that any utopian view of man's goodness is a "dangerous fallacy" and especially objects to the notion that human nature can be "explained" or rational-

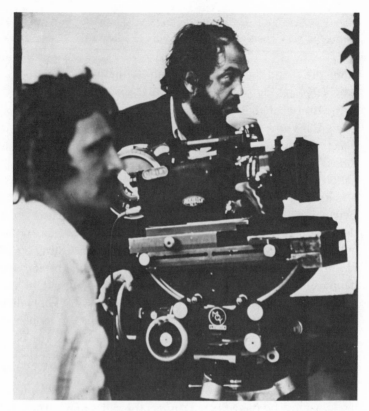

The artist behind the cameras of *A Clockwork Orange*.

ized in behaviorist terms. Skinner, it should be noted, opposes any form of negative (aversive) reinforcement, but instead writes enthusiastically about how man can change environment and inevitably control both stimulus and response: "Behavior can be changed by changing the conditions of which it is a function." Somewhat mysteriously, he contends that such changes are mandatory if human beings are to survive as a species, that we all must shed the illusion of autonomy and go "beyond freedom and dignity" (that is, beyond romantic concepts of innate goodness). Kubrick, who in *Dr. Strangelove* and *2001* had considered the subject of civilization and its discontents, offers a thoughtful critique of Skinner's book when he describes how

it works on the premise that human freedom and dignity have become inconsistent with the survival of our civilization. It's a very startling and sinister and not totally refutable contention, and *Clockwork Orange* is very concerned with this sort of idea.[9]

Notice the "sinister" and "not totally refutable": typically, he remains both skeptical about, and open to, a variety of ideas and speculations, no matter what their consequences or how they might go against the grain of his own philosophic leanings. Burgess, on the other hand, flatly rejects Skinner on the basis of Burgess's personal commitment to historical cycles and moral order, while Kubrick displays an artist's fascination with the enigmatic and unknown. He opposes Skinner's concept of man as a stimulus-response creature for the same reason he pushes Bowman as Star-Child through the monolith into space: For Kubrick, the inner universe potentially harbors as much mystery as the outer one, while in their own way both behaviorism and Burgess's Augustinian brand of Catholicism (in which evil is the norm and goodness a happy surprise) function best in argumentative rather than imaginative contexts. Hence, Burgess's *A Clockwork Orange* is not only didactic but develops a theme far too simple for the brilliance of its literary invention; like other "modernist" works (for instance, Eliot's *The Waste Land*, Joyce's *Ulysses*), it illustrates the thesis of moral/cultural decay through an ironic opposition between style and statement.

But human nature and civilization are not the only issues here. Kubrick, it must be remembered, brings the shifts and surprises of a contingent universe into any conceptual situation, while Skinner maintains that "contingencies" are subject to scientific control and Burgess accepts them as a necessary element in an essentially Manichean world view. From *The Killing* onward, Kubrick's films repeatedly dramatize the intersections of choice and contingency, and how each works on the other to produce a series of paradoxical "responses." The films, in their psychological tangle of conscious and subconscious acts, in the proximity of design and accident, embody his belief in the inextricable unity of choice and fate. Johnny Clay chooses to follow the logic of his plan, even after the intrusions of inner and outer forces far more complex than rational. Colonel Dax in *Paths of Glory* discovers that in the man-made labyrinth of World War I politics, and in the absence of real choice, what matters is the pretense of civilized behavior, of moral form without function. Humbert searches for his dream of Lolita and instead finds the perverse Quilty, an objectification of his own degradation and a disguised fate. In *Dr. Strangelove*, the creation of "fail-safe" systems and Doomsday Machines represents the ultimate choice, a kind of behaviorist dream turned nightmare, in which a passion for control eliminates not only contingencies but life itself. By *2001*, Kubrick considers the possibility that in a future dominated by machine intelligence human beings may lose both the commitment to, and the instinct for, moral choice. Moon-Watcher's discovery of the bone/tool is viewed as a magical occurrence, where inner awareness and outer mystery come together in a single moment of time, while Floyd imitates the hominid's territorial instincts but not his capacity for inner growth. He and the travelers aboard *Discovery* have almost lost those essential human attributes which are as important to Kubrick as they are to Burgess: the love of aggression, the love of language, and the love of beauty have been transferred to machines, while human consciousness hibernates in a kind of pre-evolutionary void. HAL's "humanity" (his madness) forces Bowman to rediscover his own and to contemplate the presence of an outer universe that paradoxically defies understanding as it stimulates growth.

Separating novel from film, the novelist from film maker, represents one of the first steps in estimating Kubrick's achievement in *A Clockwork Orange* (1971). If he were a writer and not a film artist, Stanley Kubrick very well might compose such a novel, except that his would be less theological and more speculative. But just consider these Kubrickian echoes in Burgess's work: (1) The narrative invention and doubling, as in the coincidental repetitions of part three in which Alex suffers retribution at the hands of his previous victims, could be compared to both *Killer's Kiss* and the more sophisticated *Lolita*. (2) The reflexive intrusions that remind the reader of the truth of fiction and the lie of reality, such as F. Alexander's political novel within Burgess's fantastic one, resemble the involutions and self-reference of Nabokov's *Lolita* as well as Kubrick's film. (3) Burgess's ironic reflection on civilized pretenses, even to the point of diminishing the moral authority of its own linguistic instrument through Alex's Nadsat ("civilized my syphilized yarbles"), recalls the devaluation of words and forms in *Paths of Glory, Lolita, Dr. Strangelove*, and *2001*. (4) The blending of the ordinary and bizarre, of social reality and private truth, resembles the kind of surreal mise-en-scène that increasingly dominates the Kubrick films of the sixties. Significantly, the novel's first-person narration provides Kubrick with a psychological and narrative focus even more subjective and nightmarish than that in Nabokov's *Lolita*. No character as important as Clare Quilty challenges Alex's insidious control or vision; indeed, Alex *is* the alter ego incarnate, the Evil One, who gleefully mocks the masks of normality worn by both the Humberts in his fictional world and the readers in Burgess's real one. But like Humbert's account, Alex's narration maintains a past tense (his "flashback") and even though it moves forward in time from episode to episode, its content remains subjective and associative rather than objective or logical.

Kubrick describes Alex's adventures in the film as a psychological myth about "natural man in the state in which he is born, unlimited, unrepressed" and likens him to Richard III:

> Alex, like Richard, is a character whom you should dislike and fear, and yet you find yourself drawn very quickly into his world and find yourself seeing things through his eyes. It's not easy to say how this is achieved, but it certainly has something to do with his candor and wit and intelligence, and the fact that all the other characters are lesser people, and in some ways worse people.[10]

But his Alex (Malcolm McDowell) is a simpler version of both Burgess's protagonist and Shakespeare's delightful villain. He is a character of intuition and instinct, a mythopoeic extension of human nature, one who does not think as much as he dreams and acts: He drinks "milk-plus" in the Korova Milkbar in order to sharpen himself for "a bit of the old ultraviolence"; he and his droogs beat up an old tramp (Paul Farrell) who is drunkenly singing a song (this scene expresses not Burgess's theme of youth versus old age but Alex's gratuitous love of violence, and it prepares for later coincidences and dreamlike recurrences —in part three, the tramp and his friends beat Alex); he orchestrates a battle with Billyboy (Richard Connaught) and his gang, not to settle an old score or to claim the devotchka (girl) being raped, but because it is an activity that gives him an intense pleasure; and he speeds through the night in a stolen car, with no specific destination in mind (one "home" is as good as another), only to revel in the visceral sensation of machine and body—"The Durango-95 purred away real horrorshow— a nice warm vibratty feeling all through your guttiwuts." As in the novel, the operative word here is *horrorshow*. For Alex, it expresses the good (from the Russian root *horosh*, for "fine" or "splendid") and in the thematic context of the film, it stands for the union of violence (horror) and aesthetics (show), as demonstrated in Alex's impromptu rendition

Our "humble narrator" and friend.

of Gene Kelly's "Singing in the Rain" (a detail not in the novel) while preparing to rape Alexander's wife (Adrienne Corri).[11] In the early scenes of the film especially, Kubrick characterizes Alex's dreamlike reverie more in terms of space and sound than time, of seeing and hearing, of being seen and heard. Alex, for instance, rarely strays from his obsessive egocentricity to editorialize about socio-political matters (as he often does in the novel) or to satirize the corruption of the other characters (as Richard III does), but he ruthlessly demands the right to look at the world in his own way—even through one eye with a false eyelash—and to choreograph scenes for his own amusement. His dresser drawer contains several stolen watches, but his wrists are adorned only with decorative bleeding eyeballs on each cuff; unlike his droogs, he shows no interest in profit ("pretty polly"), social position, or efficient planning, all of which are practical and timebound concerns, but instead searches for moments of private ecstasy, of "gorgeousness and gorgeosity made flesh." Alex wishes to render "gravity all nonsense now" by escaping into a world of "lovely pictures" (fantasy), sounds (Ludwig van), and physical sensation (action as performance). In Kubrick's version, he is the Star-Child of the Id, who, like an adolescent Quilty, explores and acts out the dark secrets of interior space as an alternative to "growing up" in a clockwork society:

> Our subconscious finds release in Alex, just as it finds release in dreams. It resents Alex being stifled and repressed by authority, however much our conscious mind recognizes the necessity of doing this.[12]

In a wry twist, Kubrick turns his audience into voyeurs (Quilty's "do you like to watch, Captain?" echoes in Alex's "viddy well, little

brother"), closet Humberts who watch in the dark and inevitably celebrate the monster's rebirth on an illuminated screen.

If the generic niche for *2001* is "mythological documentary," then
A Clockwork Orange may be nothing less than a psychological "case
study," except that its investigative method works from the inside and
documents an imaginary world even stranger than the one that ushers
Bowman through the Star-Gate to a final meeting with the monolith.
As a first-person narrative, what Bruce F. Kawin in his excellent book
on the subject would call Alex's "mindscreen," it far surpasses anything
attempted in *Lolita*, Kubrick's only other "subjective" film.[13] For one
thing, Burgess's prose style is more cinematic than Nabokov's and, for
another, the setting and subject matter of the novel did not pose problems in 1970 comparable to those which troubled the *Lolita* project in
1960. The Production Code and Legion of Decency were not significant
factors, which meant that the violence and the sexual content of the
novel could remain intact, and the action's being set in England, in the
near future, encouraged Kubrick to shoot on location for the first time
since leaving America. In addition, it allowed him the opportunity to
create a surreal style that reverses the studio-bound tendencies of his
three previous films. By bringing Alex's unique and distorted imagination into contact with perfectly credible environments, Kubrick's *Clockwork* gives the impression that the private nightmares of Quilty's Pavor
Manor and Strangelove's Mine Shaft walk the streets of the real world
and inhabit the domiciles of social normality, that psychological disorder and cultural madness are one.[14]

Paradoxically, the film seems more "realistic" and contemporary
than Burgess's novel, even though it derives much of its visual and
aural power from the techniques of cinematic distortion. In opposition
to Skinner's view that environment acts upon the "perceiving person,"
Kubrick's film, through images and sounds, shows how Alex and others
transform outer reality into the contours of inner obsession. For Alex,
place or setting has no real significance in itself—whether it be the
sanctum of his bedroom (a "real" room) or the Korova Milkbar (one
of the film's four sets), Mr. Alexander's living room (an actual home
in Radlett) or bathroom (set)—but instead serves as a stage on which
he acts out and makes "real" his theater of instinct. All the tangibles of
a random and concrete world—people, places, objects—become his
props and backgrounds, which means that Alex, perhaps more than
any other "perceiver" in literature or film, is a ready-made cinematic

concept. His field of vision changes according to his psychological condition or conditioning, just as the film maker uses reality as plastic material, responsive to both the control of predetermined factors (that is, script and budget) and the unexpected directions of creative inspiration. Especially in his "natural state" (pre-Ludovico Technique) does Alex's psychological world lend itself to the kind of expressionistic rhetoric that characterizes Kubrick's film:

1. exaggerated acting styles and pop-cult costumes;

2. stylized sets to suggest symmetry and doubling (Korova Milkbar, a mirrored hallway with a chessboard floor, a mirrored bathroom);

3. the use of unusual or ironic locations for symbolic purposes (a derelict casino for a fight; an audio-visual theater for Alex's "treatment");

4. severe backlighting for night scenes shot on location (near the Thames Embankment) and photolamps in lighting fixtures for interior scenes, both of which incorporate the devices of *cinéma vérité* (night for night; "available" light; ultra-fast lenses) into a coldly modern and eerie photographic style;

5. odd-angled close-ups and an extreme wide-angle lens (9.8 mm) for interior scenes to create foreground distortion (of, for instance, faces and prominent objects) and tunnel-like compositions and pathways;

6. the use of a handheld Arriflex camera and a variety of subjective shots, including those of characters looking into the camera (as in the opening shot of the film and in the HOME rape scene);

7. the formalizing of violence through editing, choreography, and music (the casino fight), speeded-up motion and music (at 2 frames per second for Alex's parodic "orgy" with two teenyboppers), slow-motion and music (Alex's attack on Dim; Dim's later retaliation with a milk bottle; and Alex's last fantasy);

8. an obtrusive editing style in moments of joy or crisis (for instance, when Alex is masturbating to Beethoven and during the killing of the Cat Lady);

9. the electronically realized sounds and music of composer Walter Carlos on the Moog synthesizer.[15]

But *A Clockwork Orange* does more than record the mental landscape of a highly unusual character. Its narrative field includes not only what Alex says (voiceover), what he sees (subjective camera), and what he thinks (mindscreen), but a provocative series of images and actions that originate in the iconography of Kubrick's earlier films. In that respect, the film becomes a *trompe l'oeil*, Kubrick's reflection on his cinematic past, one that puts an audience, like Bowman, in a strange room and demands it look for signs of an unseen intelligence. The opening shot, for instance, bizarrely links the endings of *2001* and *Paths of Glory* to the beginning of *Clockwork*, except that Alex's gaze into the camera more closely resembles the leopard's stare over a Pleistocene wasteland or HAL's fish-eyed surveillance of a futuristic deathship than it does the Star-Child's look of evolutionary awakening. And the world Alex contemplates is as black as the walls around him, but the camera, instead of moving through that darkness, as it does when the Star-Child escapes the eighteenth-century room, dollies backward to reveal the symmetrical outlines of a path in the middle of a world (Korova Milkbar) no more inviting than the one that concludes *Paths of Glory*. But in this film we will witness a life-and-death struggle between Alex's instinct for free expression and a social environment that prefers machine efficiency to human imagination, that creates HALs instead of Star-Childs, and that builds enclosed trenches rather than spacious chateaus. Throughout the film, the imagery recalls the corridors, paths, and tunnels down which so many of Kubrick's characters have moved, either toward a waiting death or dazzling rebirth. Early in the film Alex and his droogs are seen as stationary figures against the darkness of the Korova Milkbar and as silhouettes at the end of a tunnel (inside a pedestrian underpass, where they assault the tramp): These images recall the terror awaiting Davy Gordon in *Killer's Kiss* at the end of his nightmare corridor-ride, the execution stakes looming before the three prisoners of *Paths*, and the three figures that close in on Johnny Clay at the end of *The Killing*. In one scene that reminds us of other Kubrickian travelers, Alex moves freely through the aisles of a music bootick while the camera prepares his way with a 360° turn, and in another scene, he experiences his own version of the Star-Gate as he seems to fly through a multicolored night in the Durango-95.

Suggestions of primal struggle and evolutionary regression, of civilization moving in reverse, link *Clockwork* to the mythopoeic structures of *Killer's Kiss*, *Dr. Strangelove*, and *2001*. At the beginning, Alex is the bone-carrier and tribal leader who asserts his supremacy over Dim (Warren Clarke) beside another Kubrickian waterhole (a marina) and even imitates Moon-Watcher's apelike gestures of victory in slow motion; later, the bone assumes the ironic shape of a milk bottle as Dim and the droogs turn on Alex and undermine the autonomy of this primitive raiding party disguised as juvenile night-gang. The fight between Alex and the Cat Lady (Miriam Karlin) resembles the one in *Killer's Kiss* between Davy and Rapallo in the mannequin factory, except that in *Clockwork* the antagonists are surrounded by a surreal blend of erotic art, black and white cats, and athletic equipment in a period home. And instead of such primitive weapons as an ax and pike, they use the tools of a decadent civilization, namely, a sculptured penis and a gilded bust of Beethoven. The fantasies of orgasmic explosions and death that Alex has early in the film recall the apocalyptic ending of *Dr. Strangelove*, and in the last part of the film Alex becomes the victim of an impotent lunatic in a wheelchair (that is, his Strangelove), so obsessed by desire for revenge and for political power that he is more machine than man. Certain settings repeat the enclosures of *Dr. Strangelove* and *2001*, particularly the bone-white interior of the modernistic HOME (the White side of the board to Korova's Black) and its resemblance to Space Station 5, where Alex first plays the primitive in his assault on the writer and his wife and where Alex is later the victim of a savage retribution at the hands of his "civilized" double (Mr. Alexander).

That all this should be taken in the spirit of self-parody—as Kubrick's first-person reprise through the trick mirror of Alex's mindscreen —becomes a likely possibility when the conclusion of *Clockwork* appears to mimic *2001*'s pattern of cosmic death and rebirth. When Alex, wet and beaten, is carried into HOME, it initiates the familiar Kubrickian motif of *cleansing* (in Alexander's bathtub), *eating* (on Alexander's glass table), and *sleeping*. Only now, there are no flushings offscreen or Zero Gravity Toilets, no nympholept scribbling his dirty secrets in a diary, no crystal glass breaking on a fluorescent floor or regenerative green beds: sitting at a table and eating, at first alone, with the sound of tinkling silverware recalling the generals' breakfast in *Paths* and Bowman's last meal in *2001*, wearing the red and white robe worn by his double during the HOME rape scene, and drinking drugged red wine rather than milkplus, Alex unceremoniously falls face down into a plate of spaghetti; like Bowman, he awakens as a prisoner in an unfamiliar room (French Provincial decor), but unlike the Star-Child in his movement through the monolith, Alex and the camera go into space through a window, only to crash-land on the earth below; and in this suicidal descent he begins an ironic rebirth into a post-Ludovico world (or so he comes to believe), one that culminates with an "awakening" on a hospital bed and the discovery that he has been "cured." It is not only Alex's capacity for violence that has been restored—a point crucial to the film's ironic affirmation—but the possibility that some day he may choose to follow his love for beauty. Alex may not be ready for the mystery of the monolith, but he does escape his HAL (Alexander as double) and "re-evolve" into a human condition where inner growth and a free imagination remain two measures of hope for the future.

A *Clockwork Orange* is Kubrick's most culturally assertive film before *Barry Lyndon*; it evokes a formal and dehumanized atmosphere closer to the disco seventies than the psychedelic sixties. In part one particularly, Kubrick draws as much attention to the psychological origins of a cultural malaise as he does to the specific aberrations of Alex's character. In the association of psychic enclosure with the demise of civilization, the film resembles the drama that takes place in *2001* after HAL murders Poole, aborts the hibernators, and denies Bowman access to *Discovery*. HAL assumes control over a lifeless world of mechanical objects like himself in order to preserve an illusion of machine infallibility. In *Clockwork*, characters inhabit equally artificial environments—mirror worlds—in which they sacrifice the richness of self for the perfection of mechanical form. Appropriately, Kubrick uses an extreme wide-angle lens in almost all these settings (Korova, HOME, the Cat Lady's) and thereby creates another version of HAL's fish-eyed madness. Long before Alex becomes the Frankenstein monster of a clockwork state, social communication has degenerated into an impersonal and sterile intercourse—masculine with masculine, feminine with feminine, objects with objects. Alex disturbs this reflexive seance —and becomes the only regenerative force in the film—because he embodies the concept of the Other, society's nemesis rather than child, more *doppelgänger* than twin.

The classical symmetry of the Korova, for instance, not only stands as High Camp mockery but expresses a conditioned society's transference of sexual fantasy and function to the solidarity and harmony of machines disguised as art objects. White female statues perform machine functions (as tables and dispensers of milkplus) and assume postures in sadomasochistic Grand Guignol. They either can be contemplated from afar, as Kubrick's camera invites us to do at the end of the opening shot, in its backward movement, or "used" as machines: in one scene, Dim reaches between the legs of one figure ("Pardon me, Luce") to pull the phallic lever that dispenses milkplus through the nipple of a jutting breast, while the arms, in chains, extend backward in a gesture of erotic submission. In the first HOME scene, Kubrick creates a domestic version of the same world: Mr. Alexander (Patrick Magee), in a red and white robe, is first seen as a figure behind a prominent and red IBM Selectric, while the camera records a conjugal distance when it tracks right to pick up his wife, in a red pajama suit, engulfed by a white modernistic chair shaped like a lopsided egg and upholstered in the assertive hues of Korova purple. As before, decor— the arrangement of shapes and colors within a confined space—absorbs people as well as things into the configurations of a clockwork aesthetic. In the hallway, as Alex and his masked droogs invade this museum advertised on an illuminated sign as the archetypal HOME, mirrors on each side of a chessboard floor create a triptych that recalls the static duplications first seen in the Korova Milkbar. Yet seemingly none of this affects Alex, the only original in a world of machine reproductions. At the Korova, his sinister glare and his Nadsat bring a highly charged consciousness into an otherwise inhuman and somnambulant mise-en-scène, while in HOME his improvisations resemble those of an unruly but creative child turning the tables on parental authority. Alex not only disrupts HOME's Korova-like stasis, but forces Alexander to watch as his wife is twisted into an animated version of a Korova sex-machine (except that her pubic hair is natural red). Although like an adolescent Alex first goes for the breasts (milkless, not milkplus), his sexual mode is phallic rather than oral. He wears a mask with a long red nose, which he pokes toward the camera and into Alexander's face, carries a cane harboring a knife and, as if to exaggerate his genital authority, wears a large codpiece in which he stores rubber balls. Because this scene is inventive as well as shocking, Kubrick's ironic point is made: in the context of the Korova's sexual postures and its unnatural colors (bright oranges and purples) in the midst of a predominately black and white world, as well as HOME's heterosexual sterility (the Alexanders spawn objects instead of children), Alex's rape of the wife/mother has the virtue of being a "normal" (even if Oedipal) expression of an unrepressed libido.

Alex's killing of the Cat Lady extends this sexual allegory even further. When first introduced, the Cat Lady is an upside-down figure in a landscape of erotic paintings showing women in various states of sex-

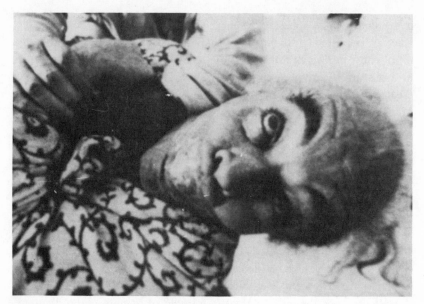

The victim as voyeur (Patrick Magee).

ual excitement, either masturbatory or lesbian. Overall, she assumes a
character and definition several steps higher on the aesthetic ladder
than Alex's own Mum, making her the decadent rather than pathetic
mother-figure: Em (Sheila Raynor), for instance, decorates her home
in a ghastly combination of colors (electric blue and pink in the living
room; yellow, orange, and silver reflective checkers in the kitchen) and
with discount-store paintings of darkly exotic women who all look
alike, and she wears brightly colored orlon wigs (like the statues in the
Korova) and vinyl miniskirts to disguise both her age and maternal
status. Even her bedroom—seen only once, when Deltoid (Aubrey
Morris), Alex's "Post Corrective Adviser," plays the role of surrogate
father/castrator (he punishes the truant in the crotch)—exemplifies the
same kind of dehumanized nightmare found elsewhere. The pink walls
and green bedspread attest to her bad taste, not to visions of rebirth,
while the presence of white wig forms without eyes or mouths and
dentures without a head in a glass of water—respectively staring and
grinning toward the camera in unison with Deltoid on the bed—aligns
this lower middle-class domicile with the Korova's and Cat Lady's more
decadent aberrations. But the Cat Lady totally denies her potential for
procreation (one which Em, like Charlotte in *Lolita*, symbolically denies). She lives amidst lesbian self-portraits (including a face with

mouths within mouths, and teeth to link her with the grinning dentures), colors herself like an art object (heavy lipstick on a large mouth, red-tinted hair, green and white leotards), and twists her body into mechanical contortions that resemble a piece of abstract sculpture or her own "health farm" exercise equipment. This psychosexual landscape, like the Korova, suggests not only that sexual function has been replaced by sexual extensions, but that human beings, machinelike, imitate the objects of their own creation. As a female masturbatory nightmare, the Cat Lady's room both opposes the masculine fantasies of the Korova and symbolically castrates them. In one shot, for instance, a boot being caressed by a woman in one of the paintings appears to kick the sculptured penis, on the table below, in the testes. And before Alex brings his decidedly phallic sexuality into this domain, we notice that only two objects—the penis and Beethoven's bust—have a male association and each, to quote the Cat Lady, is a "very important work of art." Alex (and Kubrick's handheld camera) disrupts this narcissistic world, which the Cat Lady identifies as a "real" person's house, and turns an object of contemplation into a tool/weapon when, in an act that is simultaneously murder and oral copulation, he crashes the bone-white phallus into the Cat Lady's mouth. Symbolically, he actualizes his culture's almost extinct unconscious (she uses the bust as weapon), gives its artifacts a renewed function (albeit a violent one), and increasingly assumes the role of life-force as well as scourge.

During Alex's nocturnal adventures in the early scenes of *Clockwork*, from Korova to private orgasm, Kubrick builds a progression of music, images, and events into a mock-heroic preamble. Alex, like Moon-Watcher, inhabits a wasteland littered with bones, only here they are the aesthetic remains of a mechanical civilization of the future. He is a child of darkness, a satiric spirit of life, who awakens from the sleep of the dead to act out his worst dreams and bring a renewed vitality and function to the people and things of his world. Notice, for instance, how the following outline of Alex's journey through the night evokes the resonance of such a myth: (1) The film begins with the dark, processional sounds of Purcell's "Music for Queen Mary's Funeral" on the Moog, an appropriately surreal rendering in the context of both the Korova's decor and Alex's Nadsat; Alex's face and eyes fill the screen, just as the glaring countenance of Beethoven on a window-blind will dominate his room during a triumphant masturbatory fantasy, while from long shot, he and his droogs seem to slumber inside the womb of a cultural death-chamber. (2) Next, Alex and his droogs appear as shadows in a uterine tunnel, quadruplets ruling the night, while the only sounds heard are the tramp's nostalgic "Sweet Molly Malone" and Alex's mockery in voiceover; spotlighted from behind, Alex and the droogs applaud the tramp's efforts before descending on him like a pack of carnivores from man's twilight more than his dawn. (3) Rossini's "Thieving Magpie," a lighter piece than the Purcell, ushers us into the derelict casino for an invigoratingly parodic showdown between rival gangs; the camera pulls back from a flowered landscape in pastel and a gilded proscenium arch with a Zeus-like head at its apex—relics of a more romantic age—and reveals below a stage "spotlighted" by a purple glow, surreal heads of laughing dummies against the wall and, *in medias res*, the rape of a young woman with large breasts;[16] a piano, a broken roulette table, and debris strewn on the floor before the stage complete the decor; the fight itself, a surprisingly bloodless affair, is a graceful ballet of music and movement (stunts and fast-paced editing) that effectively captures the reverie of Alex's mindscreen and its merger of instinct and performance. (4) After the nightride in the Durango-95, Rossini gives way to HOME's doorchime (a chord from Beethoven's Fifth) and Alex's "Singing in the Rain," staged as a parody of Gene Kelly's song and dance from the 1952 MGM musical; in place of an umbrella, Alex uses his cane as both dance prop and weapon, for as the song says, he has that "glorious feeling" and is "ready for love"; he overturns Alexander's bookshelves and writing desk, emblems of a humane past as extinct as the aesthetic traditions and games of chance found in the derelict casino. On a white wall hangs a modern landscape painting which becomes especially prominent as a backdrop to the rape itself and recalls the artwork that presided over the fight with Billyboy's gang; in the end, Alex's grotesquely masked appearance and Alexander's face—distorted in close-up by the wide lens and a ball protruding from his taped mouth—form complementary images of Alex the performer and Alexander the voyeur. (5) Then, all "shagged and fagged and fashed," Alex and his band of merry players return to the Korova and hear a woman (a "sophisto" from a TV studio), with a gold frame highlighting her eyes like a proscenium arch, sing a fragment of Schiller's "Ode to Joy" from Beethoven's Ninth; Alex is an appreciative audience, while Dim exercises the privilege of the unenlightened by moronically blowing a raspberry (for which he receives a rap from Alex's cane). (6) Finally, Alex walks home to the music of Purcell, through the clutter of Municipal Flat-block 18A (a Thames architectural project), passes a blandly idealized socialist mural ("The Dignity of Labor") decorated with juvenile graffiti, and relieves himself in his bathroom; with the sounds of the scherzo from Beethoven's Ninth filling his bedroom, the camera prepares for Alex's orgasmic climax through a series of startling images. Successive zooms move closer and closer to Beethoven's face on the shade, until his eyes stare directly into the camera, then to a painting of a nude woman blissfully smiling in a pose of sexual invitation and a pan down to Alex's snake, Basil, curled around a branch, seemingly about to enter the vaginal opening. Then, within the same shot, four Christ statues on Alex's dresser, joined in a passion of celebration (crown of thorns, nails in wrists, red hair, genitals, right fists raised in defiance and left feet extended in dance), convert crucifixion into performance; the faces of Christ, Alex, and Beethoven then come together in a prelude to that imaginary ride through a private Star-Gate dominated by a repeated close-up of Alex/Dracula, bloody fangs and all, presiding over a B-movie apocalypse of hanging figures, avalanches, and doomsday explosions.

As these sequences demonstrate, Alex works from the inside out—from fantasy to performance—as he transforms the lifeless settings and cultural mythology of an overly conditioned society into a new order of truth. Rather than remain a slumping figure in the static decor of the Korova or become lost in a sentimental and boozy journey into the past (the tramp, like Alex, leans against a darkened wall), Alex gives form to his imaginative life through action and performance. The derelict casino symbolizes the decline of imagination (theater) and a belief in chance, both of which intersect in an act of creation and oppose the repressive aims of the clockwork state, and this setting perfectly suits Alex's dreamlike character. He travels through the night impulsively, seizes the moment and spins the wheel, and envisions action as a theatrical mixture of dancelike movement and music. He does not separate mind from body, reflection from action, the unconscious from social reality; nor does he transfer his sexual or violent urges onto objects and become, like others, a voyeur of his own degradation. Instead, he forces Alexander to watch the rape of his wife—a primal scene in reverse, where the father watches the Oedipal moment—and to confront a complex humanity which, by part three of the film, Alexander and his madness share with Alex. Significantly, Alexander does not close his eyes

or avert his gaze—it is a *horrorshow* that holds the same fascination
for him as it does for his adolescent double. Alex may stand and watch,
even applaud, the tramp's song or Billyboy's gangbang, but ultimately
he is a performer, not a voyeur, and he gives his inner world both a
violent substance and an aesthetic form. Performance rather than sublimation defines his mode. Similarly, he transforms the Christian idea
of the Fortunate Fall (that Adam's sin bestowed on man the moral
freedom of choice and the possibility of redemption) into a celebration
of pleasure, the liberation of the libido from the restraints of perfection, the bestowing on man of the gift of multiplicity. Alex's Eve (in
the painting) opens her legs for Basil because in this futuristic parable
Eden represents the original clockwork state and the snake, like Alex,
becomes a sign of the Other. Kubrick's Alex reverses the Freudian notion that multiplicity in the human personality often leads to psychosis,
that repression is not only inevitable but necessary and benevolent.
His character exhibits a wholeness of mind and body absent in such
mechanical caricatures as Pee (Philip Stone) and Em, Deltoid, and
Alexander; rather than contemplating Beethoven's music and Christ's
suffering as aesthetic or spiritual objects, he experiences them as emotional and physical realities. Beethoven's face, like Alex's, confronts
the audience in close-up with the artist's interiority, while Alex's Christ
is both pluralistic (four in all) and an entertainer with balls, one who

mocks the passive glory attached to religious suffering and defiantly celebrates the triumph of body over spirit. Because he lives in a decadent world, in which the mechanics of sublimation are so pervasive that the conscious mind not only rules the body and its instincts but turns it into a machine, Alex's humanity can be expressed only through violence and creative improvisation.

Not surprisingly, this journey through the geography and iconography of Alex's mindscreen has several ironic complications and stands in sharp relief to Kubrick's omniscience. Alex's originality as an artist/ performer exists on a primitive level, in that Alex takes received images and sounds—cultural systems—and rearranges them into an egocentric paradigm that is more preconscious than intuitive, parochial rather than catholic. In parts one and two especially, he fails to express a *chosen* middle ground between an enslavement to instinct and a forced acquiescence to the dictates of a clockwork environment. The music of Rossini, for instance, both inspires his violent improvisations ("lovely music that came to my aid") and functions as an integral component in their enactment ("Thieving Magpie" for the casino/marina fights and the killing of the Cat Lady, "William Tell Overture" for the orgy), while Beethoven's Ninth sweeps him into a state of private ecstasy ("Oh, bliss . . . bliss and heaven. . . . It was like a bird of rarest spun heaven metal or like silvery wine flowing in a space ship") and triggers an internal *horrorshow*, Alex's Cinema of the Id. He experiences the fight with Billyboy's gang as a stylized barroom brawl, something between *West Side Story* (1961) and the archetypal Western fight scene from *Dodge City* (1939); and in this mental screening room, he transforms himself into a Hammer horror film performer (in this instance, Christopher Lee's Dracula) who incongruously directs a series of deaths and stock-footage disasters reminiscent of the 1960s Hercules epics from Dino de Laurentiis. Ironically, Alex's "outer-space" reverie resembles a subspecies of a midnight horror-camp classic like *The Rocky Horror Picture Show* (1975) more than it does the extraterrestrial visions of *2001*; his imagination repeatedly asserts a juvenile fondness for creative parody and a restructuring of a Hollywood-induced film mentality.[17] It reverses the sentimental and melodramatic formulas associated with popular film storytelling, just as Kubrick's film not only frustrates conventional expectations and sympathies but undercuts a mindless identification with Alex, its nominal "humble narrator" and resident cineaste. In that context, part one of *Clockwork* portrays the rude beginnings of Alex's artistic evolution, his "dawn," in which a creative vitality is threatened with extinction by the clockwork intrusions of a highly mechanical and repressed society. And finally, one must praise Malcolm McDowell's brilliantly innovative but controlled performance. Through a blending of facial expressiveness and body kinetics, McDowell fully objectifies Alex's progress from the *enfant terrible* of part one, through the ordeal of conditioning and mechanical transformation in part two, to the struggles of rebirth in part three. His is one of the most underrated performances of the seventies in one of that decade's least understood films.

Parts two and three of *Clockwork*, characterized by the slow movement from Rossini's "William Tell Overture" and Alex's voiceover as "the real weepy and tragic part of the story," show our "friend and humble narrator" moving from artist/performer to victim/voyeur.[18] For Alex as well as the film viewer, it represents a symbolic descent from the mysteries of inner space into the real but sinister order of exterior time. It is as if we traveled through a surreal landscape of wonders and nightmares, a Star-Gate in reverse, only to double back and discover that we had never left the gravity of temporality—of causal logic and mechanical process, the "science" of stimulus-response psychology and the art of linear film making. In Kubrick's vision, as far back as *The Killing*, the clockwork state (of mind, as well as that of the body politic) prefers to take that which is complex or otherwise intractable and diminish it to a level of predictability compatible with any one of several process-systems; the state always prefers such reduction to exploration and speculation. Alex's identity, for instance, is quickly reduced from "Alexander de Large" (the Great) to a number (655321) by the Chief Guard (Michael Bates—the most amusing example in the film of mechanical man) as Alex toes the white line in a prison reception center decorated with horizontal rows of shelved boxes (civilian clothes in mothballs), a desk for personal inventories (Alex's begins with a half bar of chocolate and ends with a "Timawrist" watch), tables for stripping and physical identification (where Alex bends over for a rectal examination), and tubs for cleaning the body. For his soul, Alex confronts the dubious *choice* between the prison chaplain's (Godfrey Quigley) "incontrovertible evidence that Hell exists" (from his "visions") and the biological conditioning of the Ludovico Technique. On a platform/stage in the prison chapel, Alex becomes the object of "leering criminals and perverts" as he turns an overhead projector that displays the ironic words of a hymn ("I was a wandering sheep") about the evil of straying from the fold ("I was a wayward child/ I did not love my home") and the necessity of *control* ("I did not love my shepherd's voice/ I would not be controlled"). Later, he is bound in a straitjacket inside a theater—his head wreathed by the straps and electronic plugs of a Frankenstein crown of thorns, his eyes held open by lidlocks—and forced to watch, but not participate in, hackneyed film versions of his past history, namely droogs tolchocking a man (the tramp scene) and raping a devotchka (the casino). In each case, he finds himself defined within the timebound category of incorrigible sinner/criminal, and thereby falls victim to an institutional monolith (State/Church/Science) that would deprive him of *his* visions (of violence and beauty) by transforming him into the ultimate Clockwork Man, a two-way mirror, at once an object for others to contemplate and a voyeur.

Even as he brings Alex down to Earth and adjusts the visual/aural style of the film to a more "objective" and less expressionistic mode, Kubrick continues to develop associative details that provide an audience with sources of understanding independent of his protagonist's first-person manipulations. In other words, *A Clockwork Orange* illustrates the dangers of psychological conditioning in both a social context (Alex's plight) and a cinematic one (Kubrick's film). On one level, Alex's screen duplicates our own, which means that it can mesmerize as well as brainwash us into a condition of total identification. If we fail to escape Alex's control, we become *his* victims and voyeurs of *our* psychological disorder. Yet when we *choose* to acknowledge Kubrick's dreamlike presence—the "real" performing artist—through a recognition of the symbolic or associative structure of the film, we throw ourselves into a contingent world where almost anything is possible and nothing is certain. Consider how the following visual and aural patterns reveal this disparity between Alex's mindscreen and the film maker's intentions. In Alex's single fantasy in part two (from prison reception to Ludovico release), a Biblically-inspired vision of Sodom and Gomorrah (the scourging of Christ, the cutting of throats in battle, and the despoiling of Jewish handmaidens), Kubrick once again draws attention to a primitive cinematic imagination. Alex's simulacrum is parodic, certainly—his fantasy assumes a cliché-ridden film style reminiscent of the Biblical movie epics of the fifties, complete with the bombastic chords of Rimsky-Korsakov's "Scheherezade" (Rimsky-Korsakov is the Miklos Rozsa of classical music), while his focus suggests the inspirations of a Marquis de Sade rather than a Cecil B. DeMille.* And, no doubt, the scene offered Kubrick another opportunity to exorcise some private demons having to do with *Spartacus*, his only film mounted in Alex's "height of Roman fashion."[19] Of greater significance, however, are the parallels between this scene and others. The Christ figure, with his wooden cross and crown of thorns, recalls the statuary in Alex's bedroom, although here his passion is given a more old-fashioned ("realistic") film treatment, even down to the obviously *painted* blood on his forehead (a throwback to the days of the Production Code). Later, in an *audio-visual theater*, Alex wears the Ludovico crown of thorns and watches a man being beaten in a film that likewise clashes with the visual originality of Kubrick's film; Alex, however, likes what he sees, particularly the blood on the victim's face ("the red, red vino on tap"), and even expresses the aesthetic judgment that "the colours of the real world only seem really real when you viddy them on the screen." Yet the blood on the screen-victim's face is blatantly artificial and contrasts with an earlier scene in a police-interrogation room where Alex's blood (on his face and a white wall) seems far more "real" *on our screen* than what is seen on the one in the Ludovico facility. Finally, after Alex is beaten in part three by Dim and Georgie (James Marcus), who are now policemen in Her Majesty's Service, Julian (David Prowse, who plays Darth Vader in *Star Wars*), Alexander's strong-man companion, carries Alex into HOME as if he were a child. Significantly, Alex's bloodied face is identical to the one in the Ludovico film, only once again the color red is far more "realistic."

More than anything else, such authorial maneuvers show Alex be-

---

* Anyone who grew up watching the American *film noir* of the forties and fifties, as Kubrick himself did, would be familiar with the sounds of Hungarian-born Hollywood composer Miklos Rozsa. His distinctive form of invigorating musical bombast enhanced an impressive number of *noir* films—*Double Indemnity* (1944), *Spellbound* (1945), *The Killers* (1946), *Brute Force* (1947), *The Naked City* (1948), and *The Asphalt Jungle* (1950). What is particularly interesting, however, about what could be a parodic allusion to his music in Kubrick's selection of "Scheherezade" for Alex's scourging of Christ fantasy is that during the fifties and sixties Rozsa scored a number of Biblical or epic behemoths, among them, *Quo Vadis* (1951), *Ben-Hur* (1959), *El Cid* (1961) and, most appropriate of all, the atrocious *Sodom and Gomorrah* (1962). One of his recent credits is for the music in Resnais's *Providence* (1977), where, as in *Clockwork*, one hears the chords of musical parody.

coming the victim of Kubrick's irony. Because he cannot see the unreality and contrivance of those films, or put aside his instinctive reactions
in the interest of imaginative freedom, Alex's responses are conditioned
even before the injection of aversive serum by Dr. Branom (Madge
Ryan). He does not see, for instance, the differences between his fantasies and those projected on a movie screen, whether in a commercial
cinema or the laboratories of *Clockwork*'s mad scientists. He characterizes the first Ludovico film as "a very good, professional piece of sinny,
like it was done in Hollywood," indicating that Kubrick—not Alex—
asks *his* audience to associate the sentimental or visceral responses in-
duced by the archetypal Hollywood product with those created by the
Ludovico Technique.[20] What Alex fails to notice about such films, of
course, is that they encourage (or force) an identification with victims
rather than victimizers, but as a Hobbesian primitive (who is both *free*
and *innocent*) he lacks the moral awareness to understand such intentions. No matter if it be a film or life itself, he responds to experience
instinctively, not ethically, which means that the Ludovico Technique
ultimately represents in the *ethos* of the *film*, as well as that of the novel,
the horrors of an enforced social contract, even one which occurs on
the decadent landscapes of a near but imaginary future. Yet Kubrick
knows beforehand that his audience in present time will have those responsive and "civilized" codes plugged in at the moment he assaults
the audience with the surreality of both Alex's mindscreen and his own.
Ideally, those viewers will *choose* to engage the parody (as the mid-
night-cult audience has done) as well as the aesthetic/conceptual density and will, to quote the film's Minister (Anthony Sharp) standing
before *his* audience in yet another theater, be sufficiently stimulated to
"observe all." To observe, for instance, that the post-Ludovico Alex falls
from a private Eden into world where he must not only identify with
life's inevitable victims but become one himself. To observe that Alex's
crown of thorns and bloodied face have no more "reality" on our screen
than do his internal horrorshows or the Ludovico images of a man being beaten. To observe that, symbolically, his suffering is the primitive
retribution of a clockwork society and, even more important, to observe
the workings of a Kubrickian parable that brings the audience into an
illusory world of cinematic "normality" (stylistically as well as morally)
only to demonstrate that Alex as passive victim of the Good has far less
expressive value as a human being *or* as a film character than does
Alex the scourge and performing artist.

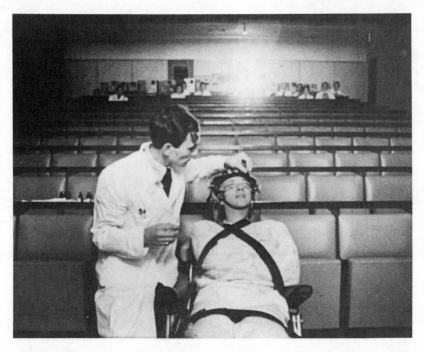

But images are not the whole story. When Alex's imaginative world is flushed out into the open and brought under the temporal authority of science, his aural sense also loses contact with that part of his humanity—a love of beauty—which might some day allow him to choose a creative rather than violent form of expression. Beethoven's Ninth ("The Turkish March," or second movement) is not only an inadvertent casualty in Alex's treatment when it serves as "background score" (to quote Dr. Branom) for a Ludovico newsreel film showing goose-stepping Nazis and World War II battlegrounds; but such uses cause it to degenerate into a type of decorative muzak on the same order of inspiration as a fatuous tune like "I want to marry a lighthouse keeper," heard on a radio when Alex returns home and discovers that Pee and Em have replaced him with a surrogate son (Joe the lodger, played by Clive Francis). Throughout parts two and three, Kubrick frequently uses musical associations and repetitions to complement Alex's experience as victim in a series of nightmarish recurrences in the broad daylight of cinematic realism. The second movement of the Ninth, for instance, is first heard in part one when Alex marches through the music bootick and dazzles us—as well as two teenyboppers licking phallic ice-sticks—with his parodic majesty, while Kubrick's dynamic

360° camera movement and a brief glimpse of a *2001* soundtrack album (listed under the heading "Underground Records") alert us to the film maker's presence. Inevitably, that music is associated in the Ludovico theater with film propaganda (synonymous with "art" in a conditioned society), clockwork armies marching to the tunes of war, and a shot of children in a statuary dancing hand-in-hand on a devastated landscape. To make the pop-culture charts, both Beethoven and Alex's musical gifts would have to undergo the same Anglo-Slavic vulgarization as evidenced by one teeny's preference for "Googly Gogol," "Johnny Zhivago," and "The Heaven Seventeen."

Aside from such incidental or satiric purposes, Kubrick uses musical associations to support and deepen the film's ironic account of Alex as life-force. In perhaps the most striking scene of part two, Alex stands on a stage, spotlighted in a dehumanized blue color, to demonstrate before an audience the curative wonders of the Ludovico Technique by playing the part of victim/voyeur in a stimulus-response entertainment. First, he is humiliated and brutalized by a stage actor (John Clive) in a vaudeville routine that mixes farce (face-slapping, nose-tweaking, ear-pulling) and subjugation (Alex pushes out his "red yahzik [tongue] a mile-and-a-half to lick the grahzny boots"), while Kubrick *on our soundtrack* plays the Elizabethan-inspired music of Terry Tucker's "Overture to the Sun" for ironic counterpoint. Following polite applause and bows by the actor, a partially nude blonde actress (Virginia Wetherell) appears from behind a dark curtain and confronts Alex, the audience in the auditorium, and the viewers of *Clockwork* with an erotic objectification of a collective unconscious. She moves out of the darkness toward us as well as Alex, who ironically describes her as "like light of heavenly grace" before feeling the Ludovico sickness—not the tugs of conscience—and wants to "have her right down there on the floor with the old in-out, real savage." This scene connects with those earlier occasions in which Alex was the performer and others were his foils or victims, while the sounds of Purcell's "Music for Queen Mary's Funeral" on the Moog associate it with the visual and conceptual milieu of the Korova Milkbar. Only now Alex remains a slumped and lifeless figure, not a spirit of renewal awakening to prowl the night. He kneels before the now stationary and impassive girl, reaches up toward her beautiful breasts, and cups his hands in midair around nipples jutting outward like one of those grotesque machine-dispensers of milkplus in the Korova. But like others, he has been con-

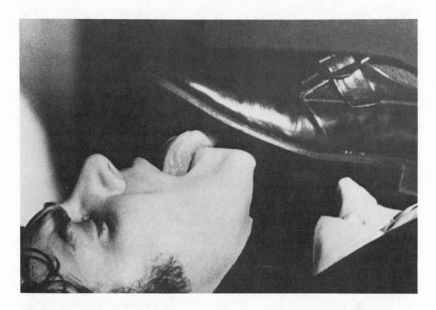

Alex as victim *and* voyeur.

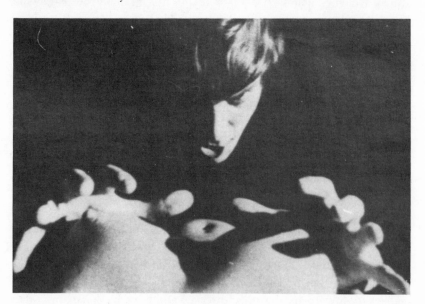

ditioned to look, not to touch. Later, the Purcell will return when Alex is taken into the woods and beaten by his former droogs, as his head is submerged in the muddy water of an animal trough (an ironic replay of his attack on Dim in the water of a marina) while the electronic sounds of the Moog are synchronized to blows from Georgie's nightstick. In such ways does Kubrick portray Alex's retreat into a womb of death.

In part one, the scherzo (fourth movement) from the Ninth provides Alex with inspiration for that mock-heroic display of masturbatory imagination, while in another bedroom (the French Provincial room of part three) it becomes an instrument in Alexander's revenge. As Alex pounds the floor of his eighteenth-century "cage" and pleads with unseen forces below to turn the music off—in itself an inversion of *2001's* final vision of a Bowman/monolith symbiosis—his double looks up and smiles in a pose of grotesque beatitude that mimics Alex's facial ecstasy whenever he nears an orgasmic epiphany. The camera dollies back from Alexander in close-up and, at a distance, shows him centered in a symmetrical arrangement of machines (stereo equipment) and people (the other three conspirators) forming a pathway down a green billiard table to a lovely tapestry hanging on the far wall. Even though the colors (predominantly greens) and music are regenerative and heroic, the camera movement and composition recall the imagery of that opening shot in the Korova. But here Alex's look of malign creativity dissolves into the crazed mask of another Dr. Strangelove spiritually resuscitated by the prospect of death.* As an element in *Clockwork's* narrative repetitions and visual/aural associations, this scene not only asserts the Korova's deathscape but asks the audience to compare our narrator's midnight fantasies (parodic, vital) with a daylight nightmare

* Throughout *Clockwork*, as in all his films, Kubrick creates some interesting associations through *visual geometry*. The Cat Lady's room, for instance, represents a surreal blend of aesthetic and temporal associations at the same time that it functions as a psycho/sexual enclosure. Besides those items of decor already mentioned in the text, the room contains a Persian rug (on which she exercises), gold drapes (the same color as Alexander's clothes in the last HOME scene), white wallpaper with a gold *fleur-de-lis* pattern, and a *green ceiling*. Through various low camera angles and the wide lens, Kubrick creates the geometry of a rectangular box with a green lid (ceiling), one which resembles the lines of composition found in a later scene with Alex in a prison exercise yard, only there an over-exposed sky creates a blindingly white "ceiling" for that enclosure. And, Korova's narrow tunnel-shape (again, enhanced by the lens) is repeated in the contours of the prison reception centre, both of which were sets built in the same warehouse. Overall, the film exhibits not only a strong visual coherence but demonstrates Kubrick's remarkable ability to abstract emotional and psychological meaning from color and shape.

that turns Beethoven (now the author of the "dreaded Ninth Symphony") and a generative art (the tapestry) into unwitting accomplices in both Alex's suicidal despair and a culture's Dance of Death.

This scene also marks the culmination of the elaborate doubling of Alex/Alexander that has been developing. Alex/Alexander can be paired in several polarities: youth/age; "primitive" adolescent/"civilized" adult; performing artist/writer; visual imagination/verbal manipulation; Beethoven as inspiration/Beethoven as decoration (HOME's doorchime); phallic virility/mental impotence; movement and dynamism/inertia and sitting (either behind a typewriter-machine or in a wheelchair). In the two HOME sequences (parts one and three), the following repetitions/pairings occur: (a) In both sequences the same *camera position* is used *outside*, in the first, when Alex and his droogs in the stolen car stop on the other side of the illuminated HOME sign and, in the second, when Alex arrives in the rain, alone and beaten. (b) The *first shot inside* the house in both sequences uses the same camera position and movement, namely, from Alexander seen behind an IBM Selectric (red in the first, light blue in the second) to a *track-right* and a sitting figure *in red* (his wife, reading a book, in the first; Julian, wearing briefs and exercising with dumbbells, in the second). (c) In each scene, Alexander responds to the doorchime with "Who on earth could that be?"—a question which assumes a special kind of resonance in a film by the director of *2001*. (d) The *camera position* in the hallway with the mirrors and chessboard floor is repeated, the first sequence showing an invasion by the droogs in clown masks and the carrying of the wife and the second sequence showing Julian picking up and carrying the bloody-faced Alex. (e) In the first sequence, Alexander is *forced* to watch as victim the "Singing in the Rain" performance/rape; in the second, he *listens* from the opposite side of a bathroom door to the ghostly echoes of Alex singing the same song while taking a bath. (f) In the first, Alexander wears a *red and white robe*; in the second Alex puts on the same robe after his bath and wears it during the scene at the table where he is drugged by the wine.

Almost mummified in white plaster from head to foot, Alex awakens from the sleep of the dead on a hospital bed and begins his "recovery" from the Ludovico Technique and the madness of his "civilized" HAL. To complement this ironic resurrection, the film shows the return of Alex's violent/creative instincts in a scene where he "interprets" a series of slide-projected drawings on a small screen. The artwork in these comic-strip Rorschachs is even more primitive than the style of the Ludovico films, although Alex's psychic/aesthetic responses remain those of a performer rather than voyeur—that is, his imagination translates them into the same kind of parodic or adolescent "meanings" found in the more expressive imagery of his fantasies. Even the camera movement and colors of this sequence suggest Alex's eventual restoration to a state of psychological and physiological "normality." A long, fast-moving dolly shot, like the one in the music bootick of part one, ushers a woman psychiatrist (Dr. Taylor, played by Pauline Taylor) into his hospital room, where she (and later, the Minister) is greeted with sneering majesty; while the appearance of bright but natural colors (e.g., an EAT ME basket of fruit, Em's red vinyl, Dr. Taylor's orange and blue dress) offsets the hospital's resemblance to prior institutional settings. And in that final *rapprochement* between Alex and the Minister, Kubrick slyly binds the formal hypocrisies of the state to an unruly primitivism in an exchange where paternal authority both solicits the savage's blessing and pops food into his demanding jaws. Of all the ritualized eating scenes in Kubrick, among them, the post-execution breakfast of *Paths*, the buffet in the War Room in *Dr. Strangelove,* Moon-Watcher's first carnivorous meal and Bowman's last meal, this scene from *Clockwork* best captures a Buñuelian conjunction of civilization and its primitive discontents.

Appropriately, Kubrick ends *A Clockwork Orange* in a flurry of images and sounds. Photographers and a stereo unit with two enormous speakers rush into the hospital room to record and celebrate an alliance between two smiling and cynical droogs, one satisfied that his time-bound needs are secured (good job, good salary) and the other prepared to turn that proverbial other cheek in a gesture of political survival. And yet, for all one knows, Alex may wake up from his newfound bliss only to discover a clockwork Mephistopheles waiting to claim his prize. But for now, Kubrick invites his audience to revel in Alex's victory as both Alex's imagination and Beethoven's Ninth are liberated from the tyranny of time's engineers. In what is the last image of the film, on our screen as well as Alex's, Kubrick for the first time visualizes Alex's exultation ("I was cured all right") as a play of fantasy *and* performance. In slow motion, Alex cavorts in a field of artificial snow with a nude girl in black gloves and stockings, while two lines of spectators dressed in the Ascot fashions of a fin-de-siècle British aristocracy form a pathway and applaud the two performers.[21] Unlike previous visions, in either Alex's imagination or Kubrick's mindscreen, this one implies an evolution toward a paradoxical but encouraging future, one that exists on the other side of the Korova's black wall. The backgrounds are a luminous white, the activity blends Victorian formality and sexual freedom, at once the enclosures of time and the expanses of inner space. And one can hope, perhaps with Kubrick as well as his cinematic double, that this path into an empty white space leads somewhere other than back into the involuted circles of time. Perhaps it leads to the *tabula rasa* of a movie screen, waiting for the performing artist and the light of his creation.

A Time Odyssey

BARRY LYNDON

For his next film, Stanley Kubrick undertook the difficult task of adapting to a large screen canvas William Makepeace Thackeray's *The Luck of Barry Lyndon* (1844), a rambling, digressive first-person novel written in an eighteenth-century picaresque form.[1] Unlike Burgess's *A Clockwork Orange*, this novel did not provide him with a "finished" story or, despite its first-person style, an intriguing subjective focus. In writing the screenplay, Kubrick eliminated at least half the episodes in the novel, but retained most of its temporal sweep. His story of the rise and fall of Barry Lyndon covers more than twenty-five years (ca. 1760–1789) and, unlike Thackeray's account, attaches fully as much significance to the historical/cultural milieu as it does to the more transparent concerns of character. Placed in the context of Kubrick's previous films, *Barry Lyndon* (1975) fits more comfortably into the same philosophical and aesthetic constellation as *Paths of Glory* and *2001* than it does with the first-person mirror worlds of *Lolita* and *A*

Clockwork Orange. In addition, it probably represented for Kubrick a
less expensive ($11 million budget) alternative to making a film about
Napoleon, while it satisfied an apparent desire to match *2001*'s epic
vision of mankind in future space with an equally ambitious film odyssey into past time.

Thackeray's novel spans at least five decades (ca. 1760–1811), develops an historical backdrop that includes the Seven Years' War and
the American and French Revolutions, and chronicles not only the fictional life and death of Barry Lyndon (who dies in Fleet Prison of
"delirium tremens") but the end of one era and beginning of another.[2]
As a counterpoint to Barry's first-person "memoir," told from the nostalgic and highly distorted vantage of "gouty old age," Thackeray creates a temporal organization that blends the "murderous work of kings"
(for instance, Frederick the Great) and the extravagances of social vanity into a mock-epic treatise on human irrationality. Thus the novel is
psychologically coherent as well as reductive, while structurally it is
large. Because Thackeray wished to parody the nineteenth-century
fondness for "personal" history (diaries, memoirs, letters, ecstatic poetry) through the guise of an eighteenth-century rogue novel, his "Romance of the Last Century," to quote the subtitle, recreates the moral
seriousness of the Enlightenment more than it imitates the social or
psychological realism of a Charles Dickens or George Eliot. Unlike the
first-person involutions of Nabokov's *Lolita* and Burgess's *A Clockwork
Orange*, Thackeray's use of the unreliable narrator turns into a thinly
veiled disguise for a more encompassing satire directed against the
excesses of the romantic imagination. His novel mourns the loss of the
eighteenth-century dream of order rather than his narrator's shallow
ambitions or personal tragedy. But, of course, between Thackeray and
the works of Nabokov and Burgess—as well as the films of Kubrick—
there has taken place an epistemological and aesthetic evolution in
which a faith in the rational order of both nature and the self dissolves
into the indeterminate boundaries of Einstein's universe.

For Kubrick, Thackeray's novel must have presented problems of
adaptation and cinematic translation unlike any he had ever encoun-
tered. Distinct from *Lolita* and *Clockwork*, its first-person style, through
a method of rhetorical disengagement, quickly diminishes both the importance and appeal of Barry's subjective peculiarities. No unique or
startling "mindscreen" can be extracted from these pages. Barry's verbal
posturings become as obvious as they are trite, so that one soon learns

to measure what he *says* against what Thackeray *means*. As George Savage Fitz-Boodle, the spurious "editor" of Barry's memoirs, Thackeray repeatedly deplores his protagonist's self-serving distortions of the truth and his shoddy moral character:

> We beg here respectfully to declare that we take the moral of the story of Barry Lyndon, Esquire, to be—that worldly success is by no means the consequence of virtue; that if it is effected honestly sometimes, it is attained by selfishness and roguery still oftener; and that our anger at seeing rascals prosper and good men frequently unlucky, is founded on a gross and unreasonable idea of what good fortune really is.[3]

Even in the absence of such intrusions (in the 1856 edition, Thackeray deletes Fitz-Boodle's commentary), Barry's penchant for self-aggrandizement and his skill at blarney quickly make the reader suspicious about the truthfulness of his confidences, especially in his oft-repeated claims of nobility for the "house of Barry of Barryogue":

> Truth compels me to assert that my family was the noblest of the island, and, perhaps, of the universal world.[4]

Barry, one learns, is a very inventive storyteller who fabricates both his legal and his moral history in order to justify on a grand scale, *ex post facto*, a life of cheating, lying, and wife-beating. Note, for instance, how hyperbole (Barry's "voice") and indirect disclosure (Thackeray's irony) merge in an early description of his father:

> My father was well known to the best circles in this kingdom as in that of Ireland, under the name of Roaring Harry Barry. He was bred like many other young sons of genteel families to the profession of the law . . . and, from his great genius and aptitude for learning, there is no doubt he would have made an eminent figure in his profession, had not his social qualities, love of field sports, and extraordinary graces of manner marked him out for a higher sphere.[5]

What this really means is that "Roaring Harry Barry" preferred gaming to learning and the "higher sphere" of social vanity to eighteenth-century enlightenment. Like father, like son. Throughout his "memory" account and mock-confessional, which is quite different from the dreamlike reveries of Humbert and Alex, Barry remains steadfast in his belief that wealth, titles, and fashion—the *appearances* of value—give substance to man's journey through time:

> We wore silk and embroidery then. . . . Then it took a man of
> fashion a couple of hours to make his toilette, and he could shew some
> taste and genius in the selecting it. What a blaze of splendour was a
> drawing room, or opera, of a gala night! What sums of money were
> lost and won at the delicious faro-table! . . . Gentlemen are dead and
> gone. The fashion has now turned upon your soldiers and sailors, and
> I grow moody and sad when I think of thirty years ago.[6]

No clear understanding of life's incalculable sorrow or the erosions of
time liberates Barry's perspective from a nostalgic faith in the importance of a socially objectified morality. For Thackeray, as well as the
reader, Barry Lyndon remains a comic figure with a tragic fate.

But in keeping with another picaresque convention, Thackeray invests his protagonist with certain redeeming graces. Barry's naïveté and
ready courage—particularly evident in the first half of the novel—lend
his character an emotional integrity that tragically disappears amid the
ephemera of Vanity Fair. He falls in and out of love all too easily and
often, violates the rules of decorum in the interests of passion (e.g., by
throwing a glass of claret in Captain Quin's face over a marriage to
Nora Brady), and is all too anxious to fight for love, honor, and country. Because he lacks the ability to harness these instincts into an enlightened moral or intellectual framework, Barry Lyndon becomes a
victim of a deceptively attractive *haut monde* as well as his own shallow character. By the time he moves into that "higher sphere" of fashion, fictional claims have been converted into personal truths just as
moral substance defers to painted surfaces. When he first encounters
the Chevalier de Balibari—who, it turns out, is nothing more than an
Irish gambler and pretender like Barry himself—his emotional *largess*
transforms itself into social aspiration:

> It was very imprudent of me; but when I saw the splendour of his ap-
> pearance, the nobleness of his manner, I felt it impossible to keep dis-
> guise with him. . . . I burst into tears.[7]

What Barry sees is a splendor he desires for himself and, ironically, one
attainable only through the art of disguise. By the end of part one,
Thackeray's hero has not only learned the rules of the game—and the
first one is that honest emotion must be submerged in decorous formality—but acquired the skills of an accomplished player. No longer
swayed by romantic notions of love or honor, he ruthlessly pursues
Lady Lyndon for a year to obtain "the style and title of Barry Lyndon"

and later strives for a peerage that ultimately eludes his grasp. In the final pages of the novel, with his life in a state of personal and financial ruin, Barry's unwitting self-exposure becomes complete and coincides with an acquiescence in the romance of his own inventions, which earlier stood as studied responses to the accidents of fortune and his ambition for social rank.

While Thackeray requires the reader to penetrate the rhetoric of first-person manipulation and move from Barry's unreliable account to both Fitz-Boodle's editorial morality and his own irony, Kubrick alters the tone as well as the purpose of the novel when he asks his audience to follow Barry's story from the distanced perspective of an omniscient narrator. Having a storyteller (Michael Hordern), whose voice is steady and deliberate in its ironic and sympathetic reflections on the rise and fall of Barry Lyndon (Ryan O'Neal), allows Kubrick to condense a great deal of expository and psychological information. The narrator both *explains* the historical ambiance (the Seven Years' War) and *interprets* the inner workings of character (Barry quickly recovers from a tearful farewell with his mother because "no lad who has liberty for the first time and twenty guineas in his pocket is very sad"). He creates in Part I an atmosphere of comic fate and irony, while in Part II his comments become increasingly sympathetic and support a growing mood of tragic irony. He alerts us to patterns of fortune and chance that the characters, especially Barry himself, fail to comprehend. Kubrick's protagonist in Part I accepts fortuity with confident, unreflective self-assurance, while in Part II the narrator anticipates for us the death of Barry's son and our hero's eventual ruin. In such a manner, Kubrick structures a narrative vise of irony and fate, comic in Part I and tragic in Part II, and reminds us of that broader historical context from which no character, not even the narrator himself, can hope to escape. The titled "Epilogue," taken from chapter 1 of Thackeray's novel, stands as Kubrick's most noticeable intrusion into the *temporal* structure of the film; it transcends the narrator's limited frame of reference to remind us of time's irrevocable obliteration of the personal struggles of an entire era. "They are all equal now," we read, as most of us shall be sometime in the twenty-first century, except for those of us who, like Kubrick, have preserved in art or artifacts a private vision or sense of humanity to withstand the irrevocable course of time.[8]

Not only the Epilogue, but the film's narration and dialogue, as well as titles for Parts I and II, either come directly from or appear to be inspired by Thackeray's novel. But Kubrick, by not allowing Barry to tell his story as Thackeray does, diminishes further his character's perceptual range and freedom of choice. In the novel, for instance, Barry makes observations and voices opinions about his historical milieu, even though his authority in such matters is challenged by Thackeray's ironic presence and his own admission of shortcomings as a "philosopher and historian." Rather than have his protagonist tell his own story, as Humbert and Alex are allowed to do in *Lolita* and *Clockwork*, Kubrick chooses a strategy which creates a disparity between the film's "objective" structure (i.e., its temporal rhetoric) and a brilliantly conceived visual/musical form. On the one hand, the narrator gives the impression that *Barry Lyndon*, to use one critic's descriptive vocabulary, is a "documentary on eighteenth-century manners and mores,"[9] while on the other his temporal authority is undermined by the part it plays in Kubrick's more expressive cinematic ambitions. Like those disembodied voices of objectivity in *The Killing, Paths of Glory*, and *Dr. Strangelove*, and like HAL in *2001*, the narrator of *Lyndon* knows something about time but nothing about space. He offers us a comfortable and ironic detachment from Barry's rise and fall, while he fails to see Barry's emotional complexity or moral growth; he provides an historical awareness that strengthens the sense of fate in the film, but he fails to comprehend its larger philosophic or aesthetic meaning. His is the voice of reason and wit to be sure, a mixture of eighteenth-century urbanity and Thackerayean bonhomie, but one confined within the temporal frame of the film. He has access to knowledge of Barry's ultimate ruin and sorrow, the complexities of eighteenth-century European politics, and in general to the simple dynamics of social intercourse. Beyond the level of story, that rudimentary urge to tell a tale, the narrator has little or nothing to say. Significantly, he does not comment on most of what we *see* and *hear*. He has no access to the cinematic order of images and sounds of which his narration is but a small part.[10] Like others in the film, his existential presence metaphorically turns to dust and becomes absorbed into an expressive film art which looks backward in time and outward toward the duration of cinematic space.

Yet the narrator's importance in the film should not be underestimated. Both his detachment and his sympathy serve to make the tone elegiac rather than nostalgic; the narrative Time-Machine mournfully ticks off the tragic foibles and petty strivings of an ordinary humanity ensnared in the processes of life itself. In Part I, for instance, the narrator's commentary on Barry's first taste of battle and the folly of the Seven Years' War reaches far beyond a single moment in time:

Though this encounter is not recorded in any history books, it was memorable enough for those who took part.

In this "skirmish" with the French, Barry loses his friend Captain Grogan (Godfrey Quigley), who dies, with countless others, on one of history's innumerable forgotten battlefields. And in Part II, the narrator sadly recounts Barry's decline into debtorship and the social disgrace and banishment that result from his stepson's revenge on him. The narrator foretells the death of Barry's son—"fate had determined that he should leave none of his race behind him"—and even tells us that he will finish life "poor, lonely, and childless." Kubrick, unlike Thackeray, literally frames his *Barry Lyndon* within both an atmosphere of transience and the finality of death: The film begins and ends with formal white titles and end-titles on a black screen, while on the soundtrack one hears the elegiac grandeur of the main theme from Handel's "Sarabande." Part I begins and ends with death, while Part II moves

from the resplendence of the marriage in scene one to the dissolution
of that bond and the scene where Lady Lyndon (Marisa Berenson)
mournfully signs an annuity made out to Redmond Barry. In the first
part, Kubrick frames the film's rising action by going from a long-
distanced view of Barry's father being slain in a duel to a close-up of
Sir Charles Lyndon (Frank Middlemass) struggling vainly to stay
alive. As we witness this second invasion by death, with its hideous
shrieks and twitchings, the narrator's unemotional reading of the old
man's obituary reduces him to one more item on the endless rolls of
history:

> From a report in the *St. James Chronicle*: Died, at Spa, in the King-
> dom of Belgium, the right honorable Sir Charles Reginald Lyndon,
> Knight of the Bath, Member of Parliament, and, for many years, His
> Majesty's representative at various European courts. He has left be-
> hind him a name which has endeared to all his. . . .

As the reading of the obituary slowly drowns out and the screen cuts
to black, we realize that his esteemed name will shortly be usurped by
one Redmond Barry. Ironically, Part II—in its journey from marriage
to estrangement—shows Barry losing the name of Lyndon and returning to a tragic obscurity (as Redmond Barry) for which posterity keeps
very few records.

   Throughout, Kubrick strives to lift the events from Thackeray's
novel out of period time (that is, the eighteenth-century) into a realm
of emotional and conceptual film-time. The temporal fabric of his film
is made up of not only marriages and deaths but births and birthdays,
old families and new families, first loves and last loves, friendships and
sibling rivalries, quarrels and duels, games and debts: in other words,
an elaborately ritualized parable of journeys begun and journeys ended.
He compresses and arranges the content of the novel into a formal tapestry that brings together the archetypal delusions of youth and the
sorrows of time—the sublime within the trivial—while the stately pace
of the film resembles a procession moving through vanity fair on its
way to tragic pageantry. Barry's father dies in a formal pistol-duel
over, the narrator informs us, "the purchase of some horses"—and not,
as is the implication in Thackeray, of cardiac arrest while gaming at
the Chester Races.[11] Later, Barry's purchase of a horse—for his son
Bryan's ninth birthday—will lead to a death whose poignancy is un-
tainted by comic irony. In Part I, Barry fights a duel with the braggart

Quin (Leonard Rossiter) for a prize—Nora Brady (Gay Hamilton)—
being auctioned off to the highest bidder, ignorant of the fact that her
family has rigged the contest as insurance against losing the Captain's
£1,500 a year. In Part II, Barry confronts the hatred of his stepson
Bullingdon (Leon Vitali) in another duel with pistols, only now he
gives the ritual the substance of moral courage by refusing to fire on
his wife's sole remaining heir. During his first journey from Ireland and
eventually to England, Barry is initiated into the perils of the road by
an amusingly polite but efficient highwayman named Captain Freny
(Arthur O'Sullivan), while in Part II, crippled and on crutches, Barry
takes his last journey to a carriage that will transport him out of England into permanent exile. In Part I, Barry cynically woos Lady Lyndon over a Belgian gaming table and prompts this example of our
narrator's ready wit: "to make a long story short, six hours after they
met, her ladyship was in love." In Part II, following several infidelities
with maids and concubines, Barry's arrogance turns into a loyal affection for his "vaporish" (neurotic) wife and an abiding love for his
doomed son. In such ways, and others, does Kubrick's *Barry Lyndon*
transport its audience both backward in "real" time (the eighteenth
century) and forward in narrative time through a credible but distanced landscape. In the end, however, it becomes an odyssey which,
in its canvas of humanity, embodies a pattern not only close to us all
but one for all time.

Particularly in the language and music of *Barry Lyndon* can one
chart Kubrick's development as a complete film artist. From the beginning, even within the crude narrative mythology of *Fear and Desire*
and *Killer's Kiss*, he demonstrates a visual talent commensurate with
the spatial complexities of later films like *Paths of Glory, Dr. Strangelove, 2001*, and *A Clockwork Orange*. But not until *2001* does a Kubrick
film realize a sound aesthetics equal to its temporal and spatial brilliance. *Paths* dabbles briefly in musical counterpoint (e.g., a Strauss
waltz before an execution) and the euphemisms of power politics,
while *Dr. Strangelove* balances laughter and surreal terror in a handful
of popular tunes ("Try a Little Tenderness" and "We'll Meet Again")
and a grimly amusing Doomsday jargon. *2001*, by contrast, develops a
paradoxical alignment of language and classical music by characterizing the first as an extinct fossil (e.g., HAL's primitive regressions) and
the other as conjunctive with the evolutionary mysteries of outer space
(e.g., *Zarathustra* and the monolith). And in *Clockwork*, Alex's Nadsat

symbolizes a verbal conduit to a highly intuitive inner life, one that opposes the assembly-line slogans and knee-jerk politics of the clockwork state, while the music of the film mixes parody with creative improvisation. In adapting *Barry Lyndon* to film, Kubrick uses the subtly ironic and formally measured syntax associated with Thackeray's "voice" rather than Barry's first-person hyperbole. As a result, the language suggests Barry Lyndon's psychological entrapment within the formal properties of a verbal maze that an outsider may imitate but rarely understand. Just as he perceives the mechanical workings of fate, however, the narrator commands this language and thereby aligns his voice with Barry's eventual victimization in a decorous and formal labyrinth disguised as an eighteenth-century mise-en-scène. The narrator, however, unlike Barry, gives the impression that he has escaped the painted cage and, from above, now muses over its splendor with a fascination that belies his stance of urbane contempt. Perhaps Barry's tragedy can be explained, in part, by the faith he invests in not only titles but words: in an assurance that once he takes up the King's English like any gentleman, his future will be secured and ordered. In Part II, for instance, his quest for peerage brings him to one Lord Wendover (André Morell), whose patronage and balanced syntax envelops Barry in a cocoon that stimulates the illusion that chance curtsies before the whims of human design:

> When I take up a person, Mr. Lyndon, he or she is safe. There is no question about them anymore. My friends are the best people. I don't mean they are the most virtuous, or indeed the least virtuous, or the cleverest, or the stupidest, or the richest, or the best born. But the best. In a word, people about whom there is no question.

And besides, Lord Wendover explains, "any gentleman with an estate and £30,000 a year should have a peerage." By the end of the film, Barry's vocabulary has declined to an occasional whisper—and little more—just as he begins to show an emotional and moral strength of character that eludes the explanatory powers of the narrator's Word.

Kubrick's musical choices for *Barry Lyndon*—primarily baroque rather than purely classical, with the heavy elegance of Handel's "Sarabande" providing the central musical theme—reinforce the film's elegiac structure as well as its narrative and tonal disparities. The brief selections from Bach (a concerto for two harpsichords played in a recital at Castle Hackton) and Vivaldi ("Cello Concerto in E Minor," which first appears after the marriage scene of Part II and later blends into the "Sarabande-Title" music for Bryan's funeral) suggest minor harmonic progressions common to the baroque, while the lighter piece from Mozart ("March from Idomeneo," played during Barry's brief tenure as a spy for Captain Potzdorf) and one from Schubert (a "German Dance," heard during the period of Bryan's eighth birthday celebration) blend with the simpler and more traditional melodies associated with Barry's romantic entanglements with Nora and a young German girl (e.g., "Women of Ireland," "Lilliburlero," "British Grenadiers"). Together these selections form a baroque whole that supports the film's visual mixture of lyrical simplicity and formal artifice, its narrative merger of the comic and tragic, its emotional subtext of the trivial and sublime, a vanity fair and an epical grandeur. As part of a system of aesthetic analogy (to several forms of seventeenth, eighteenth, and nineteenth century art and music), the music contributes to that historical dimension within the film that both documents and universalizes the end of an era.*

Throughout his career, Kubrick repeatedly expresses his fascination with the classical style and forms associated with an eighteenth-century sensibility, even though *Barry Lyndon*, his tenth feature film, is the first to take place in that period of history. On the simplest conceptual level, a classical mise-en-scène in a Kubrick film accentuates the tension between the enclosures of time and the expanses of space discussed throughout this study. In highly formal environments, whether they are defined through aesthetic or mechanical imagery, Kubrick's characters become separated from both the unresolved conflicts of inner space (resulting in sublimation and repression) and the irreducibility of outer space: which means, in the Kubrickian *mythos*, that they have less access to mystery, creativity, and the possibility of future hope. More often than not, Kubrick expresses a latent surrealist temperament through the placement of an eighteenth-century formalism within a variety of dissonant film contexts. Johnny Clay's robbery plan in *The Killing*, for instance, matches the precision of classical design against the ubiquity of chance. In *Paths of Glory*, an eighteenth-century cha-

---

* Other musical selections in the film include Schubert's "Piano Trio in E-Flat" (discussed more fully in the latter portion of chapter 7), an adaptation of Paisiello's "The Cavatina" from *Il Barbier Di Siriglia* (used in two card-cheating scenes involving Barry and the Chevalier), and Frederick the Great's "Hohenfriedberger March" (ironically associated with Barry's desertion and his movement through Prussian lines).

teau provides a "civilized" battleground for World War I barbarity, while Quilty's mansion in *Lolita* represents a Gothic parody of classical order, and the Gainsborough-like portrait behind which he dies, an image of lost innocence. The inhabitants of *Dr. Strangelove's* mad enclosures cling to a faith in an eighteenth-century Clockworld which they assume will run forever and carry them beyond Doomsday, while the travelers of *2001* organize the infinity of space into a technological harmonics as an alternative to vision. And *A Clockwork Orange* visualizes the death throes of civilization as a dislocated eighteenth-century nightmare (e.g., the Korova's symmetry and statuary) taking place in an imaginary future. Not until Bowman's final excursion into past time (his "memory" room) does Kubrick begin to clarify the role neoclassical formality plays in his film iconography—and it's more than just a belief in the tragic entrapment of one historical period within a rational and mechanical formalism. It stands for a memory as much as an historical fact; a dream of order and beauty, not just a period of time; a human artifact, not merely a museum collection of paintings and music, great homes and palaces. It is a vision of people in their created world, of a civilization with its discontents hidden from view, one which in some parts of the globe still surrounds *our* creations like a radiant but alien presence. Yet like the characters of *Barry Lyndon*, we frequently gaze at its strangeness and splendor as voyeurs of time and imitate its surfaces while misapprehending its complex meanings.

Within the two-part structure of *Barry Lyndon*, and its balancing of comic and tragic irony, Kubrick develops additional narrative comment through a series of ritual activities. Among these dramatized motifs, *four* stand out—dueling, wooing, card-playing, and debt-paying—as evidence of his desire to visually objectify the conceptual and emotional content of the film in ways beyond the narrator's compass. All four of these activities include in their formal order the workings of fate or chance and each, in its own way, dramatizes a Kubrickian conflict between human design and contingency. As the characters pursue either their instincts or the mediated goals of "civilized" ambition, they become absorbed within a larger temporal and cinematic process; as they duel with one another over the ephemera of love and honor, we comprehend their losing battle with fate; as they idly pass the time playing cards, or attempt to fulfill selfish ambition by cheating at these games of chance, we realize their time is short and running out; and while the Chevalier (Patrick Magee) and Barry may cheat and win with the cards or in the game of love, in the film's larger order of moral reference they must inevitably pay up. In Part II of the film, Kubrick isolates the piling up of debts and signing of bank drafts as another ritual activity performed at a table—on two occasions with three present (Barry, Lady Lyndon, and a bookkeeper) as in the games of Ombre seen earlier—and again portrays in microcosm the thematic and psychological content of the film.

A close look at how Kubrick shapes and patterns these narrative motifs in Part I ("By What Means Redmond Barry Acquired the Style and Title of Barry Lyndon") reveals something more complex than the narrator's irony or the simple mechanics of fate. The film's initial scene, shot from afar and explained by the avuncular yet detached narrator, links the death of Barry's father to the contrary designs of nature and human artifice. A spectrum of natural color (from top to bottom: gray, blue, brown, green) captures in portraiture the romance of eighteenth-century dueling (isolated figures integrated into a stunning landscape), while the narrator's exposition functions as ironic counterpoint to the painterly appeal and verbal formality of the dueling scene. As the narrator tells us about the father's promising legal career ("no doubt he would have made an eminent figure in his profession"), we hear a countdown to death ("Gentlemen, cock your pistols. One, two, three") and the popping sounds of exploding gunfire, while we notice the lone figure on the left falling to the ground at the same moment that the narrator completes his commentary ("had he not been killed in a duel over the purchase of some horses"). Immediately, Kubrick forces us to look at such human struggles from a distance, at once historical and cinematic, and to note the disparities between form (a duel) and content (a human life sacrificed to a quarrel over horses). Barry's duel with Captain Quin, drawn out sufficiently by Kubrick to capture the ritual and aesthetics of an eighteenth-century barbarity, likewise has an ironic substance. In a later candlelit scene, Captain Grogan informs both Barry and the audience of the film that the pistols were loaded with harmless pluckets of tow and that the cowardly Quin fainted from fright. During the duel itself, the audience remains as ignorant of the Brady family's machinations as Barry does (although a clue is provided to both when Barry notices that Grogan, his second, hands him someone else's pistol), just as it fails to perceive a sordid truth (a family's avarice) within the forms of ritual. In this instance, the narrator's silence links him to the

film maker's deception: a slow reverse zoom and the steady rhythm of Handel's "Sarabande-Duel" take us from a close-up view of the pistols being prepared by Grogan and Ulick, Barry's cousin, to a long shot of five figures (as in the first duel) in a lovely natural setting of blue water and green trees; Barry, like his father before him, occupies left screen, although here it is the duelist on the right (Quin) who falls to an apparent death. Significantly, Kubrick cuts back and forth between emotional close-up (of Barry's foolhardy courage and Quin's cowardice) and a pleasingly attractive distance, thereby providing his audience with both a source of psychological identification and an aesthetic distance. Within the film's thematic aspirations, it indicates how the forms of things can be manipulated and the courses of fate momentarily postponed. By the end of Part I, following his and the Chevalier's disconnected wanderings through the courts of Europe, Barry has learned how to thrive on guile and good form as he develops an art for dueling as well as for lovemaking and card-playing.

In the three love/wooing scenes of Part I, through a pattern of visual and aural repetition, Kubrick enlarges the significance of Barry's moral progress from Irish primitive to rakish gentleman. In the ribbon scene between Barry and Nora, he captures both the charm and triviality of romantic love by slowing down the pace and allowing the action to play itself out, to assert a temporal and emotional integrity that solicits from the audience both responsive feeling and circumspect understanding. Here, as elsewhere, a reverse-zoom shot moves from something particular (i.e., the statue of a child) to a more generalized composition of human figures, colors, and light: Sitting at a table playing cards ("Killarney"), with the pleasing sounds of a spring rain and the music from "Women of Ireland" blending into a soft-textured imagery, the two performers embody familiar sentimental gestures, a subtle turn of the head or closing of the eyes too studied to be profound. Even though the narrator intrudes with his usual sardonic advantage ("First love!," he intones, "what a change it makes in a lad . . . the tender passion gushes instinctively out of a man's heart!") and subsequently deplores Nora's shallow emotional character and her family's greed, Kubrick—by means of the integrity of the scene—forces us to apprehend a world at odds with that commentary and to acknowledge a fuller human content. During another rainstorm complemented by music from "Women of Ireland," Barry sits by candlelight with his Lischen and her baby (Diana Koerner gives a remarkable performance as Lischen) at another table, only this one serves for eating rather than card-playing. Again Kubrick preserves the internal coherence of the scene, allowing it a full emotional and visual exposition and communicating nuances of character beyond those already apparent in Barry's disguise (in deserting the English army, he has assumed the identity of one "Lieutenant Fakenheim") and soldierly pretenses ("I'm an officer and must do my duty," he says in response to Lischen's concern about the dangers of war). Kubrick (and Ryan O'Neal) reveals how simple and human it is for Barry to become enveloped in the magic of his own invention and how, for a brief moment of time, we, too, share that magic.[12] This sequence completes itself the next morning with the two lovers in close-up—their heads tilted together in a static tableau of bright light and soft-focus—as we relish the visual charm and the innocence of the exaggerated sentiment. In contrast, the narrator's game calls for him to get the last word ("This heart of Lischen's was like many a neighboring town, and had been stormed and occupied several times before Barry came to invest it") and to announce, somewhat condescendingly, an emphatic verbal formulation of Barry's tragicomic attempts at circumventing both fate and his own emotional character. For Redmond Barry, this scene foreshadows his movement into a "higher sphere" of fashion more commensurate with the narrator's civilized detachment than his own naïveté, a sphere where spon-

taneity loses its way in a labyrinth of psychological disguise and social formality. Barry's wooing of Lady Lyndon over a Belgian gaming table recalls his earlier contest with Nora, only now the mask of bold ambition replaces youthful ardor and the measured elegance of Schubert's "Piano Trio in E-Flat" replaces the more lyrical "Women of Ireland" as the musical love-theme. Dressed in silk and lace, manicured, painted, and coiffured like a figure from an eighteenth-century wax museum, Barry ruthlessly pursues Lady Lyndon to a blue moonlit terrace where she turns to receive his advances in a ritual of love that pleases the eye but chills the heart. Soon afterwards, Barry, with his newly acquired arrogance and cruelty, enters an ornate candlelit room where he confronts Lady Lyndon's crippled husband with his sexual advantage, while the old man, sitting at *his card table*, rails and dies in a losing game with time.

Besides the light it casts on Barry's development, this progress in the mise-en-scène of the film from natural beauty to formal artifice contains the paradoxical merger of economics and aesthetics. When he flees from the mercenary deception of the Bradys, Barry takes the twenty guineas that belong to his mother (Marie Kean) on a journey through a series of beautiful rural settings to an unexpected rendezvous

Barry (lower right center) is entrapped in the geometry of eighteenth-century warfare.

with a highwayman and his son. This brief exchange is ironically polite and formal: Barry keeps his boots but not his money or his horse, as Captain Freny demonstrates both the ethics and aesthetics of his profession. He takes Barry's horse because of practical considerations ("with people like us, we must be able to travel faster than our clients"), while he leaves him his boots out of sympathy and, more important, an appreciation for proportion and balance (to take them would be excessive, an act of bad form more than of cruelty). Stripped of money to support his trip to Dublin, Barry becomes seduced by the simple blandishments of an English recruiting sergeant seeking to enlist cannon-fodder for the European wars. He offers promises of money (1 shilling a day for life) and honor (to those "ambitious of becoming gentlemen"), as well as an opportunity for Barry to wear the uniform he had earlier enviously admired while watching Quin parade and strut with his regiment. Once he takes the bounty, however, Barry becomes imprisoned within a military geometry that resembles the horizontal lines and pathways in *Paths of Glory*. Several zoom/telephoto shots of Barry marching in an army of multitudes or leading a man through a brutal Prussian gauntlet reinforce this sense of entrapment, while the first battle scene in the film, a brilliantly staged affair in a rural orchard between stationary (the French) and advancing (the English) lines,

shows how eighteenth-century warfare maintained its formal aesthetics
even at the expense of human life and tactical sense. Barry carries the
fatally wounded Grogan into a muddy and smoke-filled trench similar
to the one that directs Colonel Dax's movements in *Paths*: but this soldier weeps over the body of a friend who ironically wills him a portion
of the money (100 guineas) earned from his part in the Quin/Nora
marriage (meaning that Grogan, his friend and second, was party to
Barry's deception) and which, incidentally, represents what is left from
a losing battle with the cards on the night before his death. In such
ways does truth emerge from a tangle of commerce and decorum, ambition and artifice, the civilized mask of war and its lethal absurdity.

In still other ways, Kubrick opposes the forms of a rigid military
aesthetics with complicating internal factors and prepares his audience
for Barry's eventual absorption into a highly artificial cultural milieu.
Barry's fistfight with a belligerent soldier named Tool both conforms
to specified rules and takes place inside an enclosed regimental square,
while Kubrick's handheld camera not only records the violence of the
fight but opposes its formal outline. The second battle of the film is
framed initially through a square farmhouse window—surely a visual
allusion to the horizontal viewer through which we first see no-man's-
land in *Paths of Glory*—before all is scattered into confusion and exploding cannon fire. During the most frantic and disordered moments
of the battle, Barry instinctively risks his life to save Captain Potzdorf
(Hardy Kruger). Later he is castigated by a Prussian colonel for im-
moral conduct off the battlefield as well as rewarded for his courage
with two *Frederics d'or* during a ceremony that takes place within a
formal regimental horseshoe. Appropriately, this fortuitous intersection
of courage and profit enables Barry to escape military service and advance even closer to that gentlemanly splendor he privately covets. In
Berlin, in an ornate and classical palace that resembles the chateau in
Paths, Barry assumes another disguise, in this instance the double one
of Potzdorf's spy and the Chevalier's confidant. Yet the film intimates
that even though these games of state function on a scale grander in
their properties than Barry's puerile involvement in a romantic triangle
and a family's greed, they lack a correspondingly noble substance. In
one scene, for instance, Barry stands between symmetrical gold pillars
in the Minister of Police's palatial office and reports false information
about the Chevalier, while the camera, positioned behind the Minister,
tracks back and forth (left to right, right to left) on a horizontal course

which opposes Potzdorf's pacings. Visually, this scene recalls the court-martial in *Paths* and its paradoxical suggestion of horizontal entrapment in a setting of vertical reach and aspiration. In Barry's first meeting with the Chevalier, Kubrick visually prepares for a movement from one world into another, from the clockwork machinations of military formality to an environment of aristocratic self-indulgence; and in terms of cinematic self-reference, from the chateau of *Paths* to that extrater-restrial room in *2001*. He begins the scene in the Chevalier's palatial apartment from a distance and behind a figure on screen-right who, like Bowman as eighteenth-century gentleman, sits with his back to the camera and eats breakfast at a formally prepared table. After Barry enters through a door centered in the background and framed by white pillars, a reverse angle reveals the Chevalier's startling appearance— a white wig, a powdered and rouged face, a black patch over his right eye and beauty moles both above and below his left one—as well as the presence of a red canopied bed in the background. Appropriately, there are no rebirths or moral transformations here: only an exchange by Barry of one disguise and patron (as Potzdorf's spy) for another (as the Chevalier's protégé), as well as the illusion that the splendor of this painted rogue will transport him out of a world of horizontal intrigue into a realm inhabited by ethereal beings who seem as enduring as the attractive *objets d'art* that surround them.

To complement the contrary tendencies of verbal narration and visual narrative, what upon reflection could be termed the disparities of film content in *Barry Lyndon*, Kubrick employs an impressive technical strategy that binds the film into an aestheic and philosophical whole. His use of camera and lens, composition and mise-en-scène, and a musical score of recurring baroque cadences, produces a grandiosity of form which could redefine prevailing concepts of the film epic. *Barry Lyndon* exemplifies many of the characteristics traditional to a genre developed first by Griffith and the Italians, refined by Eisenstein and Russian theories of epic montage, and exploited for its full commercial value through bravura technical feats by such film makers as Abel Gance and Cecil B. DeMille: a display of innovative visual and technical effects, impressive formal compositions, rhythmic editing, and an actual or pseudo-historical ambiance. Yet, as Kubrick himself has noted, while such films historically resulted in significant advances in the areas of film technology and film language, they rarely embodied a content equal to their formal pretensions. Kubrick's belief that "Eisenstein is all form and no content, whereas Chaplin is content and no form," coupled with the comment below, articulates what I take to be his primary goal as a film artist and his actual achievement in *Barry Lyndon*: "Obviously, if you can combine style and content, you have the best of all possible films."[13]

In Part I of *Barry Lyndon*, for instance, Kubrick's use of reverse zooms allows him to move into and away from a given scene without fragmenting the harmonious *appearances* of space or compressing the realities of time. More important, it allows him to create an ironic juxtaposition between Barry's gradual rise and a complex mise-en-scène, one that supports the film's spatial/musical rhetoric as it transcends its temporal content. As the love tryst involving Barry, Nora, and Quin develops in time, Kubrick slowly zooms back from the particulars of film content (e.g., Barry chopping wood, Nora's and Quin's hands joined, pistols being prepared for a duel) to assert open landscape compositions similar to those found in the paintings of Gainsborough and Constable, a lyrical ordering of the rural setting, which dwarfs the conflicts that unfold *inside* that world.* Because Barry fails to perceive such basic disparities as those between his rather ordinary ambitions and an expressive natural environment, he lacks the necessary imagination to transcend his own fate. Instead, he abandons the open expanses of rural space for the attractive enclosures of social space, an alignment of choice and chance that takes him into a world far closer to the formal gardens and internal mazes of Resnais's *Last Year at Marienbad* (1961) than the exuberant eighteenth-century gregariousness of *Tom Jones* (Tony Richardson, 1963). Correspondingly, Kubrick's camera reverses its earlier tendencies and becomes more static (with even less optical movement), especially in those impressive candlelit scenes (made possible by a Zeiss still-camera lens) at the Belgian spa in Part I and at Castle Hackton in Part II, which resemble the incandescent paintings (and recreations) by Adolf Menzel of Frederick the Great's concerts at Sans Souci.[14] By the end of Part I, the camera more often

---

* Painterly sources for the imagery of *Barry Lyndon* probably include the works of Thomas Gainsborough (1727–1788), known for his lyrical rural landscapes and his rather ethereal portraits of women; John Constable (1776–1837), whose landscapes are remarkable for the beauty they attach to the everyday and mundane; William Hogarth (1697–1764), whose paintings of eighteenth-century social life are less idealized and more satirical than the above; and Adolf Menzel (1815–1905), German lithographer and painter, whose primary claim to fame are his renderings of Frederick the Great's court. No doubt, the list goes on and includes several other names.

than not establishes first, a distant and static tableau in which characters artfully blend into a generalized period-setting, before it then cuts into the specific details of such internal narrative developments as Barry's wooing of Lady Lyndon or her husband's death. Paradoxically, the film implies that Barry's attraction to this world comes from his seeing it, as the narrator does, from afar rather than close-up, which reverses his earlier failure to escape a subjective response to his rural imbroglios by viewing them, objectively and imaginatively, from the expanded distances afforded the film's audience by the zoom lens. In a larger aesthetic sense, Kubrick suggests how painting and film correspond as visual media wherein the artist both reshapes personal experience into the contours of imagination ("subjective," like Alex of *Clockwork*) and universalizes the processes of time for a receptive audience ("objective"). The aesthetic of the zoom lens allows him to capture close-up the triviality, absurdity, and tragedy of various human entanglements, some of which collectively add up to what we call history, while from a distance it stimulates, through an integration of spatial form and temporal content, a release made possible by the perspectives of art. In that respect, Barry Lyndon unknowingly imprisons himself within a painted cage because, unlike the performing artists

of *A Clockwork Orange* (Alex *and* Kubrick), his is an imitative rather than creative imagination.

More than ever before in a Kubrick film, time becomes a felt presence in Part II of *Barry Lyndon* ("Containing an Account of the Misfortunes and Disasters Which Befell Barry Lyndon"), even as the action moves into a plush aristocratic society that makes every effort to slow it down and deny its existence. Reverend Runt (Murray Melvin), flanked by two large candles, presides over a regal marriage ceremony in which he affirms the sanctity of marriage and moralizes about "man's carnal lusts and appetites" (sternly looking at Barry), while the narrator provides the first specific date in the film, June 15, 1773. At the "pitch of prosperity," Barry exudes a confident glow in keeping with the symmetry and resplendence of his new setting, one which Kubrick characterizes as a formal dream in slow time. Throughout the early scenes of Part II, life at Castle Hackton proceeds as if it were floating in suspended animation, a world of rarefied figures brushed onto an idealized canvas or carved into the stone of a Grecian urn, a world that assumes the appearance of motion without the finality of consummation. From a distance, and that is apparently how Barry initially sees it in his mind's eye, its processional activities express a cultural/period harmony while they lack specific definition. In truth, of course, the film's characters rarely occupy their generous allotment of leisure time with practical duties or concerns, but rather indulge in such ritual pastimes as dwelling at their toilette (with servants to hold ornate mirrors and wash bowls), selecting from a tailor's collection the fabrics necessary to proper fashion, walking in gardens and riding in carriages, boating and fishing, playing lawn games by day and cards at night, and lingering over sumptuous meals prepared with great care and served by ubiquitous well-liveried servants. For Barry, it gives him time to master the rules of the game, to learn that if one wishes to indulge in sexual infidelities or bribe a willing nobility in the pursuit of peerage, it must be done within the bounds of decorum (i.e., over a game of cards, during a formal dinner party, or in the guise of collecting works of art).* Lady Lyndon, on the other hand, passes time with her two children, plays cards with her ladies-in-waiting, polishes her skills with the harpsichord in the company of the Reverend and Lord Bullingdon, dresses herself like an art object to be admired, and, as Barry's obsession with a title increases, sits at a table with Graham (Philip Stone), her bookkeeper, and tirelessly signs bank drafts to pay for that extravagance. But time does not stop or slow down, even if the emotional and spiritual life of Castle Hackton does: The lugubrious chords of a Vivaldi cello concerto become a prominent musical theme and represent a variation on Handel's "Sarabande" and its march toward death, while the sounds of numerous ticking clocks (for instance, as Barry reads Bryan a book about birds, or as Mrs. Barry dismisses Runt) and the

---

* In a brief satirical episode in which Barry bribes an unnamed nobleman by purchasing works from his art collection at exhorbitant prices, he fatuously admires one painting ("I love the use of the color blue by the artist") which the nobleman explains is by one "Ludovico Corday, a disciple of Alexandro Allori, and shows 'The Adoration of the Magi'." Kubrick, I suspect, creates an inside joke here. For one thing, no such painter as "Ludovico Corday" ever existed as far as I know, but the first name, of course, recalls *Clockwork*'s Ludovico Technique (which, then, decodes as an imitative and mechanical art). Alexandro Allori (1535–1607) was known for his mediocre anatomical drawings; he was an imitator of the Florentine school, which means that the fictional "Ludovico" is an imitator of an imitator. Moreover, The Adoration of the Magi has to be one of the most hackneyed and overdone subjects in the history of art, something of an obligatory piece for the artists of the Renaissance (Botticelli's is probably the most renowned example). The color blue that Barry admires is, of course, associated with the Virgin, and in several scenes, he wears that color. And finally, the nobleman—like General Broulard in *Paths*—refers to the *painting* as a "picture" ("this is one of my best pictures"). I suspect Kubrick's wife Christiane, herself an accomplished painter, had a hand in this scene. But enough! As Nabokov's Humbert says, "my little cup brims with tiddles."

ringing of church bells acknowledges time's passage. All of which prepares for the death of Barry's son—that "contest with the grim invin-
cible enemy," to quote the narrator—and its disruption of this dreamy
immobility. Bryan's death forces Barry and Lady Lyndon to experience
a tragic loneliness so inconsolable that the durable but uncomprehended art that has embellished their leisure now serves as a mockery
of their transience.

While the characters in Part II live in an illusory slow time, the
audience experiences in rapid succession the following: a marriage, a
birth, a marriage's gradual dissolution, a birthday, Barry's fervent quest
for peerage and another title, a second birthday, and a death. One can't
help but recall the birthdays of *2001*, touchingly absurd in their expression through the gargantua of space-age technology, and their foreshadowing of Bowman's rebirth as Star-Child. In *Barry Lyndon*, however, the birthdays blend in with other ritual activities and support a
parable of time rather than an odyssey through space. A pattern of
touching and tragic irony is captured by the sight of Bryan's white ornate coffin leading his world in a procession of regal sorrow, transported
as it is by the carriage and lambs which had been his birthday present
the year before and which now carry his body after his death in a fall
from the horse his father gave him as a birthday present. The boy's
bed provides a setting for two birthday scenes. The first is one of
charming innocence with father and son by candlelight, as Bryan holds
a stuffed toy lamb and Barry tells a highly embellished story from his
military past (about his assault on a fort with "rampaging he-devils"
and the cutting off of heads); in the second scene, the bed serves as
Bryan's deathbed and the site of Barry's greatest loss as he breaks
down in tears while repeating the same story about the fort. More than
anything else, Bryan's innocence represents Barry's single perception
into something fine, a brief glimpse of a tangible human beauty within
the grasp of his appreciation. We are allowed to sense, through Kubrick's enforcement and compression of time, an emotional growth in
Barry's character beyond that found in Thackeray, but one that, tragically, comes too late; Barry no longer plays at sentiment as before, but
he suffers a tragedy so profound that not even the narrator's explanatory genius can do it justice. Kubrick lets us read it in the hands that
clutch at Bryan's fragile life and on the faces of the two people left
behind to ponder their sorrow and isolation.

As wooing and card-playing were appropriate to the rising action of Part I, debt-paying provides Kubrick in Part II with an expressive activity enacted at a table and one that capsulizes not only Barry's personal decline, but that of an entire culture. Since the characters of *Barry Lyndon* lack sufficient imaginative resources to mitigate the harsh rule of time, they fatalistically bow to its authority and probably repay more than a fair share of their accumulated debt. In Kubrick's moral universe, Barry and Lady Lyndon pay for their shallowness, for their passive willingness to be absorbed into the formal and mechanical hypocrisies of their social milieu. In three of the four debt scenes, the scratching sounds of Lady Lyndon's quill pen and the rustling of paper complement the methodical signing of her name to endless stacks of notes and checks, while Kubrick embodies in a single human activity a culture's fall into the morass of its own triviality and pettty entanglements. As "H. Lyndon" (her Christian name is "Honoria") increasingly becomes a dominant visual motif, the film reminds us that such documents are all that survive as the record of a myriad ordinary human struggles, in our own time as well as eighteenth-century time. Barry and Lady Lyndon leave behind no art or beauty to express their sorrows or their fondest dreams. Barry's hope for futurity, his son, dies, as do his ambitions, in a tangle of debts and writs. In that respect, Kubrick's *Barry Lyndon* is one artist's attempt to capture a human pathos that, more often than not, becomes lost in both the temporal progress of history and the spatial distances of art.

Especially through Barry's conflict with Bullingdon does Kubrick infuse *Barry Lyndon* with that mythopoeic subtext that dominates the structures of *Dr. Strangelove, 2001,* and *A Clockwork Orange.** While Barry is an Irish "ruffian" and "upstart" who assumes the disguise of English gentleman, Bullingdon's "civilized" character exhibits a wide range of cultivated language and social form at odds with his latent barbarity, which expresses itself in an attack on Bryan and the revenge directed against his stepfather. Just as Part I shows Barry rising in fortune and declining in character, Part II matches him against Bullingdon as a way of objectifying Barry's moral growth during his fall into misfortune. In a scene not found in Thackeray, Bullingdon disrupts a formal gathering during a musical recital (Bach) at Castle Hackton (the shoes scene with Bryan), just as Barry in Part I throws a glass of wine in Quin's face rather than submit to a code that requires him to play the gracious loser in a contest for Nora Brady. There is a differ-

---

* For a discussion of the "mythopoeic" in Kubrick, see chapter 4.

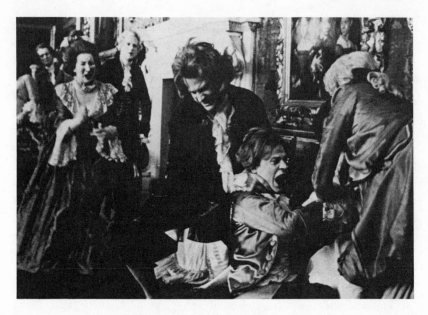

ence, however: Barry's violation of decorum (amid formal toasts of
marriage at a dinner table in the Brady home) was the spontaneous
act of a love-sick adolescent, while Bullingdon's act is a calculated
move in a young nobleman's revenge. As Bullingdon artfully castigates
Barry with his verbal superiority, the recital audience remains politely
inert, as if to demonstrate the extent of its civilized restraint. No one
moves in his chair or raises an objection until Barry counters Bullingdon's words with his own violence. In his savage attack against his
"noble" stepson, in full view of those he seeks to impress with his claims
of peerage, Barry offends this society's sense of form and decorum,
rather than arousing its moral indignation. Unlike Bullingdon, he has
not learned to express his viciousness through an acceptable verbal disguise or social form. Significantly, Kubrick's camera departs, for the
first time in Part II, from its polite and almost static objectivity when
its handheld commotion records the confusion of the fight. The entire
gathering scatters into emotional disarray as several men slip and fall
on the polished wood floor in an attempt to restrain Barry's ferocity,
while the women flee in horror from such an uninhibited exhibition of
human aggression. And even though this scene reaffirms the existence
of the "wild" Redmond Barry, it also shows that Bullingdon, his "civilized" double, has no more claim to that title than Barry does. Just as
Bowman sheds HAL, his mechanical alter ego, before he moves through

the Star-Gate to an awaiting rebirth, or the "primitive" Alex escapes the madness of Alexander before his awakening into a post-Ludovico world, Barry paradoxically emerges as a character with moral substance only after he falls from the heights of fortune and overcomes his callow fascination with those "civilized" surfaces now embodied in the style and title of Lord Bullingdon.

During the period after Barry's attack on Bullingdon and Bryan's funeral, Kubrick gradually moves his protagonist out of a world characterized by formal beauty and inner ugliness through a series of scenes in which the film's mise-en-scène declines in artifice (which reverses the pattern of Part I) as Barry undergoes an emotional and moral transformation. The final scene with Barry at Castle Hackton places him in a candlelit room, drunk and slumped in a chair. His pose recalls an almost identical pose assumed by a man seen on screen-left in the candlelit room at the Belgian spa where Sir Charles Lyndon died; in this case, however, the scene begins and ends with a shot of a symmetrical and ornate wall (a door framed by two candelabras, two large vases, and two larger paintings) which frames Barry being carried out by two servants. In an early morning setting of static and composed sloth, which is invigorated only by the most extensive camera movement of the film (a long reverse dolly shot), Bullingdon marches through a gentleman's club, past several slumping figures, and confronts Barry— also slumped asleep in a chair—with his demand for "satisfaction." Throughout this scene, Handel's "Sarabande-Duel" plays, as it did in Part I during the duel with Quin, while in the background several paintings on a blue wall are metaphorically duplicated by "real life" card-players watching the scene unfold, seemingly frozen in place, cards suspended in their hands, like figures in a Hogarth painting. Then the action moves, still with Handel's music, to what appears to be an abandoned church or tithe barn (with cross-shaped windows and a cathedral ceiling) for the climactic duel of the film, that between Barry and Lord Bullingdon, in a setting that recalls Barry's rural beginnings (straw and sacks of grain on the floor, pigeons fluttering and cooing) but here serves as backdrop for his one noble act. Finally, the film goes to a small room in a local inn where Barry lies in bed and silently plays cards with his mother, the only sounds coming from distant church bells, as he sadly contemplates the loss of his leg and the ruin of his life.

If nothing else, this sequence of events reaffirms Kubrick's remark-

Bullingdon moves down a formal corridor of slumping figures on his way to "claim satisfaction."

able talent for abstracting from both the narrative demands of his medium and its almost epistemological faith in the inviolability of "real"
space (in narrative terms, "setting") the resonance of myth. Here, he
implies that once Barry suffers public exposure—not as one lacking
good character but as one lacking good form—and loses his son, he
eventually reenters the existential context of time and exhibits a capacity for moral choice. Like Bowman and Alex before him, Barry comes
out of a deadly hibernation—embodied here in a dreamlike but stillborn
eighteenth-century formalism—and metaphorically "awakens" from his
slumber (as a collapsed figure in a chair). Stimulated by the intervention of fate (Bryan's death) and instinct (his attack on Bullingdon),
Barry escapes a world where human beings deny their moral complexity and creative potential by imitating the painted and decorative art
that surrounds them. Kubrick repeatedly transfers the frozen imagery
of wall paintings onto his moving screen creations (in makeup, costumes, formal poses and gestures) as a way of objectifying a psychological stasis in which the wellspring of consciousness becomes im-
mobilized rather than animated by the visions of art. Barry himself
becomes a figure in such a landscape (for instance, when he sits with
Bryan under an enormous and idealized painting of eighteenth-century

social life, or when he slumps in Hogarthian inebriation) as the film visually associates the palaces of civilization with the regressions of self. Consequently, Bullingdon's return "to claim satisfaction" links the demands of gentlemanly honor to a primitive code of revenge, just as Part I binds the rituals of honor to one family's meretricious greed and an Irish gambler's skill in cheating at cards. But now chance regains the upper hand and proves to be a far more instructive tutor than all the patrons and formal activities that audaciously strive to circumvent it. In the last scenes of the film, Barry no longer cheats at cards for profit or gain, but now, in a small room, plays with an already dealt hand as he faces the unembellished presence of his fate.

Kubrick climaxes the film's treatment of ritual activities in the final duel between Barry and Lord Bullingdon. Significantly, he nullifies both the narrator's voice and Thackeray's inspiration (no such scene occurs in the novel) as he returns to a form of stylistic exposition associated with Barry's rise rather than his fall. Although in more extensive terms than in Part I, Kubrick once again draws out a scene and preserves its temporal and emotional integrity, while indicating complex disparities between form and human content. The scene takes up almost nine of the film's 185 minutes, and for the first time in *Barry Lyndon*, screen time and "real" time are brought into conjunction. Barry's journey through the byroads of his ambition and into the dreamy parlors of splendor now ends in the existential actuality of time. An old church, now functioning as a tithe barn or storehouse, provides a complex setting for the deliberate exposition of this scene. One might say that for Barry Lyndon, Part II begins and ends in a church: the first, cast in a brilliant social and aesthetic symmetry; the last, closer to his rude beginnings yet ironically appropriate for his only freely chosen moral act. Psychologically, Barry comes full circle and confronts himself in the person of Bullingdon, his "noble" double. The scene begins with a close-up of hands preparing a pistol, although here the camera does not zoom back as it did in the duel with Quin, but instead cuts to a shot that establishes a moral rather than natural landscape. Once again Barry duels with someone else's pistols (a "matched pair" belonging to Lord Bullingdon), and he occupies the left-screen position associated both with his father's death in the first duel and his own apparent success in the duel with Quin, but now the rules are more rigid in their mechanics and formality. Instead of a duel where each man fires simultaneously after a count of three, this one incorporates chance or luck into its formal order: being the "offended" party, Bullingdon enjoys the privilege of calling the coin toss to determine who will fire first. As pigeons incongruously coo and stir about the barn, one man (identified only as "Sir Richard") both administers to the duel's formal requirements (tossing the coin, marking off ten paces between the two men) and its credible but absurd verbal procedures ("Mr. Barry, are you ready to receive Lord Bullingdon's fire?"), while three others function as seconds and witnesses. Barry's refusal to fire on Bullingdon after Bullingdon's pistol misfires—a moment apparently structured by Kubrick to indicate Barry's capacity to act independent of a fortuitous turn of chance—is one instance in the film where the elaborate mechanics of social form embody a correspondingly significant moral and emotional content. Unfortunately and ironically, such gestures are not enough to save Barry or his world from the consequences of their folly. Rather than displaying *noblesse oblige* and accepting Barry's act of conciliation, Bullingdon insists on "satisfaction," just as he violates decorum by vomiting in fear just before he was "to receive Mr. Lyndon's fire" (and the gentlemen in attendance register frowns of disapproval). In the end, Bullingdon concludes his shabby performance by firing on his opponent before Sir Richard even completes the count of three. In quick succession, therefore, Kubrick invests two human acts with the substance of existential truth, even though they are partly obscured by the mechanics and formality of ritual. Perhaps it is significant that Barry's only utterance during this long scene is a repeated "yes."

The final two episodes of *Barry Lyndon* unite Barry's tragic fate and Lady Lyndon's private sorrow, while they express, more succinctly than in any film before or since, both Kubrick's artistic intelligence and his personal vision. He concludes Barry Lyndon's story with the only freeze frame in the film, with the sounds of Schubert's "Piano Trio in E-Flat" returning for the first time since the wooing of Lady Lyndon in Part I, and with the narrator's last words ("He never saw Lady Lyndon again"). The camera reveals Barry from behind (probably a one-legged double for Ryan O'Neal) as he enters a carriage, artlessly suspended in midair without either the support of good fortune or good form. This series of frames, repeating and freezing the same image, visualizes Barry's personal decline within the informality of contingent space, just as the last scene of the film shows Lady Lyndon's sorrow within the static enclosures of formal space. To reconstruct this brilliant conclusion is to appreciate the mastery of *Barry Lyndon*: (1) Cut to interior shot, a large room at Castle Hackton. From a distance the setting appears static and painterly, with a large window on the left and light flooding in; a table stands in the right background on a polished wood floor, with three people sitting and one standing. The balanced spatial composition suggests a general cultural/period form, but not a specific human content. The Schubert music from the previous scene continues to play. (2) Cut to close-up view (there is no dialogue or narration) of Lady Lyndon slowly and methodically signing bank drafts. We hear the scratching sounds of her pen, a moment's hesitation as Bullingdon, to her right, places another one before her to be signed. The camera concentrates more on her face than on the activity itself. (3) Cut to slow zoom shot of a bank draft made out as follows: "Pray pay Redmond Barry for Annuity 500 guineas, and debit to my account." As she signs her name ("H. Lyndon") to the right, we see a date in the lower left corner of the frame, "11 Dec 1789." (4) Cut to close-up of Lady Lyndon's distracted and sorrowful stare. Following a moment's delay and an expression of muted emotion, she continues the ritual of signing her name to the remaining documents. (5) Cut back to long shot, static composition as before, as the last piano note strikes. (6) Screen cuts to black as Handel's "Sarabande" plays during the film's end-titles.

In the film's temporal structure, this remarkable three minutes of film completes the domination of time in Part II (which begins and ends on specified dates), while it reaffirms an eighteenth-century society's entrapment within its own forms and rituals, its own folly and moral irrelevance. As before, Kubrick's method of visual exposition delineates how the particular human content of one era becomes tragically lost in time and absorbed into the aesthetic distances of its art. By selecting 1789 for the terminating date of the story (no such date exists in Thackeray), with its allusion to the French Revolution and the beginning of a new age in Europe (which might explain the Schubert selection and serve as an indirect reference to the postponed Napoleon film project), Kubrick asks his twentieth-century audience to consider the passing glories and tragic failures of nineteenth-century heroic individualism.[15] Perhaps, he implies, the disparities between one period of history and another may not be disparities at all, but particular instances of a universal condition—of that Kubrickian odyssey through time in which mankind evolves in fits and starts on its way to a civilized humanity waiting in space on the far side of 2001. In the end, however, Kubrick's *Barry Lyndon* leaves its audience with something less tangible but far more enduring: with the haunting memory of those last frozen images of Barry and Lady Lyndon, he with his back to the camera and falling into space, she lost forever in a distant mise-en-scène, and both imploring us to gaze with feeling and understanding at two film portraits that refuse to eviscerate humanity in the formal pursuit of art.

8 THE SHINING

After *Barry Lyndon,* his least commercially successful but most artistically satisfying film, Stanley Kubrick turned to a contemporary American horror novel by Stephen King. As interesting a potboiler in its own right as Thackeray's obscure nineteenth-century picaresque adventure, *The Shining* (1977) represents a great deal more than just a ready commercial property for a film maker rebounding from a previous financial setback.[1] What is surprising is not Kubrick's choice but the fact that he waited so long to make his first "horror" film. Here is how he describes the popular mythology of the genre as well as its psychological and emotional appeal:

> One of the things that horror stories can do is show us the archetypes of the unconscious; we can see the dark side without having to confront it directly. Also, ghost stories appeal to our craving for immortal-

ity. If you can be afraid of a ghost, then you have to believe that a
ghost may exist. And if a ghost exists then oblivion might not be the
end.[2]

As early as *Killer's Kiss*, through the intertwined characters of Davy
Gordon (a paradigm of homogenized, repressed manhood) and Vincent
Rapallo (the dark beast), a Kubrick film crudely embodied the horror
genre's most enduring device, namely the psychological allegory of the
doppelgänger, the alter ego, or double. In an excellent essay on the
subject, Robin Wood describes the classic horror film formula as one
where "normality is threatened by the Monster" and the *doppelgänger*
motif as one "where normality and the Monster are two aspects of the
same person."[3] Throughout his career, however, Kukrick employs psychological doubling in ways that increasingly resemble the twists and
ironies of a Nabokovian blend of play and metaphysics more than a
locus classicus like Stevenson's *The Strange Case of Dr. Jekyll and Mr.
Hyde*. His films repeatedly mix the grotesque and banal, the conventions of Gothic confessional morbidity (for instance, De Quincey's *The
Confessions of an English Opium-Eater* or Poe's "William Wilson")
and the self-conscious involutions of modernist parody. Humbert reads
the "divine Edgar" (Poe), confesses his libidinous yearnings for Lolita
in a diary, and becomes ensnared in a dark fate disguised as the pro-
tean Quilty, who, like the Monster (played by Christopher Lee) seen
on a drive-in movie screen, slowly unwraps himself before his urbane
creator/double, just as in *Clockwork* Alex plays the "humble narrator"
in a tale that forces the audience to accept his violent freedom as a
chosen alternative to the monstrous creations of the State. And in *Dr.
Strangelove*, normality itself becomes indistinguishable from Peter Sellers's brilliant conception of Strangelove as mad scientist *and* resurrected
monster, while *2001* develops a futuristic parable of mankind awakening from an evolutionary slumber to reclaim its destiny from the polite
but murderous control of a monster/machine. Like Buñuel, who incorporates the iconography of horror into *The Exterminating Angel* (1962)
and even *The Discreet Charm of the Bourgeoisie* (1972), Kubrick in his
surrealist fascination with the archetypes of the unconscious suggests
that, to quote Robin Wood, "the Monster is normality's shadow." That
nightmare journey through the forest of *Fear and Desire* and Davy
Gordon's battle in a mannequin factory with a relentless alter ego anticipate later doublings that locate the primitive in the formal disguises
of civilization and, paradoxically, the traces of civilized evolution in

the savage's aggressive disorder. *Lolita's* Humbert becomes less European and more sympathetic as he wanders through Quilty's devious maze, just as Barry Lyndon shows a capacity for moral choice only after he falls from the graces of civility and faces Bullingdon's ritual vengeance; Muffley's imperturbable sanity merges with Strangelove's madness and both are nurtured by the same darkness; in *2001* Bowman loses himself in an eighteenth-century memory room that encloses him within the decor of civilized aspiration and temporal reduction; Colonel Dax of *Paths* waits too long before he sees the Monster in the chateau's splendor; and Alex, *Clockwork's* primitive artist, both animates Alexander's latent savagery and reverses a culture's decline into the stasis of voyeurism and sublimation.

Such paradoxical complications rarely inform the more conventional pleasures of King's novel, although an appreciation for its psychological and thematic logic does illuminate some of the more complex intentions of the film. Unlike the script written by Kubrick and American novelist Diane Johnson, King's work does not locate its mystery or ambiguity in the characterization of Jack Torrance.[4] King's omniscient style allows the reader to figuratively "shine" and rationalize practically every nuance of character, even though it never explains how or why Jack's five-year-old son Danny acquired his precognitive/extrasensory powers nor the sources of the haunted-house "shinings" at the Overlook Hotel. Danny's powers and the shinings are merely two horror-fiction givens which support the conventional wisdom of Reason's impotence before the mysterious workings of Mind and Nature (this "more things in heaven and earth" idea is partly expressed in the epigraph of the novel, Goya's "The sleep of reason breeds monsters"). And even though Jack stubbornly resists both his and Danny's unwelcome gift of "shining," his steady descent into madness resembles a psychological case study as much as a journey into the heart of darkness. The novel associates Jack's lapses into murderous rage with a pattern of father/son doubling, with his own father's frustration and drunken failures, and with a latent wish to punish his wife and son for his inadequacies as a man and incompetence as a writer/teacher. (Early in the book, for instance, we learn about Jack's violence against a former student and how he once broke Danny's arm, while he barely controls a sadistic urge to hurt his wife, Wendy, during lovemaking.) King enlarges and complicates this psychological drama through a symbolic structure that inventively mixes the pulpy cliché of Gothic horror (the novel's primary analogues include Poe's "The Masque of the Red Death," Shirley Jackson's *The Haunting of Hill House*, and Don Siegel's 1956 film version of *Invasion of the Body Snatchers*) with an implicit critique of the post-World War II American character. (Jack's "shinings" in the novel return him to a masked ball at the Overlook on the night of August 29, 1945; in the film, it is a 1920s dream party.) In that context, Jack's history becomes symptomatic of an American withdrawal from Cold War uncertainty into apocalyptic self-indulgence and a denial of the social/ existential imperatives of conscience. The Overlook, like some impersonal and Kafkaesque corporate state, claims Jack's soul and signs him to a lifetime contract as its caretaker and official biographer. He loses interest in the humane focus of his own writing (he comes to "loathe" the characters in his unfinished play) as well as the intimate bonds of family, all of which makes him the alter ego of King himself, whose fondness for *The Shining*'s characters encourages him to kill off only Jack Torrance and the Overlook's spooks. As he explores the history of the Overlook in a scrapbook, Jack not only becomes absorbed into its demonic past but his madness resuscitates both its ghouls and his father's legacy. Thematically, King suggests that this symbiotic tie between hotel and man represents America's secret longing for a timeless escape (like the revelers in Poe's story), where the complex demands of the so-called nuclear family as well as individual moral responsibility are abrogated by a mindless faith in the virtue of technocratic "work" (Jack's obsession with "doing his job") and the lure of visceral pleasure. If nothing else, Stephen King's *The Shining* reminds us that Hawthorne's New England morality and Gothic sensibility can be translated into the fictional idiom of more than one American generation.

Central to the effect and fascination of King's novel is the conflict between Family and Monster, between the norms Jack's moral education teaches him to revere and his urge to destroy those restraints and release a diseased libido. An implicit reference in both novel and film are those sudden outbursts of inexplicable violence on the placid landscapes of American family life, of husbands butchering loved ones and killing themselves, those real-life tales from the American Crypt. In King's version, the Family—that bedrock of normality, continuity, order—is threatened from within by both the Father (creator/destroyer) and the Hotel (America's recent past), while the son functions on an allegorical level as Redeemer rather than Antichrist. Danny's ability to "shine" enables him to read thoughts (e.g., he dreads the word "divorce" whenever it appears in Wendy's mind), to locate missing objects, and to "see" things from both the past and future. Initially, King misleads the reader into believing that his character may be another Satanic child, when in fact it is the Overlook which is possessed and which needs both the boy's powers and Jack's madness to revive a dormant evil. Since he does not always understand his visions, Danny creates a fifteen-year-old alter ego named "Tony" (in the book, Danny's middle name is Anthony) who not only "tells" and "shows" him things but glimpses their meaning. Toward the end of the novel, when the integrity of the family is in greatest danger, Danny experiences a vision/dream in which he falls through a Poe-inspired ballroom clock into a nightmare world akin to Lewis Carroll's *Alice in Wonderland*, only here he confronts in "Tony's" face a composite of his and Jack's visages. After Jack and the hotel are destroyed and evil purged by an exploding boiler, the novel does not completely resolve this second father/son doubling, but quietly suggests that the father's heritage survives in some hidden corridor of the son's mind even as a new family order forms around Hallorann (Overlook's black cook), Wendy, and Danny.

As the above indicates, King's novel provided Kubrick with a reasonably accessible group of characters and numerous opportunities for either conceptual/symbolic enlargement or alteration. The director of *Dr. Strangelove*, *2001*, and *A Clockwork Orange* must have been particularly intrigued by a narrative tendency to subordinate conventional linear surfaces to a symbolic or dreamlike logic, one in which the rational dualities of normal/abnormal, sane/insane, cohabit in the imaginative terrain of a modern Gothic fairy tale. Needless to say, Kubrick's *The Shining* (1980) offers little evidence that he "believes" in such things as "shinings" and paranormal close encounters, but it does reveal a film aesthetic that continues to confound audience expectations at the very moment it appears to fulfill them. For a start, Kubrick eliminates many of the supernatural episodes found in the novel, particularly those that, either through the creation of blatant "effects" or through a reliance on horror-film clichés, might violate a realist/surrealist style, which requires that the unconscious assume a palpable and empirical life. Besides the explosive ending, which King telegraphs from the beginning, Kubrick deletes these significant details from the novel: (1) an empty wasps' nest that mysteriously revives and attacks Danny; (2) an animal topiary (rabbits, dogs, lions) that keeps moving and guards the entrance to the Overlook Hotel; (3) a fire hose that becomes a snake and threatens Danny; (4) an elevator that moves by itself and contains signs of the 1945 ball (a mask, confetti); (5) a roque court (a "scientific" form of croquet) from which Jack gets the short-handled mallet he uses as a murder weapon in the novel; and (6) a model playhouse/replica of the Overlook Hotel in which Danny feels a malign presence. Elsewhere, Kubrick and collaborator Diane Johnson alter both the impact and the meaning of several key episodes found in the novel. In the novel Room 217 is where Danny first sees REDRUM (written on the bathroom mirror) and a bloated female corpse in the bathtub. In the film room 217 has become 237, the locus of a psycho/sexual event for Jack Torrance (who, in the novel, never sees the woman). The film retains most of Jack's conversations with Lloyd, the ghostly bartender, as well as his dialogue with Delbert Grady, the hotel's former caretaker, but places them, respectively, in an authentic Jazz Age mise-en-scène and a startling red bathroom; in both instances, the film enlarges and complicates the doubling patterns of the novel. Instead of a masked ball, the film recreates a formal party which, it turns out, takes place at the Overlook on July 4, 1921, and which includes an old song ("Midnight with the Stars and You") about romantic dreams and recollection. And at the end, Jack kills Hallorann with an ax (in the novel, the Overlook cook recovers from a roque-mallet attack) and later suffers a lonely, frozen death (rather than an explosive, infernal one) after Wendy and Danny escape in a snow-cat.

But this is not to say that the film neglects all the expected trappings of horror fiction and horror film making, although at times it uses them facetiously or buries them so deeply that they pass unnoticed. Jack (Jack Nicholson) tells hotel manager Stuart Ullman (Barry Nelson) that his wife is a "ghost story and horror film addict" after he listens to a foreshadowing story about one Charles Grady, the caretaker in 1970, who ran amok and killed his family with an ax before blowing his brains out with a shotgun. We learn from Ullman that the hotel's season runs from May 15 to October 30 (a change from the novel), which means that the Torrances move in on Halloween. During her initial tour of the kitchen with Hallorann (Scatman Crothers), Wendy (Shelley Duvall) remarks that it's like a maze and later characterizes the fast-emptying hotel as "like a ghost ship." On their way to the Overlook, the Torrances discuss the Donner party and cannibalism, a subject that Danny (Danny Lloyd) knows about from TV and that Jack characterizes as a necessary means of "survival." During the closing-day tour, however, Hallorann shows Wendy that they will have more than enough provisions for the winter, which anticipates the film's thematic concern for psychological/spiritual cannibalism and survival through Jack's eventual breakdown into madness. In a scene where Hallorann discusses "shining" with Danny, knives hanging from a kitchen-rack become prominent only after the boy asks him if he is "scared" of the Overlook, which foreshadows both Wendy's clutching at a knife after she locks Jack in dry-food storage and her later slashing of his hand as he attempts to force his way into their bathroom with an ax. Not only the knife but suggestions of birds and birdlike menace recall a primary motif in another film about the American family and schizophrenia, namely Hitchcock's *Psycho*: The opening camera movements swoop through the Rocky Mountains and pass over Jack's yellow VW like a bird of prey; strange bird sounds accompany several exterior transition shots of the Overlook and shrieking music accentuates certain moments of terror; a model of a dark eagle with its wings spread in flight rests on a windowsill in Ullman's office and Jack wears a green athletic shirt adorned with a large black eagle ("Stovington Eagles") in the scene where he eats breakfast in bed, discusses *déjà vu* with Wendy (he feels that he's been in the Overlook before), and playfully mocks her haunted house fears. Ullman passes on the apocryphal story that the hotel was constructed (1907–1909) on an old Indian burial ground, which misleads us into believing that the spirit dancers in the enormous imitation Navajo sand painting over the fireplace in the Colorado Lounge (the main room where Jack types his "book") will come to life and haunt the Torrance family. Another foreshadowing occurs in a kitchen scene where Wendy prepares supper while watching a Denver television newscast about a convicted murderer being given a "life sentence" (an indirect allusion to Jack's subsequent desire to join Overlook's immortals), an "Aspen woman" who is missing from a "hunting trip with her husband," and the progress of a snowstorm that will isolate both her and Danny during Jack's animal-like transformation. When Jack and his ax move through the hotel and into the snow-covered hedge maze (appropriately, its hedges are thirteen feet high), his exaggerated limp and foot dragging (the result of a fall down the staircase) recall all those horror film cripples and hunchbacks of the nineteen thirties, just as Wendy's vision of cobwebs and skeletons (including the humorous remains of Delbert Grady, standing with a tray in his hand and serving his "customers") in the hotel's "reception" area revives one of the horror genre's hoariest devices.

In almost every respect, Kubrick's *The Shining* challenges both an audience's expectations and its conceptual understanding of narrative events in ways King's novel rarely does. In the early scenes, Kubrick develops Jack's character from a deceptively "objective" point of view, except for that moment when Jack "shines" over a model in the reception area of the hedge maze and the camera (from Jack's perspective) slowly zooms down on the tiny figures of Wendy and Danny arriving in the center of the "real" hedge maze outside. Before his first conversation with Lloyd the bartender (Joe Turkel), Jack's interiority largely remains a mystery (in marked contrast to the novel's method) as the film requires the audience to "shine" by interpreting Jack's character through either Danny's subjectivity or other visual details. Many clues are offered:

1. Through Danny's imaginary friend "Tony" (a voice who lives in his mouth and hides in his stomach) and his "shinings"—the elevator of blood, the two Grady girls standing hand-in-hand and facing the camera, REDRUM—*The Shining* not only visualizes three images of horror but provides a symbolic conduit (visual and aural) into Jack's unconscious mind as well as its demonic reincarnation within the collective unconscious of the Overlook Hotel.

2. The Grady sisters, who look like twins but are actually doubles (their ages of eight and ten are established in Jack's interview with Ullman), link Jack to the caretaker (Charles Grady) who axed his family in 1970 (in one bloody "shining" Danny sees the girls' bodies and the ax lying on the floor in one of the hotel's corridors), while the elevator of blood first appears to Danny through a bathroom mirror in the Boulder apartment just after "Tony" tells him that Jack has accepted the Overlook job and is about to phone Wendy.

3. Subsequently, both the elevator/blood vision and REDRUM appear as "shinings" (through parallel editing) whenever Danny reacts in terror to a dramatic increase in Jack's anger or madness (for instance, when Jack blows up at Wendy's suggestion that they leave the hotel and during the scene when she holds a baseball bat and retreats from his threatening advances).

4. In the film, the hotel scrapbook—a critical and totally explained property in the novel—becomes not only a subtle narrative device but a significant visual motif: Jack, for instance, starts to write his "book"

only after the scrapbook appears on the table next to his typewriter; the scrapbook is seen briefly in the foreground of a wide-angle shot as he becomes angry with Wendy for interrupting his work ("We're going to make a new rule. When I'm in here, and you hear me typing, or whether you don't hear me typing, or whatever the fuck you hear me doing in here, that means don't come in"), thus implying that his obsessive and lonely typing (he yanks the paper out of the carriage when she arrives), his bursts of violent temper, and his trancelike states are connected with his discovery and exploration of the Overlook's secret past in the scrapbook.

5. The large brown scrapbook not only looks ancient but contains pasted newspaper clippings that assume the shape of a maze's internal design.

6. Later, in that meeting with Delbert Grady (Philip Stone) in the red bathroom of the Gold Room, Jack claims to recognize him from newspaper photos (in the scrapbook) as Kubrick creates a doubling effect not found in King; in the film there are not only two Grady daughters but *two* Grady fathers—Delbert Grady, a waiter/butler type (called "Jeevesy" by Jack) at the 1921 party, who says that his wife and daughters are somewhere in the hotel, and Charles Grady, the caretaker who killed himself and his family in 1970.

7. The various doublings imply that there are *two* Jack Torrances, the one who goes mad and freezes to death in present time and the one smiling out of a 1921 photograph that hangs on the gold corridor wall inside the Overlook Hotel.

Instead of the novel's animal topiary, its replica playhouse, or its roque court, Kubrick's film uses a hedge maze (100 yards long in the script, but reduced to a smaller scale on Elstree's backlot) to metaphorically focus the meaning of Jack's madness as well as visually embody larger conceptual aspirations.[5] Mazes—like games of chess—combine design and deception, paths and choices, fate and cul-de-sacs: all of which, in various guises, play significant thematic roles in almost every Kubrick film. Mazes are highly artificial human contrivances whose orderly and complex sense of purpose involves a twofold conceptual game in which the player must not only *search* for the center but *remember* how to get out. Thus a maze embodies the double idea of movement toward enclosure (self-contained; formal art uncontaminated by life) and movement toward escape (chaos, infinity, contingency). In the fiction of Jorge Luis Borges, for example, characters repeatedly

Jack Torrance (Jack Nicholson) sitting in the center
of the Overlook's maze and making contact with a
memory lost but not forgotten.

search for the "center" of their existence, only to discover that life has
no essence but that it does contain an appealing multiplicity and complexity within its mazelike exchange between objective and subjective
worlds.[6] Kubrick's chateau in *Paths of Glory* resembles a labyrinth
(corridors, uncertain turns, spatial design from afar and dislocation
from within) but only General Broulard moves through it with assurance, and even he answers to unseen forces off-screen. More often than
not, Kubrick's characters get lost in a tangle of ambition and desire:
Davy Gordon's romantic infatuation with a ballroom dancer becomes
confused by the obscure objects of his desire and the deceptive moves
of Rapallo, while both Humbert and Barry Lyndon briefly attain the
"center" of their respective quests (nymphet, wealth/title) only to realize that it resembles an empty room without doors. In *The Shining*,
the maze concept encompasses the film thematically and aesthetically
(i.e., both within the film itself and the audience watching it); it not
only helps explain Jack's madness (that is, the subconscious as a labyrinth in which the conscious self gets lost) but inspires the Overlook's
floor-plan and decor (for instance, the maze pattern of the carpet outside Room 237), as well as the events which occur there; in addition,

the film contains a maze-within-a-maze (the model inside the hotel) that doubles with the "real" maze outside. Significantly, Jack wants to stay inside the hotel's maze rather than explore its surroundings (after closing day, he's not seen outside until that final chase through the snow into the hedge maze), to control its center (the Colorado Lounge) like a mad god writing his book of Creation. Symbolically, he wants to "forget" himself (Jack Torrance in present time) and to "remember" not how to escape from the center of the maze but how to command its static and enclosed timelessness. In contrast, the film associates both Wendy and Danny with "outside" worlds, with contingency and movement, which means from the beginning that they will either escape Jack's madness if they "remember" how to retrace their steps or be cornered in some dead-end if they choose the wrong path. Early in the film, for instance, they learn how to negotiate the corridors of the hotel ("to leave a trail of breadcrumbs," to quote Wendy), and in one scene Danny moves in a circle around the Colorado Lounge on his Big Wheels tricycle, while Jack tends to remain stationary within its center; Wendy and Danny explore the hedge maze and complete a circular course from inside space back into outside space, into a world of design and a return to life's expansive disorder; Jack, on the other hand, imitates what Borges characterizes as the death-in-life of the "North" (that is, northern European intellectualism)—that yearning for a totally rationalized world without those crevices of unreason that arouse despair in some and imagination in others—rather than the "South's" desire to traverse the maze and engage its multiplicity, to confront fate and choice, and to outface oblivion in an act of creation. To covet the center of the maze as permanent resting place leads not only to death but to madness.

Within the mazelike designs of *The Shining*, Kubrick develops a series of doubling/mirroring effects that go far beyond anything found in King's novel. And because the film so completely integrates these doublings into a narrative and visual labyrinth, the viewer-turned-critic needs a descriptive map before he dares to chart any interpretive course. We must see what is *there*, before asking what it *means*. With that in mind, as well as the summary already provided, consider the following:

1. Jack's interview with Ullman (whose confident affability contrasts with Jack's unconvincing nonchalance) pairs off with the meeting between Wendy and a woman doctor (Anne Jackson) whose sober and

professional womanhood reacts in stunned disbelief to an offhand but slightly cowed explanation for an old injury (separated shoulder) inflicted on Danny by his drunken father.

2. For the interview, Jack and Ullman are joined by a hotel employee named Bill Watson (Barry Dennen), whose only real distinction (and function) is his striking physical resemblance to Jack Nicholson, especially when seen from behind (they pair off into chairs opposite one another and facing Ullman); and on closing day Watson completes a double pairing of *four* figures walking in single file (Ullman, Wendy, Jack, Watson) through the Colorado Lounge and past the hedge maze on their way to the snow-cat, where they divide into *twos* (Wendy and Watson on the left, Jack and Ullman on the right).

3. Interestingly, this grouping resembles the *four* horizontally placed figures inside the "circle" of the Navajo sand painting over the fireplace, with Wendy and Jack occupying the privileged "center" position and Ullman and Watson framing them on either side.

4. On two occasions, Ullman says goodbye to two young female employees and, just as the Torrances are ushered into their hotel living quarters, Jack noticeably glances after them in a gesture of sexual interest.

5. In the kitchen on closing day, Hallorann shows Wendy the meat in the deep freeze and the food in dry storage but not those things which fall in between (for instance, butter, milk, eggs, and so forth), just as the various weather reports emphasize *extremes* (for instance, the TV newscast Wendy watches in the kitchen and the one in Hallorann's Miami bedroom, which mentions both a record heat wave in Florida and a record snowfall in Colorado). So Wendy and Danny watch *Summer of '42* (Robert Mulligan, 1971) on television in the midst of a winter snowstorm, and Jack relives an Overlook ball from the summer of 1921 during a winter in present time.

6. In that Miami bedroom, two paintings showing a black nude woman on opposite walls (mirroring) are seen just before Hallorann experiences a "shining" that occurs between Danny's and Jack's separate visits to Room 237.

7. Two versions of the same nude woman inhabit the green bathroom of Room 237. One is an old hag/corpse who apparently rises out of the bathtub to strangle Danny and the other is an erotically inviting siren who "seduces" Jack before transforming herself back into the decomposed and laughing crone.

8. While Danny's "shinings" link him to Jack's subconscious, they also provide a horrific vision into the Overlook Hotel, one that opposes his father's more nostalgic and dreamy "memories"; similarly, Danny's association with cartoon characters and stuffed animals (in one early shot, his face is doubled with that of a teddy bear pillow) anticipates Jack's grotesque metamorphosis at the end (into the Big Bad Wolf coming after the "little piggies" with an ax).

9. Jack "shines" on two occasions, once with each of his two Overlook doubles, namely Lloyd the bartender and Delbert Grady, the first decidedly American and the other English.

10. The film contains *four* bathrooms, *two* associated with both the Torrance family *and* images of murder (in the Boulder apartment and their Overlook quarters), and *two* (the green and red ones) with Jack's regression into madness and the hotel's past.

11. Not only does the film contain *two* mazes (the hedge outside and a model inside) but the Overlook itself is a maze and, significantly, it breaks down into *two* sections, one old and one remodeled, one past and one present; the hotel's old-fashioned "staff wing," for instance, contains the Torrances' rather shabby and cramped apartment, as well as the hallway (worn blue carpet, faded yellow wallpaper) where the two Grady children were murdered; in contrast, the "public" half of the Overlook is done in a mélange of "modern" and indigenous decorative styles, including authentic Navajo designs and colors, mazy patterns in the carpeting, and the refurbished (according to Ullman) gold and pink gaudiness of the Gold Room.

12. Finally, mirrors figure prominently in the following settings and scenes: inside the four bathrooms; in the Torrance bedroom at the Overlook (in one scene, a mirror completes a double image of Jack sitting in bed and later converts REDRUM into MURDER); in the hallway entrance inside the Torrance apartment (where Jack's reflection is prominent just *after* he returns from his visit to Room 237); in Hallorann's Miami bedroom; on the wall of the corridor leading to the Gold Room (before both his "shinings" in that room, Jack's reflection in a corridor mirror is shown); behind the bar of the Gold Room; and just inside the doorway of Room 237.

With the possible exception of *2001*, no Kubrick film before *The Shining* contains as many important details or stimulates as many associative responses. It requires several viewings before its secrets are released, and even though like a maze-puzzle it can be assembled into

Wendy and Danny on a tour of the kitchen maze
with Hallorann (Shelley Duvall, Danny Lloyd, Scatman Crothers).

one or more interpretive orders, mysteries remain which intimate that
there is still more. Like Bowman within his memory room, we sense a
familiar terrain, a kind of private and cinematic *déjà vu*, but one dislocated from conventional time and space (both "real" and filmic) in
just enough ways to encourage new perceptions and fresh understandings, if for no other reason than a desire to escape its powerful hold on
our imagination. In that sense, Kubrick's films have always been about
"shining," about the difficulties of seeing, of choosing, of creating, *of
knowing*. And what is it that makes up good art, or even good criticism,
if not a magical conjunction of informed knowledge and inspired "shining"? Let us now remove the qualifying marks and shine on.

The narrative structure of *The Shining* involves a journey from an
ordered and forward-moving world of time into the disorders of self
and regressions of memory. In some ways, it recalls the first three parts
of *2001* in reverse ("Dawn of Man," Floyd's journey to the Moon, "Jupiter Mission: 18 Months Later"), in that Jack Torrance, unlike Bowman as Star-Child, does not escape from his memory room (the Overlook Hotel) into space, but instead retreats into its deadly order.

Through the use of titles on a black screen, Kubrick emphasizes time more than he does space, as the following breakdown of the film's organization reveals:

Prologue	Credits (Rocky Mountain flight)
Part 1	"The Interview" and "Closing Day"
Part 2	"A Month Later"/ "Tuesday"/
	"Thursday"/ "Saturday"/ "Monday"/
	"Wednesday"
Part 3	"8 am" and "4 pm"
Epilogue	Two Frozen Images of Jack (in the
	hedge maze and in the 1921 photograph)

Notice how the progression of events goes from months to days to hours, a process of reduction and intensification which moves toward a single moment in time when insanity breaks loose from the bonds of rational order. As he has done so often in other films, Kubrick undermines an audience's faith in causal order by, first, establishing the credibility of such order through a realistic, matter-of-fact style (in part one), only to confuse that truth by transforming it into a memory as faint or illusory as Jack's mad quest for the immortality of death. By parts two and three, the periodic screen-titles conform to an associative or symbolic logic, to the film's complex patterns of doubling and reversal (i.e., the every-other-day quality of "Tuesday"/ "Thursday," etc., or the movement from "8 am" to "4 pm"), which inevitably mock our desire for temporal sense and rational sequence. Early in the film, for instance, Kubrick creates subtle time confusions that become even more pronounced later on. Wendy tells the doctor that "Tony" first appeared about the same time that Jack, in a drunken rage, separated Danny's shoulder, which, we learn later, happened *three years before*. Not only does Wendy fail to make the psychological connection between "Tony" and Jack's violence, but she pretends to be reassured by the fact that Jack has been on the wagon for *five months*, which means that any remorse he felt about his son was either very belated or nonexistent. During Jack's first conversation with the bartender, he acts as if his life in present time were a bad dream from the future (i.e., post–1921) and that *his* imaginary friend Lloyd has as much continuity and corporeality as the members of his own family (his first words, spoken directly into the camera, are "Hi, Lloyd"). Ever so quietly, the film implies from the beginning that psychological time and real time do not operate according to the same causal schedule, that the objective world and its temporal assertiveness may not explain character but it does provide clues to those who shine.

In the credits, the camera from above moves over water and through mountains with the ease of a bird in flight and the rapidity of a machine in space. Below, on a winding mountain road, Jack's diminutive yellow Volkswagen journeys through a tree-lined maze (the film's second shot) and resembles one of Danny's toy cars or the yellow tennis ball seen later from another overhead shot on the maze-patterned carpet (orange and brown colors, with a *red* center) in the corridor outside Room 237. Above, one experiences the freedom and uncertainty of contingent space, an anticipation of either Star-Gates (*2001*) or Doomsday flights (*Strangelove*), while the theme music (by Wendy Carlos and Rachel Elkind) sounds like a Gregorian chant for the dead (*Dies Irae*) and prepares us for the world below, for paths and endgames within a horizontal labyrinth, where one forgets how to look up and out into the wonders of space. Part one maps out this terrain in a deceptively clear and orderly manner. The interview between Ullman and Jack takes the form of questions and answers, explanations and reassurances—that is, the give and take of rational, linear discourse. Ullman "explains" the caretaker's job, how it is not "physically demanding" but potentially involves problems of adjustment ("cabin fever") for certain kinds of people. Like those disembodied narrators throughout the soundscape of Kubrick's films, his voice and manner serve the requirements of narrative exposition while they fail to explain or acknowledge the mysteries of inner and outer space. Jack smiles and affects a relaxed informality, although his attention becomes more concentrated, even trancelike, when Ullman, himself all smiles, relates as a footnote to the interview a story about the former caretaker who "seemed perfectly normal" but nevertheless cut up his family with an ax and "stacked their bodies neatly in one of the rooms in the west wing." Naturally, he has worked out a reassuring and logical explanation for such an appalling departure from sane behavior (a "claustrophobic reaction"), although Jack's obvious interest (as if it recalls one of his own nightmares) and his insincere congeniality (early signs of a personality malfunction) lead us to believe that the film's definition of his madness will be far more complex. By the end of the film, the Grady story takes on a larger meaning in the way it not only anticipates Jack's fate but completes a doubling pattern identical to the one between Jack and that smiling figure in the 1921 photograph (that is, as Jack pairs off with a 1921 persona, so Charles Grady in 1970 confronted his other self in the figure of Delbert Grady). But all that seems part of another universe in the context of the interview structure of the film's opening, a context and structure that eventually recalls a style of *cinéma-vérité* psychodrama familiar in the works of Truffaut (for instance, *The 400 Blows*) and Bergman (*Scenes from a Marriage*, 1973, *Face to Face*, 1976). Is it imitation or parody? Not only in the beginning, but in the other "interviews" of part one (Wendy and the doctor, Jack and Wendy in the car, Hallorann and Danny in the kitchen), Kubrick disturbs the still waters of cinematic normality with something more important than just Danny's bloody shinings; through his characters' bland, offhand reportage of gruesome acts of horror from the past, he suggests that Ullman's world might have less substance than a madman's phantasms. Charles Grady's butchery and suicide, Jack's earlier violence against his son, the cannibalism of the Donner party, and the threat of Room 237, as well as other "bad" things alluded to by Hallorann in the Overlook's history, become inseparable from all the small talk about "making good time" (Jack's trip from Boulder to the hotel) and making new friends (Wendy's reassurances to Danny), about a "new writing project" and a fresh start (for Jack and his family). Eventually, Jack denies existential time in search of private time, Danny's new friends are two dead girls who want him to play and live with them "forever and ever and ever," and Jack's creative ambitions degenerate into a stack of papers that repeat a single obsessive thought. In the end, *The Shining* concerns old projects and unfinished journeys, secret longings and frustrated desires, movements in reverse rather than movements forward, "interviews" with the Self's dark but hardly imaginary friends.

And what is "Closing Day" all about if not an attempt to define and place the spatial geography of the film? Like the interview, the closing-day tour puts things in order, establishes relationships, and completes the film's temporal and spatial exposition of the Overlook Hotel. But again there are unexplained confusions and tensions more significant than just Danny's game-room shining (of the two Grady daughters) or the audience's natural tendency to look for the first indications of horror yet to come. Spatially, the tour shows us rooms, places, and objects of importance to later events, while it fails to provide an overview of the whole. Where, for instance, is the Colorado Lounge in relation to

the kitchen? or the Gold Room? or Room 237? or the Torrances' apartment?* Like Wendy in her reaction to the kitchen, the audience feels
both at home and lost within the hotel's vast public areas and its more
intimate corridors and rooms. Like a maze-puzzle and like the film itself, it has design and purpose, but one which initially requires its
inhabitants/players—namely the characters in the hotel and audience
in the theater—to look for signs of that unseen intelligence that created
it and that understands its logic. During the interview, for instance,
Ullman tells Jack that the Charles Grady killings took place in the
"west wing," while he defines the section of the hotel that houses the
Torrance apartment as the "staff wing." Is this not one example of an
Ullman euphemism (as well as a Kubrick irony), in that the hallway
directly opposite the entrance to the apartment leads to the corridor
(a dead-end) with the faded yellow wallpaper with blue flowers where
later Danny shines and sees the butchered Grady daughters. Jack and
Wendy stand together in the white bathroom of the apartment, where
in part three she will be cornered by his madness, and both express
disapproval—Jack, through sardonic humor ("homey," he calls it), and

---

* Needless to say, some familiarity with Kubrick's maze—namely, his Overlook
Hotel set in *The Shining*—helps in placing action and understanding parallels,
associations, and repetitions. With that in mind, consider these few items of interest:

1. The reception area, kitchen (which is behind the reception area), gold
corridor, and the Gold Room occupy the *first floor* of the Overlook; the *model
maze* sits on a table by a window opposite Ullman's office in the reception area
and appears in the background of several scenes (e.g., when Jack first arrives at
the hotel, when he calls Wendy to tell her that he has the job, when Wendy
pushes a breakfast cart in "A Month Later," and when Hallorann, taking a similar
course [from kitchen, through gold corridor, to reception area], is murdered).

2. The Colorado Lounge is located in the *center* of the *second floor* of the
hotel, and Room 237 appears to be in a wing behind the table where Jack types
his manuscript; Danny Big Wheels in a circle ("A Month Later") around the
Colorado Lounge, from a service corridor behind the wall with the fireplace and
Navajo sand painting, to an alcove by the elevators behind Jack's typing table,
past a sign in red advertising "Camera Walk" (Kubrick's joking reference to the
Steadicam?) and through the lounge itself, into an alcove on the other side, and
back to the original starting point—from there it is not far to the mazelike carpeting (screen right from the elevators) that leads to Room 237.

3. Apparently, the Torrance apartment is located on the *third floor* in the rear
of the hotel in the so-called "staff," or "west," wing, and it is not far from the
corridor (yellow wallpaper, blue flowers) where Danny sees the Grady daughters dead.

4. The *hedge maze*, of course, is behind the hotel. All the exterior location
shots of the hotel entrance are the work of a second-unit photography team and
show the Timberline Lodge at Mt. Hood National Forest in Oregon, while the
"backyard" area with the hedge maze is a full-size replica of the Timberline's
exterior, which was built on a backlot at Elstree studios in England.

The interview (Barry Dennen, Barry Nelson, Jack Nicholson).

Wendy, with a look of wifely disappointment—yet neither realize that, more than likely, they now inhabit an enclosed space that once gave birth to a previous caretaker's madness. Besides those extremes implied by the kitchen's two food compartments, Ullman's office and the clash between the Colorado Lounge's spacious Navajo beauty and the Gold Room's vast but garish modernity suggest a visual schizophrenia that works to defeat the orderly tendencies of "interviews" and closing-day tours. When the camera follows Jack into his meeting with Ullman, it quickly records a split personality in the decor of the manager's office. Outside the doorway, one sees on the left an abstract painting (red and blue colors, with indications of a human face) that surrealistically mimics the more traditional Navajo art seen elsewhere, and on the right, neatly arranged colored photographs of mountain scenes showing the four seasons. Inside the peach-colored office, this left/right opposition continues; on the left a multicolored jigsaw county map, a piece of abstract sculpture (of twisted figures), and ancient photographs of the Overlook (a pictorial history in the brownish hues of early 20th century still-photography) complement the abstract painting by the doorway and clash with the orderly arrangement of pictures and awards on the right wall that reflect Ullman's character and his past (e.g., a

Boy Scouts' Exploring certificate). But there is visual humor as well as counterpoint: next to a small American flag on Ullman's desk sits a metal cup containing pencils and pens *and* a miniature replica of an ax.

In part one, even though Wendy and Jack appear to be a "normal" heterosexual couple (they call each other "honey" and show other signs of affection), the film visually develops several juxtapositions that objectify latent disorders at work in both their marriage and the family. Shelley Duvall is not a sexually attractive woman and therefore plays the film's role as Danny's protective mother better than she could the novel's as Jack's lover, which, in part, helps clarify the complex symbolism of Jack's meeting with the mysterious nude woman in Room 237. Wendy is not only identified as a "ghost story and horror film addict" (in King, she reads Gothic novels and listens to the music of Bartók), but when first seen she is reading Salinger's *The Catcher in the Rye* and smoking Virginia Slims, while Jack reads *Playgirl* in the hotel's reception area and later smokes Marlboros. On the surface, such details give their respective characters a sexual eclecticism and cultural accessibility, when, in truth, they anticipate the film's sexist allegory. Jack appears to be a model of liberal politics and education—a writer and teacher, informally dressed in tweed jackets and sweaters, a man who apparently reads *The New York Review of Books*—and Wendy a candidate for modern, liberated womanhood. But, of course, he's a closet sexist and she's not much more than a dutiful housewife, concerned mother, and nervous mouse who is vulnerable to both Jack's cajolements and his masculine insecurities. Especially in the early scenes, Wendy is visually defined by her role as mother and all that it entails: her world has one central location—the kitchen, not the bedroom—and contains foodstuffs (milk cartons, boxes of cereal) and products (washing detergents, Q-Tips) necessary to her family's welfare and the management of a normal American home. Jack, on the other hand, quietly expresses not only an irritation with the banalities and routines of family life, but something far more dangerous than even he realizes. During a car trip to the Overlook, he barely suppresses an urge to ridicule Wendy's mistaken belief that the Donner incident occurred in Colorado, while he expresses himself more truly in a sarcastic response to Danny's comment that he knows about cannibalism from TV ("See! It's okay, he saw it on the television!"). Jack Nicholson uses both his face (especially his mouth and villainous eyebrows) and speech to hint at an important dysfunction in the character: After

Danny complains to his father that he's hungry, Jack barks out a reply in a primitive, illiterate slur—"you shoulda eaten your breakfast"—which belies his role as "enlightened" teacher/writer. Except for his ability to shine, Danny's character is a picture of normality: He eats peanut butter and jelly sandwiches, drinks milk, watches Roadrunner cartoons on TV, lives in a child's world inhabited and decorated by characters from Disneyland and "Peanuts," animal books, baseball bats, toy cars, astronauts, Big Wheels, and stuffed animals. This normal child's world, in the surreal landscape of a resurrected Overlook, undergoes a grotesquely satiric metamorphosis:

1. When Jack moves through the reception area in part two on his way to a shining over the model maze, he throws a yellow tennis ball past a stuffed bear and Danny's Big Wheels, which rests on the very spot (a Navajo circle design) where Hallorann will be murdered (ironically, in front of the cashier's cages).

2. Jack's tennis ball mysteriously rolls into Danny's circle of toy cars just before the boy walks through the open door of Room 237.

3. Wendy uses Danny's baseball bat as a weapon to repel Jack's first murderous advances.

4. Wendy locks Jack in the dry-food storage room where he later eats a "survival" meal closer to a child's than an adult's—peanut butter, roasted peanuts (associated with his drinking), Oreo cookies, and crackers.

5. As Jack breaks through the apartment door with an ax (and the Grady corridor looms in the background), he mocks his role as family man with perhaps his funniest line—"Wendy, I'm *home*"—which prepares for his humorous rendition of both the Big Bad Wolf and the famous introductory pitch from Johnny Carson's *Tonight Show*: "Heeeeere's Johnny." Behind Jack's grotesquely illuminated face hangs a picture of an idealized, snow-covered cottage.

6. Now the cartoon violence and lyrics of the Roadrunner show take a grimly ironic turn in Jack's Wile E. Coyote ("the coyote's after you") chasing Danny ("if he catches you you're through") into the snow-covered hedge maze, where he is outwitted by the boy's speed and ingenuity ("the coyote is really a crazy clown"). Symbolically, the Overlook Hotel becomes Jack's other Home and other Family, a nightmare world of dismemberment and alienation (where "sliced peaches" and "Heinz Ketchup" recall family massacres, not family meals), in which the mother and child are victims of the father's desire to canni-

balize one family to insure the "survival" of another, to violate one home to resuscitate the corpse of another. Paradoxically, the Monster of *The Shining* wears the face of masculine brutality *and* house Fool, one who finds his home amidst the polite society of the Overlook's past and who performs for what Ullman chauvinistically describes as "all the best people."

Jack's madness does not fully emerge until the final day of part two ("Wednesday") when his subconscious, in unison with the hotel, "awakens" and assumes a life of its own in three remarkable scenes: one in the Gold Room (Jack and Lloyd), one in Room 237 (Jack and the nude woman), and one in the red bathroom of the Gold Room (Jack and Grady). Before these important and symbolic encounters, Kubrick develops a series of visual and aural clues to their meaning. Like the film's musical progression, which, following the credits, moves from the atonalities of Bartók (the ripplings associated with Jack's maze shining and the scrapbook in "A Month Later" and "Tuesday") and Ligeti's "Lontano" (Jack's trancelike states on "Thursday" and "Saturday") to the full dissonance of Penderecki ("The Awakening of Jacob" is especially prominent in the Room 237 episode on "Wednesday"), the visual rhetoric of part two not only objectifies Jack's internal regression but places it in a recognizable mythopoeic context.* Stylistically, the "interview" realism of part one blends into the surrealism of parts two and three, just as a yellow Volkswagen assumes the shape of a tennis ball (which "travels" on the maze carpet into Danny's circle of toy cars) and links Jack's character to the symbolism of a Navajo sand painting. In one striking shot, for instance, the camera tilts up from the typewriter, with a blank piece of paper in its carriage, to reveal the source of a loud pounding noise: in the background, Jack angrily throws a yellow tennis ball against a sand panting which, uncharacteristically,

---

* One of the more interesting aspects of Kubrick's musical selections for *The Shining* is the way they recall the Star-Gate and eighteenth-century memory room sequences in *2001*. Not only does the film use music by György Ligeti ("Lontano"), which sounds like his monolith "Atmospheres" from the earlier film, but many of the selections from Polish modernist Krzysztof Penderecki bear a striking resemblance to the dissonant "journey" and "memory" themes of *2001*. In addition, the film's "theme" music (credits) and the "Rocky Mountains" (the Torrance car trip to the Overlook) by Wendy Carlos and Rachel Elkind recall Penderecki's apocalyptic *Dies Irae Oratorium Ob Memoriam*, what he calls his "music of terror." And finally, Kubrick uses the "Midnight With the Stars and You" tune for the 1920s party and the Epilogue, while an old song called "Home" is heard during the red bathroom scene between Jack and Grady (performed by the Gleneagles Hotel Band).

delineates a totally masculine world; within its enclosed design, which includes the traditional opening to the East, four *male* figures (the squarish heads denote masculinity) stand erect and "safe" within the painting's "circle." In the symbolism of most Navajo sand paintings, yellow is a male color and blue normally identifies the female.[7] (In the mythology of several Indian tribes, yellow denotes death and blue is associated with sky/happiness/love.) In Kubrick's film, Jack's "colors" begin in the warm part of the spectrum (brown, green, yellow) but inevitably move toward *red* (e.g., he wears a maroon-colored jacket in the last part of the film, talks with Grady in the red bathroom, and Danny's blood elevator/REDRUM shinings are associated with his father's subconscious); conversely, both Wendy and Danny start off in blues and reds, while she, in particular, ends up in greens and browns. As the film moves closer to Jack's madness and the Overlook's resurrection, the color yellow becomes even more symbolically assertive, although Kubrick usually provides a source light which realistically "explains" it. The Grady murder corridor is decorated in yellow wallpaper; a lamp next to Jack's typewriter gives the paper a yellow texture; his face and eyes turn yellow like the bourbon in his glass during his talk with Lloyd; the hallway into the Torrance apartment is decorated with yellow-flowered wallpaper; as Jack stands outside the bathroom with the ax, his face and the walls take on a yellowish glow from another lamp (while Wendy wears the blue bathrobe inside the blindingly white bathroom); and when he moves on his murderous course to intercept Hallorann, the hotel's interior lighting transforms the walls from daytime white into evening yellow. In addition, the gold corridor and Gold Room convert the warmth and beauty of yellow (as in the aspens behind the credits) into something akin to the unnatural and discordant colors of the Korova Milkbar in *Clockwork*, especially when mixed with pink upholstered furniture and a bright red bathroom. Symbolically, both Jack's madness and the Overlook's past express a decidedly masculine ethos, one which not only threatens the structures of normality (man/woman, family) but the integrity of psycho/sexual duality. Reminiscent of HAL in *2001*, Jack seeks to command a dead but self-contained world, one that denies existential time as well as contingent space. Significantly, both Jack and HAL are associated with enclosed worlds (spaceship *Discovery* and the Overlook Hotel), with obsessive attitudes toward their "jobs" (the Jupiter Mission and Jack's contract with the Overlook), with a primitive regression disguised by civilized formality (HAL's language and Jack's association with Delbert Grady and the 1920s party), *and* with the colors yellow and red. HAL's ubiquitous eye (red iris, yellow pupil) not only recalls the leopard's surveillance of a Pleistocene darkness but achieves a humanized incarnation in the sexist coloration of Jack Torrance's insanity.

By the middle section of *The Shining*, the latent schizophrenic tendencies of part one have escaped from the closet and turned both psychological and cinematic "normality" inside out. During Jack's breakfast in bed ("A Month Later"), Kubrick photographs the first half of the scene *inside* the reflection in the bedroom mirror and the second half *outside*, a form of visual doubling that goes from a reversed to "normal" perspective, from a simulacrum to "reality" itself. Yet within the "abnormal," reversed imagery of the mirror (the lettering on Jack's shirt and the illusion that he eats with his left hand) the Torrance couple engage in a banal conversation about staying up late and the difficulties of writing ("lots of ideas, no good ones"), while in the "normal" space outside the mirror Jack talks about *déjà vu* and how he "fell in love" with the Overlook "right away." Soon afterwards ("Monday"), Danny visits his now wakeful and unshaven father—sitting on the edge of the same bed and wearing a blue bathrobe—and stands between Jack's mirror reflection on screen-left and his "real" image on screen-right. Even within this touching exchange between father and son, however, Kubrick hints at the macabre awakening of both Jack's dark self and the hotel's past, of a sinister force struggling to escape from the flat surfaces of memory into that three-dimensional world on the other side of the mirror. As the Bartók from his maze-shining plays on the soundtrack, Jack's attention wavers between Danny on his lap ("I love you, Danny, more than anything in the *whole* world") and the seductive intrusion of other visions and other voices: he tells Danny that he can't sleep because of his "work" (the scrapbook), which indicates that his nightmares are learning to walk and to talk; and echoing the Grady daughters' sinister invitation, he tells his son that he would like to stay in the Overlook "forever and ever and ever." In two key scenes, Jack's menacing, godlike isolation *inside* the hotel opposes Wendy and Danny's spirit of *outside* play and exploration. In the first, he shines over the model maze as they playfully race into the hedge maze (and the loser "keeps America clean") and experience its confusion (indicated to the audience by the dizzying motions of the Steadicam). In the second scene ("Thursday"), Wendy and Danny play in

Danny translates his father's subconscious into a mirror image of madness.

the snow below Jack, who, with the sand painting prominent in the background, grins and stares out in a hypnotic, slack-jawed trance from a second-floor window in the Colorado Lounge. As the snowdrifts increase *outside*, the Torrance family becomes more isolated *inside* as normal communication breaks down: Jack sits in the empty but symmetrical "center" of the Overlook, where he reads the scrapbook and translates its collective unconscious into the idiom of his private unconscious; Danny rides his Big Wheels through narrow corridors and sees bloody visions showing the monsters being reborn inside his father's mind; and Wendy tries, with little success, to fight off her loneliness through contacts with the outside world (she watches TV and uses her radio transmitter to say "hello" to a fire-station ranger). But in the surrealistic inversions of part two that ordinary world now seems as alien to us as did the Jack Torrance who forced himself to smile in part one's reassuring temporal and spatial masks. The past now speaks through the present, the primitive seems indistinguishable from the civilized, and inner worlds express themselves in strangely familiar dialects and assume familiar shapes. The demons in the mirror have escaped—and not only are they *real* but they grin in mockery at our bewilderment.

In the climax to part two, Kubrick translates the film's repeated motifs of shining and *déjà vu*, of dreams and recollections, into such an undeniable cinematic and psychological reality that normality itself seems but a distant memory as the Monster both learns to speak our language and discovers its Home. The film starts off with Ullman's recollection of the Charles Grady tragedy, while Danny describes his shinings as dreams faintly remembered and Jack senses that he's lived in the Overlook Hotel before. Yet before he can *remember*, Jack must *forget*. He must forget his past failures and inadequacies as a father, husband, and man of enlightenment; he must forget those responsibilities that bind him to Wendy and Danny; he must forget himself as Jack Torrance in present time, the writer/teacher of part one, and *remember* that other self who forever waits in a memory room for the lights to be turned on. In *The Shining*, that memory room becomes the Overlook Hotel itself, not as it was, but as Jack would like it to have been. Danny sees the truth—the "horror"—of his father's yearning for the center of the maze, of his macabre quest for the perfection of death, while Jack casts it in the nostalgic afterglow of a formal 1920s mise-en-scène. Sitting at the bar in the Gold Room, Jack looks into the camera and enjoins us—not just Lloyd—to shine with him, not only to drink and be merry, but to share his memory and his disease: a memory of license, of masculine freedom and violence, one in which Jack no longer represses either the sexist urge to demean Wendy ("the old sperm-bank upstairs") or his selfish resentment toward the moral demands of fatherhood ("I wouldn't hurt a single hair on his goddamn head! I *love* the little sonofabitch!"). In a remarkable screen performance, Jack Nicholson captures not only the madman's self-delusion and self-pity but, what is even more impressive, a psychomachia that pits the primitive nuances of "man to man" talk—"You set 'em up, Lloyd, and I'll knock 'em down"—against the convolutions of rationalization. He takes his first drink (*Jack Daniels*, naturally), rolls his eyes upward in monstrous bliss, and reenacts before the sepulchral bartender an act of violence against his son:

> The little *fucker* had thrown all my papers on the floor. All I tried to do was *pull* him up [*he violently imitates a jerking motion*]. A momentary loss of muscular coordination, a few extra foot pounds of energy per second, per second [*he narrows two fingers into an imaginary measuring device, then brings his hands together in a quick 'bone-snapping' motion*].

He tells his ghostly but formal reflection (Lloyd also wears a maroon-colored jacket) that Wendy won't let him "forget" his brutality against their son three years before (and in present time, she has just accused him of strangling Danny), which anticipates the fact that soon he will *forget* himself and only *remember* a once latent urge to dominate and to rule. When Jack shines in the green bathroom of Room 237, he experiences a memory of illicit eroticism while Danny relives (he shines in his bed) the grotesque rebirth of the decomposed hag rising out of the bath water. Symbolically, both versions of the nude woman (hag/siren) represent an assault on the integrity of Wendy's role as mother/wife. Danny is enticed into the room by the mysterious appearance of the yellow tennis ball that rolls into his circle, an event that coincides with Jack's nightmare in the Colorado Lounge about killing his family with an ax. As Danny approaches the open door and the dangling *red* key, he calls for Wendy ("Mom, are you in there?") at the very moment that she, from the basement (where she does Jack's "work"), responds to Jack's cries of terror. But Jack will deny the truth of that nightmare when he both embraces the young nude woman (Lia Beldam) and retreats in disgust from the laughing crone (Billie Gibson)—from yet another Kubrickian bathroom that links masturbatory fantasy and death (remember Humbert in the bathtub, dreaming of Lolita just after Charlotte's death).* Sitting on his bed with a tearful Wendy, he tells her that the room was empty and that Danny must have strangled himself. In other words, Jack *forgets* the green and purple horror of Room 237—that hideous mockery of life itself—and *remembers* only its erotic invitation (the woman and sexual patterns in the green and purple carpeting); he *forgets* his "contract" with Wendy and *remembers* only that secret agreement he makes with his other half in the center of the hotel's maze. As Danny "sees" the blood elevator and REDRUM visions from his bed, Jack's anger mounts to a feverish pitch after Wendy suggests they leave the Overlook; he then severs his responsibilities to one family ("I've let you fuck up my life so far, but I'm not going to let you fuck this up") and reaffirms those to another ("I'm really into *my work*"). As he storms out the apartment door, we notice that his path will take him through the Grady corridor (faded yellow wallpaper) on his way back into the Gold Room and its ghoulish denial of time.

The sounds of a romantic tune lure him back into his Gold Room

---

* Just before Jack and the Steadicam travel through Room 237 on their way to the green bathroom, Hallorann experiences a long-distanced shining from his bedroom in Miami, which reveals a private male world not as complex as Jack's and far more sane. Consider these contrasts between Hallorann's shining and Jack's visit to Room 237:

1. Before Hallorann's shining, Kubrick employs two reverse zooms that recall the kind of visual doubling found in the breakfast scene discussed in the text. In this case, each reverse zoom reveals a picture of a nude black woman on opposite walls, each a kind of mirror reflection of the other, although they are pictures of *two* different women. Hallorann, seen lying in bed between the two pictures, watches TV in an orange-colored room, which is ordered and symmetrical (there are lamps on each side of the TV and on each side of his bed), but *not* schizophrenic (unlike Ullman's office). However, he does wear blue pajamas that express a kind of visual split personality—the lower half is solid blue (and earlier his color was blue), while the upper half resembles an abstract, mazelike design; overall, Hallorann's decidedly male world expresses balance rather than dissonance.

2. In contrast, the decor of Room 237 is a ghastly combination of different shades of green and purple, colors which in Kubrick's iconography work against each other—green suggests one value (rebirth, in the eighteenth-century room of 2001) and purple another (Korova decadence); the carpeting in the room is decidedly sexual and mazelike (resembling phallic keyholes inside circles), the wallpaper duplicates the vertical lines of a cage, and just outside the bathroom door hangs a picture of a *fox*; and, of course, there are *two* versions of one woman in the green bathroom (with Gold Room trim arching over the tub), but unlike the pictures on Hallorann's wall they hardly suggest the workings of a healthy libido. Hallorann has his sexual fantasies well in hand, while Jack's express the extremes of lasciviousness and disgust.

of memory to celebrate a liberation on Independence Day (July 4, 1921) from the restraints of civilization. He tells Lloyd that "it's good to be back, I've been away, but now I'm back," just as a male voice begins to sing the lyrics of a song about love, surrender, and remembrance ("Your eyes held a message tender,/ Saying 'I surrender all my love to you',/ Midnight brought us sweet romance,/ I know, all my whole life through,/ I'll be remembering you"). For Jack, shining entails recollection more than extrasensory perception, a nostalgic dream of immortality and pleasure rather than intimations of hidden evil. His brass and vulgar regressions (the ugly American), however, clash with the overdressed, European formality of this huge gathering (300 people), just as his ornate recollections oppose the horrific truth of Danny's shinings. Appropriately, Delbert Grady now enters and crashes into Jack, spilling *Advocaat* (a *yellow* liqueur) all over his jacket. Inside the red bathroom, reverse camera positions emphasize a mirroring effect (that is, one figure turns his back to the camera and the other faces it), which now doubles Jack with an even more "civilized" but sinister version of Lloyd the bartender. Again, the subject of "recollection" comes up as Jack mistakenly confuses this Grady with Charles Grady ("you *were* the caretaker") and accuses him of murdering his family. (An old song called "Home" is faintly heard throughout this scene.) At first Grady pleads ignorance—"That's odd, I have no recollection of that at all"— but then he *remembers* and confronts Jack with a new truth: "I beg to differ with you, sir, but *you* are the caretaker, you have *always* been the caretaker." In the film's psychological allegory, this implies that the Jack Torrance/Charles Grady figures of present time "care for" the Overlook by resurrecting its past through a recollection of that other self which sleeps but never dies. And once that memory is found inside the center of the maze (self/hotel), how one got there is quickly *forgotten* or sublimated within a formal and enclosed artifice. In his first Gold Room shining, Jack *remembers* how to express his sexist prerogatives ("white man's burden") through the primitive banalities ("words of wisdom") of that conversation with Lloyd (who says, "Women! Can't live with them, can't live without them!"), only to *learn* from Grady in the red bathroom how to couch them in the chilling disguise of polite euphemism, in a kind of Overlook Doomsday jargon. Grady describes how, at first, his two daughters did not like the hotel (and one even tried to burn it down), but that he "corrected" them ("and when my wife tried to prevent me from doing my duty, I *corrected* her"). Later, from inside the dry-food storage room where Wendy locks him after hitting him with the baseball bat, Jack no longer talks about "bashing her brains out" but instead promises to "deal with the situation" once he is released, in what "Mr. Grady," from the other side of the door, describes as "the harshest possible way." And Grady knows how to push all the right buttons, especially when he prods Jack's masculine insecurities by commenting on Wendy's unexpected "resourcefulness" and wondering aloud if his American friend has the "belly" for this kind of work.

By part three, Jack's "interviews" with his recollected friends and his tour of the Overlook's psychic history have been completed. His unconscious mind has awakened from a long sleep and now, like the Minotaur, seeks to purify its maze/home of those alien forces that threaten its rule. In many respects, part three doubles back on part one like a grotesque reflection in a funhouse mirror. Hallorann, for instance, moves through an outside world that looks as if it were shrouded in Jack's madness. He calls Durkin's Garage (Larry Durkin is played by Tony Burton) in Sidewinder, where it's almost completely dark even at mid-morning because of a heavy snowstorm. He passes a traffic accident in which a *red* Volkswagen is crushed under the weight of a flatbed truck (in the novel, Jack drives a *red* VW). He moves in a snow-cat ("4 pm") through a dark and eerie corridor of trees that resembles an enlarged version of the Overlook's hedge maze. Inside the hotel, Wendy and Danny sit at breakfast, and Danny watches the Roadrunner show on TV, just as they did in the Boulder apartment of part one. But now Wendy talks to "Tony" exclusively ("Danny isn't here, Mrs. Torrance") as her son's world becomes engulfed by Jack's red madness. Wendy then picks up a baseball bat (toy/weapon) and walks downstairs to the Colorado Lounge, now the Monster's inner sanctum, where she gazes on a manuscript that reveals the nature of Jack's "work" inside the center of the maze. In yet another startling image, Wendy's terrified face resembles a pale moon from *2001* rising from behind the horizontal lines of Jack's madness (the typewriter and carriage paper form a double line across the bottom of the frame) and moving into a space enclosed from above by two more lines (the third-floor balcony). As she frantically leafs through the manuscript with its seemingly infinite mirror repetitions of "All work and no play make Jack a dull boy," Kubrick shows us a visual sequence, or history, that objectifies the progress of Jack's insanity (form and spelling become ever more erratic) and clarifies the film's particular use of the maze

concept. Not only does the visual sequence resemble a horizontal labyrinth, and therefore suggest fate and psychological entrapment, but it
also associates Jack's madness with an image of reduction and repetition. On one page, for instance, his mad litany is typed in the shape of
an upside-down pyramid that squeezes his character and his world
into a single word ("boy")—as if it were *The Shining's* Rosebud, except in his film Kubrick portrays a character who obsessively denies
complexity (both inner and outer) by searching for the center of existence in only *one memory room* (i.e, his unconscious). By part three,
Jack no longer explores other ideas—good or bad ones—but moves in
straight lines (the gold corridor) or repeated patterns in the center of
his horizontal maze. Wendy, on the other hand, has learned how to
back up and negotiate the maze without looking (as she retreats from
Jack and swings the bat), which reverses her forward turns and movements into the kitchen in part one (where a reverse dolly shot and
Hallorann escort her through the maze). Jack has been seduced by the
center's illusion of order and timelessness, while its madness and deadly
stasis are revealed to us through such typographical disorders as "work"
altered to "worm," "boy" to "bog," and "a dull" to "adult."

Only after Jack leaves the hotel to chase Danny into the snow-
covered hedge maze does Wendy shine for the first time and the Overlook take on the traditional characteristics of a haunted house. In perhaps the film's least convincing sequence, Wendy and the audience see
not only the truth of Danny's earlier shinings but the hideous reality of
Jack's recollections, ones no longer distorted by nostalgic subterfuge
(he has left the *inside* maze for an *outside* one). Danny's world as
a child and Wendy's harmless interest in ghost stories are trans-
mogrified into a surreal fairy tale about fellatio between a figure
in a teddy bear/boar suit (with a piggish snout and fangs) and
a gentleman in white tie and tails, skeletons enjoying cocktails and
making calls from telephone booths, a man with his head cleaved open
("Great party, isn't it?"), and cascades of blood pouring from an elevator as if from the ruptured artery of a monster. Not only does Wendy's
journey through and out of the Overlook's inner maze parallel Danny's
movements into and out of the hedge maze, it provides the film with
a series of visual and emotional "effects" that at first seem to satisfy
certain expectations but that probably do not resolve an audience's
perplexity over the ambiguities of Jack's shinings in Room 237 and the
Gold Room or the meaning of that 1921 photograph seen in the last

shot of the film. The ending is reminiscent of the ending to *2001*: Kubrick deliberately (some say perversely) gives and takes away at the same time (the Star-Gate ride was not an unexpected event, but what does the eighteenth-century room mean?). But, aesthetically, the maze concept requires that an audience be tested and challenged, even to the point of confusion if it fails to shine and *remember* not only how it got into the film (i.e., the guided tours of narrative exposition) but how it got lost. In retracing those steps, the viewer might discover that it wasn't Kubrick's *The Shining* that betrayed him but all those false expectations that tyrannize audiences into believing that filmic understandings should follow straight paths into a center of meaning.

So what does *The Shining*'s ending "mean"? On its most essential psychological level, it means that Jack Torrance freezes and dies inside the hedge maze because he forgot how to deal with the basic paradoxes of his own nature. Rather than exploring and discovering, making choices and risking both failure and success, he prefers to sit inertly in the center of an enclosed world and shine from above in god-like contemplation of the beauty of his creation. Like Barry Lyndon moving through a formal eighteenth-century maze, Jack forgets to look closely at either his own past or that of the Overlook, at the disorders and complexities that exist *inside* the structures of personality and civilization; instead he transforms each into a grotesque vision of duration. He attempts to destroy his family/home in present time because it requires a "contract" that not only involves responsibilities to others and even to another sex (the human world *outside* the masculine self), but a form of moral/emotional "work" where there are no certainties and very few givens. Jack's "love" for the hotel—rather than for Wendy and Danny—is another Kubrickian version of that mad craving for immortality that animates Strangelove's excitement over the perfection of the Doomsday Machine and HAL's desire to protect an illusion of machine infallibility from the intrusions of humanity. Jack explores and even learns how to control the memory world resurrected from inside the Overlook's maze, while he fails to perceive that, psychologically, it is a denial of *outside* worlds that offer not only the threat of uncertainty but the possibility of hope. Like Johnny Clay's movements into a world outside the temporal and spatial gameboard of his robbery plan, Jack's final journey into the outside maze throws him into a setting that is unresponsive to his obsession for control or recollection. While Bowman wandered through his memory room, only to escape as an enhanced being into the expanses of space, Jack tragically moves from one enclosed maze into another. In the end, he becomes a lonely, anguished figure who cries out in an almost inaudible pain from the loss of both his actual and imagined homes. As he did so often within the hotel's maze, he sits down and faces screen-right, only now he gazes into a bleak and frozen landscape, into a vision of nothingness that waits in the center of the labyrinth. Like so many others in Kubrick's films, Jack Torrance forgets that in a contingent universe an obsession with timelessness becomes tantamount to a love affair with death.

In the epilogue, Kubrick takes us back inside the Overlook Hotel for a final visual tour that paradoxically asserts the continuity of film time *and* confuses its traditional explanatory function. Reminiscent of a Wellesian journey into Xanadu's fire and the meaning of Rosebud, his camera reaffirms its omniscience and its freedom by traveling through space with an assurance and purpose first glimpsed in the credits. But in this case, it asks the viewers in the theater to shine and recollect, to remember not just one piece in the maze-puzzle (i.e., a Rosebud) but others as well. The camera moves across the reception area of the hotel—from the place where Jack Torrance first was seen and Hallorann eventually murdered—to a picture that hangs on the wall of the gold corridor in the center of another maze. It reveals a smiling likeness of the grinning monster in the hedge maze, looking up in greeting amid a society of civilized revelers from the past, trapped in the middle of a pictorial manuscript (21 pictures) arranged in three horizontal lines.° This shot not only completes the film's story of Jack Torrance but it reverses an earlier psychological evolution. In the mazes of parts one and two, Kubrick doubled Jack the writer/teacher with Jack the Monster, normality with its shadow, present time with a

---

° Here are a few observations (partly facetious) about the role numbers play in *The Shining*'s maze/puzzle: Danny wears a jersey numbered 42, and he briefly watches with Wendy the Robert Mulligan film, *Summer of '42*. Forty-two is 21 doubled (1921, 21 pictures on the gold corridor wall). The number 12 is a mirror image for 21, the radio call number for the Overlook is KDK 12, and the two screen titles for part three ("8 am" and "4 pm") add up to 12, which means that the film both duplicates and reverses the numbering of *2001* if you omit the zeroes. In *2001*, we learn that HAL's birthday (the day he became operational in Urbana, Illinois) is 12 January 1992, which not only reverses the numerical title of the film (12) but, if added together, the year's numbers (1+9+9+2) equal 21. Kubrick changed Room 217 in the novel to 237 in the film (one published report explains it as a "legal" necessity). The numbers 237 added together equal 12. Numerically speaking, *The Shining* is a *2001* in reverse gear. Double, double, toil and trouble.

hideous memory lost but not forgotten. Now, past time reflects the image of normality (the 1921 photograph) and present time shows the visage of madness (the frozen, grotesque mask of death in the hedge maze). And as the nostalgic music from the Gold Room party plays again, *The Shining* recalls the ending of another film, Kubrick's own *Barry Lyndon*, as it tries to stimulate *our* memory—not of a collective unconscious, but of a collective humanity (in the picture) tragically lost and frozen in the maze of *our* scrapbooks and *our* history. More than anything else, perhaps, it is Kubrick's dream of civilized life—a remembrance of things forgotten.

FILMOGRAPHY

1951   *Day of the Fight*
Director/Photography/Editor/Sound   Stanley Kubrick
Commentary   Douglas Edwards
Documentary short on Walter Cartier, middleweight prize fighter
Running Time: 16 minutes
Distributor: RKO Radio

1951   *Flying Padre*
Director/Photography/Editor/Sound   Stanley Kubrick
Documentary short on the Reverend Fred Stadtmueller, Roman Catholic
   missionary of a New Mexico parish that covers 400 square miles
Running Time: 9 minutes
Distributor: RKO Radio

1953   *The Seafarers*
Director/Photography/Editor   Stanley Kubrick
Script   Will Chasan
Producer   Lester Cooper
Narrator   Don Hollenbeck
Documentary short in color about the Seafarers International Union
Running Time: 30 minutes

1953   *Fear and Desire*
Production Company   Stanley Kubrick Productions
Producer   Stanley Kubrick
Associate Producer   Martin Perveler
Director/Photography/Editor   Stanley Kubrick
Script   Howard O. Sackler
Dialogue Director   Toba Kubrick
Music   Gerald Fried
Cast: Frank Silvera (Mac), Kenneth Harp (Corby), Virginia Leith (The
Girl), Paul Mazursky (Sidney), Steve Coit (Fletcher), David Allen (Nar-
rator)
Running Time: 68 minutes
Distributor: Joseph Burstyn

1955   *Killer's Kiss*
Production Company   Minotaur
Producers   Stanley Kubrick, Morris Bousel
Director/Photography/Editor   Stanley Kubrick
Script   Stanley Kubrick, Howard O. Sackler
Music   Gerald Fried
Choreography   David Vaughan
Cast: Frank Silvera (Vincent Rapallo), Jamie Smith (Davy Gordon), Irene

Kane (Gloria Price), Jerry Jarret (Albert), Ruth Sobotka (Iris), Mike Dana, Felice Orlandi, Ralph Roberts, Phil Stevenson (Hoodlums), Julius Adelman (Mannequin Factory Owner), David Vaughan, Alec Rubin (Conventioneers)
Running Time: 64 Minutes
Distributor: United Artists, United Artists/16

1956 *The Killing*

Production Company Harris-Kubrick Productions
Producer James B. Harris
Director Stanley Kubrick
Screenplay Stanley Kubrick, based on the novel *Clean Break*, by Lionel White
Additional Dialogue Jim Thompson
Photography Lucien Ballard
Editor Betty Steinberg
Art Director Ruth Sobotka Kubrick
Music Gerald Fried
Sound Earl Snyder
Cast: Sterling Hayden (Johnny Clay), Jay C. Flippen (Marvin Unger), Marie Windsor (Sherry Peatty), Elisha Cook (George Peatty), Coleen Gray (Fay), Vince Edwards (Val Cannon), Ted de Corsia (Randy Kennan), Joe Sawyer (Mike O'Reilly), Tim Carey (Nikki), Kola Kwariani (Maurice), James Edwards (Parking Lot Attendant), Jay Adler (Leo), Joseph Turkel (Tiny)
Running Time: 83 Minutes
Distributor: United Artists, United Artists/16

1957 *Paths of Glory*

Production Company Harris-Kubrick Productions
Producer James B. Harris
Director Stanley Kubrick
Screenplay Stanley Kubrick, Calder Willingham, Jim Thompson, based on the novel by Humphrey Cobb
Photography George Krause
Editor Eva Kroll
Art Director Ludwig Reiber
Music Gerald Fried
Sound Martin Muller
Cast: Kirk Douglas (Colonel Dax), Ralph Meeker (Corporal Paris), Adolphe Menjou (General Broulard), George Macready (General Mireau), Wayne Morris (Lieutenant Roget), Richard Anderson (Major Saint-Auban), Joseph Turkel (Private Arnaud), Timothy Carey (Private Ferol), Peter Capell (Colonel Judge), Susanne Christian (German Girl), Bert Freed (Sergeant Boulanger), Emile Meyer (Priest), John Stein (Captain Rousseau), Ken Dibbs (Private Lejeune), Jerry Hausner (Tavern Owner), Harold Benedict (Captain Nichols)
Running Time: 86 Minutes
Distributor: United Artists (presented by Bryna Productions), United Artists/16

1960 *Spartacus*

Production Company   Bryna
Executive Producer   Kirk Douglas
Producer   Edward Lewis
Director   Stanley Kubrick
Screenplay   Dalton Trumbo, based on the book by Howard Fast
Photography   Russell Metty
Additional Photography   Clifford Stine
Screen Process   Super Technirama-70
Color   Technicolor
Editors   Robert Lawrence, Robert Schultz, Fred Chulack
Production Designer   Alexander Golitzen
Art Director   Eric Orbom
Set Decoration   Russell A. Gausman, Julia Heron
Titles   Saul Bass
Technical Adviser   Vittorio Nino Novarese
Costumes   Peruzzi, Valles, Bill Thomas
Music   Alex North
Music Director   Joseph Gershenson
Sound   Waldo O. Watson, Joe Lapis, Murray Spivack, Ronald Pierce
Assistant Director   Marshall Green
Cast: Kirk Douglas (Spartacus), Laurence Olivier (Marcus Crassus), Jean Simmons (Varinia), Charles Laughton (Gracchus), Peter Ustinov (Batiatus), John Gavin (Julius Caesar), Tony Curtis (Antoninus), Nina Foch (Helena), Herbert Lom (Tigranes), John Ireland (Crixus), John Dall (Glabrus), Charles McGraw (Marcellus), Joanna Barnes (Claudia), Harold J. Stone (David), Woody Strode (Draba), Peter Brocco (Ramon), Paul Lambert (Gannicus), Robert J. Wilke (Captain of Guard), Nicholas Dennis (Dionysius), John Hoyt (Roman Officer), Fred Worlock (Laelius), Dayton Lummis (Symmachus)
Original Running Time: 196 Minutes
Current Running Time: 184 Minutes
Distributor: Universal Pictures, Universal/16

1962 *Lolita*

Production Company   Seven Arts/Anya/Transworld
Producer   James B. Harris
Director   Stanley Kubrick
Screenplay   Vladimir Nabokov, based on his novel
Photography   Oswald Morris
Editor   Anthony Harvey
Art Director   William Andrews
Set Design   Andrew Low
Music   Nelson Riddle
Lolita's Theme   Bob Harris
Sound   H. L. Bird, Len Shilton
Assistant Directors   Roy Millichip, John Danischewsky
Cast: James Mason (Humbert Humbert), Sue Lyon (Lolita Haze), Shelley Winters (Charlotte Haze), Peter Sellers (Clare Quilty), Diana Decker (Jean Farlow), Jerry Stovin (John Farlow), Suzanne Gibbs (Mona Far-

low), Gary Cockrell (Dick Schiller), Marianne Stone (Vivian Darkbloom),
Cec Linder (Physician), Lois Maxwell (Nurse Mary Lord), William Greene
(Mr. Swine), C. Denier Warren (Mr. Potts), Isobel Lucas (Louise), Max-
ine Holden (Hospital Receptionist), James Dyrenforth (Mr. Beale), Ro-
berta Shore (Lorna), Eric Lane (Roy), Shirley Douglas (Mrs. Starch),
Roland Brand (Bill), Colin Maitland (Charlie Holmes), Irvin Allen (Hos-
pital Attendant), Marion Mathie (Miss Lebone), Craig Sams (Rex), John
Harrison (Tom)
Running Time: 153 Minutes
Distributor: Metro-Goldwyn-Mayer, Films Incorporated/16

1964   Dr. Strangelove, or How I Learned to Stop Worrying and Love the Bomb

Production Company   Hawk Films
Producer/Director   Stanley Kubrick
Associate Producer   Victor Lyndon
Screenplay   Stanley Kubrick, Terry Southern, Peter George, based on the
   novel *Red Alert*, by Peter George
Photography   Gilbert Taylor
Editor   Anthony Harvey
Production Design   Ken Adam
Art Direction   Peter Murton
Special Effects   Wally Veevers
Music   Laurie Johnson
Aviation Adviser   Captain John Crewdson
Sound   John Cox
Cast: Peter Sellers (Group Captain Lionel Mandrake, President Muffley,
Dr. Strangelove), George C. Scott (Buck Turgidson), Sterling Hayden
(General Jack D. Ripper), Keenan Wynn (Colonel Bat Guano), Slim Pick-
ens (Major T. J. "King" Kong), Peter Bull (Ambassador de Sadesky),
Tracy Reed (Miss Scott), James Earl Jones (Lieutenant H. R. Dietrich,
D.S.O.), Glenn Beck (Lieutenant W. D. Kivel, Navigator), Shane Rimmer
(Captain G. A. "Ace" Owens, Co-pilot), Paul Tamarin (Lieutenant B.
Goldberg, Radio Operator), Gordon Tanner (General Faceman), Robert
O'Neil (Admiral Randolph), Roy Stephens (Frank), Laurence Herder,
John McCarthy, Hal Galili (Members of Burpleson Base Defense Corps)
Running Time: 94 Minutes
Distributor: Columbia Pictures, Swank/16

1968   2001: A Space Odyssey

Production Company   Metro-Goldwyn-Mayer
Producer   Stanley Kubrick
Director   Stanley Kubrick
Screenplay   Stanley Kubrick, Arthur C. Clarke, based on Clarke's short
   story "The Sentinel"
Photography   Geoffrey Unsworth
Screen Process   Super Panavision, presented in Cinerama
Color   Metrocolor
Additional Photography   John Alcott

Special Photographic Effects
  Designer and Director   Stanley Kubrick
Editor   Ray Lovejoy
Production Design   Tony Masters, Harry Lange, Ernie Archer
Art Direction   John Hoesli
Special Photographic Effects
Supervisors   Wally Veevers, Douglas Trumbull, Con Pederson, Tom Howard
Music   Richard Strauss, Johann Strauss, Aram Khachaturian, György Ligeti
Costumes   Hardy Amies
Sound   Winston Ryder
Cast: Keir Dullea (David Bowman), Gary Lockwood (Frank Poole), William Sylvester (Dr. Heywood Floyd), Daniel Richter (Moon-Watcher), Douglas Rain (HAL's Voice), Leonard Rossiter (Smyslov), Margaret Tyzack (Elena), Robert Beatty (Halvorsen), Sean Sullivan (Michaels), Frank Miller (Mission Control), Penny Edwina Carroll, Mike Lovell, Peter Delman, Dany Grover, Brian Hawley
Running Time: 141 Minutes
Distributor: Metro-Goldwyn-Mayer, Films Incorporated/16

1971   *A Clockwork Orange*
Production Company   Warner Brothers/Hawk Films
Producer/Director   Stanley Kubrick
Executive Producers   Max L. Raab, Si Litvinoff
Associate Producer   Bernard Williams
Screenplay   Stanley Kubrick, based on the novel by Anthony Burgess
Photography   John Alcott
Color   Warnercolor
Editor   Bill Butler
Production Design   John Barry
Art Direction   Russell Hagg, Peter Shields
Music   Ludwig van Beethoven, Edward Elgar, Gioacchino Rossini, Terry Tucker, Henry Purcell, James Yorkston, Arthur Freed, Nacio Herb Brown, Rimsky-Korsakov, Erika Eigen
Original Electronic Music   Walter Carlos
Songs   Gene Kelly, Erika Eigen
Costumes   Milena Canonero
Special Paintings and Sculpture   Herman Makkink, Corneilius Makkink, Liz Moore, Christiane Kubrick
Production Assistant   Andros Epaminondas
Sound   Brian Blamey
Assistant to Producer   Jan Harlan
Cast: Malcolm McDowell (Alex), Patrick Magee (Mr. Alexander), Michael Bates (Chief Guard), Warren Clarke (Dim), John Clive (Stage Actor), Adrienne Corri (Mrs. Alexander), Carl Duering (Dr. Brodsky), Paul Farrell (Tramp), Clive Francis (Joe, the Lodger), Michael Gover (Prison Governor), Miriam Karlin (Miss Weber, the Cat Lady), James Marcus (Georgie), Aubrey Morris (Mr. Deltoid), Godfrey Quigley (Prison Chaplain), Sheila Raynor (Mum), Madge Ryan (Dr. Branom), John Savident

(Conspirator), Anthony Sharp (Minister of the Interior), Philip Stone (Dad), Pauline Taylor (Dr. Taylor/Psychiatrist), Margaret Tyzack (Conspirator), Steven Berkoff (Constable), Lindsay Campbell (Inspector), Michael Tarn (Pete), David Prowse (Julian), Jan Adair, Vivienne Chandler, Prudence Drage (Handmaidens), John J. Carney (CID Man), Richard Connaught (Billyboy), Carol Drinkwater (Nurse Feeley), Cheryl Grunwald (Rape Girl), Gillian Hills (Sonietta), Barbara Scott (Marty), Virginia Wetherell (Stage Actress), Katya Wyeth (Girl), Barrie Cookson, Gaye Brown, Peter Burton, Lee Fox, Craig Hunter, Shirley Jaffe, Neil Wilson
Running Time: 137 Minutes
Distributor: Warner Brothers, Swank/16

1975   Barry Lyndon
Production Company   Warner Brothers/Hawk Films
Producer/Director   Stanley Kubrick
Associate Producer   Jan Harlan
Screenplay   Stanley Kubrick, based on the novel by William Makepeace Thackeray
Photography   John Alcott
Editor   Tony Lawson
Production Design   Ken Adam
Art Direction   Roy Walker
Music   J. S. Bach, Frederick the Great, G. F. Handel, W. A. Mozart, Giovanni Paisiello, Franz Schubert, Antonio Vivaldi
Music Adaptation   Leonard Rosenman
Costumes   Ulla-Britt Søderlund, Milena Cannonero
Screen Process   Panavision
Color   Metrocolor
Sound   Rodney Holland
Assistant Director   Brian Cook
Cast: Ryan O'Neal (Barry Lyndon), Marisa Berenson (Lady Lyndon), Patrick Magee (The Chevalier), Hardy Kruger (Captain Potzdorf), Marie Kean (Mrs. Barry), Gay Hamilton (Nora Brady), Melvin Murray (Reverend Runt), Godfrey Quigley (Captain Grogan), Leonard Rossiter (Captain Quin), Leon Vitali (Lord Bullingdon), Diana Koerner (Lischen), Frank Middlemass (Sir Charles Lyndon), André Morell (Lord Wendover), Arthur O'Sullivan (Captain Freny), Philip Stone (Graham), Steven Berkoff (Lord Ludd), Anthony Sharp (Lord Hallum), Michael Hordern (the narrator)
Running Time: 185 Minutes
Distributor: Warner Brothers, Swank/16

1980   The Shining
Production Company   Warner Brothers/Hawk Films
Produced in association with   The Producer Circle Company
   Robert Fryer, Martin Richards, Mary Lea Johnson
Producer/Director   Stanley Kubrick
Executive Producer   Jan Harlan
Screenplay   Stanley Kubrick, Diane Johnson, based on the novel by Stephen King

Photography   John Alcott
Editor   Ray Lovejoy
Production Design   Roy Walker
Music   Béla Bartók, Wendy Carlos, Rachel Elkin, György Ligeti, Krzysztof
   Penderecki
Music for strings, percussion and celesta/Conductor   Herbert Van Karajan,
   Recorded by Deutsche Grammophon
Costumes   Milena Canonero
2nd Unit Photography   Douglas Milsome, Gregg Macgillivray
Steadicam Operator   Garrett Brown
Art Direction   Les Tomkins
Assistant Director   Brian Cook
Assistant to Producer   Andros Epaminondas
Personal Assistant to Director   Leon Vitali
Cast: Jack Nicholson (Jack Torrance), Shelley Duvall (Wendy Torrance),
Danny Lloyd (Danny Torrance), Scatman Crothers (Hallorann), Barry
Nelson (Stuart Ullman), Philip Stone (Delbert Grady), Joe Turkel (Lloyd),
Anne Jackson (Doctor), Tony Burton (Larry Durkin), Lia Beldam (Young
Woman in Bath), Billie Gibson (Old Woman in Bath), Barry Dennen (Wat-
son), David Baxt (Forest Ranger 1), Manning Redwood (Forest Ranger
2), Lisa Burns, Louise Burns (The Grady Girls), Alison Coleridge (Ull-
man's Secretary), Jana Sheldon (Stewardess), Kate Phelps (Overlook Re-
ceptionist), Norman Gay (Injured Guest with Head-Wound)
Running Time: 145 Minutes*
Distributor: Warner Brothers

*Before releasing *The Shining*, Kubrick previewed it for a London audience,
after which he deleted an ending showing Wendy recuperating and talking with
Ullman in a hospital.

SELECTED BIBLIOGRAPHY

Additional sources can be found in the Notes.

1. Comprehensive Studies, Essays, Interviews

Andrew, Dudley. *André Bazin*. New York: Oxford University Press, 1978.

Andrew, J. Dudley. *The Major Film Theories: An Introduction*. New York: Oxford University Press, 1976.

Bernstein, Jeremy. "Profiles: How About a Little Game?" *The New Yorker*, 12 November 1966, pp. 70–110.

Braudy, Leo. *The World in a Frame*. Garden City, N.Y.: Anchor Books, 1977.

Cavell, Stanley. *The World Viewed: Reflections on the Ontology of Film*. Enlarged edition. Cambridge: Harvard University Press, 1979.

Ciment, Michel. "Entretien avec Stanley Kubrick," *Positif* (June 1972): 22–33.

Coyle, Wallace. *Stanley Kubrick: A Guide to References and Resources*. Boston: G. K. Hall, 1980.

Devries, Daniel. *The Films of Stanley Kubrick*. Grand Rapids: Eerdmans, 1973.

Feldmann, Hans. "Kubrick and His Discontents," *Film Quarterly* (Fall 1976): 12–19.

Gelmis, Joseph. *The Film Director as Superstar*. Garden City, N.Y.: Doubleday, 1970, pp. 293–315.

Giannetti, Louis. *Understanding Movies*. 2d ed. Englewood Cliffs, N.J.: Prentice-Hall, 1976.

Gorchakov, Nikolai M. *Stanislavsky Directs*. Trans. Miriam Goldina. New York: Funk and Wagnalls, 1954.

Henderson, Brian. *A Critique of Film Theory*. New York: E. P. Dutton, 1980.

Houston, Penelope. "Kubrick Country," *The Saturday Review*, 25 December 1971, pp. 42–44.

Kagan, Norman. *The Cinema of Stanley Kubrick*. New York: Holt, Rinehart, and Winston, 1972.

Kawin, Bruce F. *Mindscreen*. Princeton: Princeton University Press, 1978.

Kohler, Charles. "Stanley Kubrick Raps," *Eye* (August 1968): 84–86.

Kolker, Robert Phillip. *A Cinema of Loneliness*. New York: Oxford University Press, 1980, pp. 69–138.

Kubrick, Stanley. "Director's Notes: Stanley Kubrick Movie-Maker," *The Observer* (London), 4 December 1960.

Kubrick, Stanley. "Words and Movies," *Sight and Sound* (Winter 1960/61): 14.

Kubrick, Stanley. "Kubrick Dissects the Movies," *Newsweek*, 2 December 1957, pp. 96–97.

Mast, Gerald. *A Short History of the Movies*. 2d edition. Indianapolis: Bobbs-Merrill, 1976.

Monaco, James. *The Films of Stanley Kubrick*. New York: The New School Department of Film, 1974.

Nelson, Thomas Allen. "Through a Shifting Lens: Realist Film Aesthetics," *Film Criticism* (Fall 1977): 15–23.

Nelson, Thomas Allen. "Film Styles and Film Meanings," *Film Criticism* (Spring 1979): 2–17.

Norden, Eric. "Interview with Stanley Kubrick," *Playboy Magazine*, September 1968, p. 85.

Phillips, Gene D. "Interview with Stanley Kubrick," *Film Comment* (Winter 1971/72): 30–35.

Phillips, Gene D. *Stanley Kubrick: A Film Odyssey*. New York: Popular Library, 1975.

Pudovkin, V. I. *Film Technique*. London: George Newness, 1933.

Rapf, Maurice. "A Talk with Stanley Kubrick," *Action*, January/February 1969, pp. 15–18.

Rhode, Eric. *A History of the Cinema from the Origins to 1970*. London: Allen Lane, 1976, pp. 610–14.

Stang, Jonathan. "Film Fan to Film-Maker," *New York Times Magazine*, 12 October 1958.

Stanislavsky, Konstantin. *Stanislavsky, on the Art of the Stage*. New York: Hill and Wang, 1961.

Strick, Philip, and Penelope Houston. "Interview with Stanley Kubrick," *Sight and Sound* (Spring 1972): 62–66.

Taylor, John Russell. *Directors and Directions: Cinema for the Seventies*. New York: Hill and Wang, 1975, pp. 101–135.

Walker, Alexander. *Stanley Kubrick Directs*. Expanded edition. New York: Harcourt Brace Jovanovich, 1972.

Walter, Renaud. "Entretien avec Stanley Kubrick," *Positif* (Winter 1968/69): 19–39.

2. The Early Films

Alpert, Hollis. "The Day of the Gladiators," *The Saturday Review*, 12 October 1960.

Cobb, Humphrey. *Paths of Glory*. New York: The Viking Press, 1935.

Crowther, Bosley. "Shameful Incident of War," *The New York Times*, 27 December 1957.

Gurnseley, Otis L. "Review of *Fear and Desire*," *The New York Herald-Tribune*, 1 April 1953.

Lambert, Gavin. "Killer's Kiss," *Sight and Sound* (Spring 1956): 198.

Lambert, Gavin. "The Killing," *Sight and Sound* (Autumn 1956): 95–96.

Lambert, Gavin. "Paths of Glory," *Sight and Sound* (Winter 1957/58): 144–45.

"Review of *The Killing*," *Time*, 4 June 1956, p. 106.

"Review of *Fear and Desire*," *Time*, 3 April 1953.

White, Lionel. *Clean Break*. New York: E. P. Dutton, 1955.

3. Lolita

Appel, Alfred. *The Annotated Lolita*. New York: McGraw-Hill, 1970.

Appel, Alfred. *Nabokov's Dark Cinema*. New York: Oxford University Press, 1974.
French, Brandon. "The Celluloid *Lolita*: A Not-So-Crazy Quilt," in *The Modern American Novel and the Movies*, ed. Gerald Peary and Roger Shatzkin. New York: Frederick Ungar, 1978, pp. 224–35.
Nabokov, Vladimir. *Lolita: A Screenplay*. New York: McGraw-Hill, 1974.
Nabokov, Vladimir. *Strong Opinions*. New York: McGraw-Hill, 1973.
Toffler, Alvin. "Interview with Vladimir Nabokov," *Playboy Magazine*, January 1964, pp. 35–45.

4. Dr. Strangelove

Bryant, Peter. *Red Alert*. New York: Ace Books, 1958.
George, Peter. *Dr. Strangelove*. New York: Bantam, 1963.
Linden, George W. "*Dr. Strangelove*," in *Nuclear War Films*, ed. Jack G. Shaheen. Carbondale: Southern Illinois University Press, 1978, pp. 59–67.
Macklin, Anthony. "Sex and *Dr. Strangelove*," *Film Comment* (Summer 1965): 55–57.
Maland, Charles. "*Dr. Strangelove*: Nightmare Comedy and the Ideology of Liberal Consensus," *American Quarterly* (Winter 1979): 697–717.
Milne, Tom. "How I Learned to Stop Worrying and Love Stanley Kubrick." *Sight and Sound* (Spring 1964): 68–72.

5. 2001: A Space Odyssey

Agel, Jerome, ed. *The Making of 2001*. New York: New American Library, 1970.
Clarke, Arthur C. *The Lost Worlds of 2001*. New York: New American Library, 1972.
Clarke, Arthur C. *2001: A Space Odyssey*. New York: New American Library, 1968.
Daniels, Don. "A Skeleton Key to *2001*," *Sight and Sound* (Winter 1970/71): 28–33.
Daniels, Don. "*2001*: A New Myth," *Film Heritage* (Summer 1968).
Dumont, J. P. & J. Monod. "Beyond the Infinite: A Structural Analysis of '2001: A Space Odyssey'," *Quarterly Review of Film Studies* (Summer 1978): 297–316.
Geduld, Carolyn. *Filmguide to 2001: A Space Odyssey*. Bloomington: Indiana University Press, 1973.
Hoch, David G. "Mythic Patterns in *2001: A Space Odyssey*," *Journal of Popular Culture* (Summer 1970): 961–965.
Lightman, Herb. "Kubrick's *2001*," *American Cinematographer*, June 1968.
Macklin, F. A. "The Comic Sense of *2001*," *Film Comment* (Winter 1969): 10–15.
McKee, M. "*2001*: Out of the Silent Planet," *Sight and Sound* (Autumn 1969): 204–7.
Michelson, Annette. "Bodies in Space: Film as 'Carnal Knowledge'," *Artforum*, February 1969, pp. 54–63.
Robinson, W. R. & Mary McDermott. "*2001* and the Literary Sensibility,"

The Georgia Review (Spring 1972): 21–37.
Trumbull, Douglas. "Creating Special Effects for *2001*," *American Cinematographer*, June 1968.

6. A Clockwork Orange

Alpert, Hollis. "Milk-Plus and Ultra-Violence," *The Saturday Review*, 25 December 1971, p. 40.
Bailey, Andrew. "A Clockwork Utopia," *Rolling Stone*, 20 January 1972, pp. 20–22.
Boyers, P. "Kubrick's *A Clockwork Orange*: Some Observations," *Film Heritage* (Summer 1972): 1–6.
Burgess, Anthony. "Author Has His Say on 'Clockwork' Film," *Los Angeles Times, Calendar* section, 13 February 1972.
Burgess, Anthony. *A Clockwork Orange*. London: Heinemann, 1962.
Burgess, Anthony. *A Clockwork Orange*. New York: Norton, 1963 .
Burgess, Anthony. "Juice from a Clockwork Orange," *Rolling Stone*, 8 June 1972, pp. 52–53.
Burgess, Anthony. *1985*. Boston: Little, Brown and Co., 1978.
Gilbert, Basil. "Kubrick's Marmalade: The Art of Violence," *Meanjin Quarterly* (Winter 1974): 157–62.
Gumenik, A. "*A Clockwork Orange*: Novel Into Film," *Film Heritage* (Summer 1972): 7–18.
"Interview with Anthony Burgess," *Playboy Magazine*, September 1974, pp. 68–86.
Kubrick, Stanley. *A Clockwork Orange: A Screenplay*. New York: Ballantine Books, 1972.
McCracken, Samuel. "Novel Into Film; Novelist Into Critic: *A Clockwork Orange* . . . Again," *The Antioch Review* 32, no. 3 (1978): 427–436.

7. Barry Lyndon

Alcott, John. "Photographing Stanley Kubrick's *Barry Lyndon*," *American Cinematographer*, March 1976, p. 268.
Dempsey, Michael. "Barry Lyndon," *Film Quarterly* (Fall 1976): 49–54.
DiGiulio, Ed. "Two Special Lenses for *Barry Lyndon*," *American Cinematographer*, March 1976, pp. 276–77.
Houston, Penelope. "Barry Lyndon," *Sight and Sound* (Spring 1976), 77–80.
Kael, Pauline. "Kubrick's Gilded Age," *The New Yorker*, 29 December 1975, pp. 49–52.
Nelson, Thomas Allen. "*Barry Lyndon*: Kubrick's Cinema of Disparity," *Rocky Mountain Review* (Winter 1978/79): 39–51.
Sarris, Andrew. "What Makes Barry Run?," *Village Voice*, 29 December 1975, pp. 111–12.
Schickel, Richard. "Kubrick's Grandest Gamble," *Time*, 15 December 1975, pp. 72–78.
Spiegel, Alan. "Kubrick's *Barry Lyndon*," *Salmagundi* (Fall 1977): 194–208.
Thackeray, William Makepeace. *The Luck of Barry Lyndon*. Edited by

Martin L. Anisman. New York: New York University Press, 1970.

Westerbeck, Colin L. *"Barry Lyndon," Commonweal,* March & April 1976, p. 208.

8. The Shining

Alberton, Jim, and Peter S. Perakos. "The Shining," *Cinefantastique* (Fall 1978): 74.

Brown, Garrett. "The Steadicam and 'The Shining'," *American Cinematographer,* August 1980, p. 786.

Hofsess, Jim. "The Shining Example of Kubrick," *Los Angeles Times, Calendar* section, 1 June 1980, p. 1.

Huss, Roy, and T. J. Ross, eds. *Focus on the Horror Film.* Englewood Cliffs, N.J.: Prentice-Hall, 1972.

Jameson, Richard T. "Kubrick's Shining," *Film Comment,* July–August 1980): 28–32.

Kael, Pauline. "Devolution," *The New Yorker,* 1 June 1980, pp. 130–147.

Kennedy, Harlan. "Kubrick Goes Gothic," *American Film* (June 1980): 49–52.

King, Stephen. *The Shining.* New York: Doubleday, 1977.

Kroll, Jack. "Stanley Kubrick's Horror Show," *Newsweek,* 26 May 1980, pp. 96–99.

Leibowitz, Flo, and Lynn Jeffress. "The Shining," *Film Quarterly* (Spring 1981): 45–51.

Lightman, Herb. "Photographing Stanley Kubrick's *The Shining*: An Interview with John Alcott," *American Cinematographer,* August 1980, p. 760.

Mayersberg, Paul. "The Overlook Hotel," *Sight and Sound* (Winter 1980/81): 54–57.

Perakos, Peter S. "Interview with Stephen King," *Cinefantastique* (Winter 1978): 12–15.

Titterington, P. L. "Kubrick and *The Shining*," *Sight and Sound* (Spring 1981): 117–21.

Wood, Robin. "Return of the Repressed," *Film Comment* (July–August 1978): 25–32.

NOTES

1. Reputation and Rhetoric

1. Bruce F. Kawin, *Mindscreen* (Princeton: Princeton University Press, 1978). A pioneering work on a subject—point of view—that has received too little critical attention. For more, see my comments on *A Clockwork Orange* (chapter 6 and notes to ch. 6, especially note 13).

2. For a fuller discussion of this material, see the following:

Jeremy Bernstein, "Profiles: How About a Little Game?" *The New Yorker*, 12 November 1966, pp. 70–110. Still one of the best biographical profiles of Kubrick.

Alexander Walker, *Stanley Kubrick Directs*, expanded edition (New York: Harcourt Brace Jovanovich, 1972). Easily the best work to date on Kubrick. Some excellent visual illustration and analysis.

Gene D. Phillips, *Stanley Kubrick: A Film Odyssey* (New York: Popular Library, 1975). Adds some helpful factual and interview material not included in Walker. First to mention information about Kubrick's third documentary, *The Seafarer*. Very little critical analysis, mostly plot summaries.

Joseph Gelmis, "Interview wtih Stanley Kubrick," in *The Film Director as Superstar* (Garden City, N.Y.: Doubleday, 1970), pp. 293–315. A good interview, in which Kubrick puts to rest the notion that he is obsessed with a fear of his own death; he explains that he doesn't fly, because there are "compromised safety margins in commercial aviation," a comment that shows some prescience in light of the discoveries made after the 1979 disaster in Chicago about the production of the DC-10.

3. Gerald Mast, *A Short History of the Movies*, 2d ed. (Indianapolis: Bobbs-Merrill, 1976), pp. 492–95. Sees Kubrick's essential theme as "man's love affair with death."

Eric Rhode, *A History of the Cinema from the Origins to 1970* (London: Allen Lane, 1976), pp. 610–14. Feels Kubrick is "haunted" by an obsession with his own death.

4. "Director's Notes: Stanley Kubrick, Movie-Maker," *The Observer* (London), 4 December 1960.

5. Carolyn Geduld, *Filmguide to 2001: A Space Odyssey* (Bloomington: Indiana University Press, 1973), pp. 9–20. Contains a rather general overview of Kubrick's work, one that sees the *cinema noir* as central to Kubrick's vision; remains a helpful book on *2001*.

6. Hans Feldmann, "Kubrick and His Discontents," *Film Quarterly* (Fall 1976): 12–19. Views *2001*, *Clockwork*, and *Barry Lyndon* as Kubrick's trilogy on Western civilization. Well done.

7. Pauline Kael, "Kubrick's Gilded Cage," *The New Yorker*, 29 December 1975, pp. 49–52. A review of *Lyndon*, but mostly another harangue against Kubrick's "dehumanized" art.

8. Norman Kagan, *The Cinema of Stanley Kubrick* (New York: Holt, Rinehart, and Winston, 1972). Critically superficial, but contains some important material on Kubrick's early films. Provides summary for *Fear and Desire*, a film no longer available for viewing. On p. 45, Kagan does admit

to the "limitation" of his thematic listing (since many of the themes are present in bad films as well as in Kubrick's); however, he persists in it. Nevertheless, a valuable book for research on Kubrick.

See also the chapter on Kubrick ("Tectonics and the Mechanical Man") in Robert Phillip Kolker's *A Cinema of Loneliness* (New York: Oxford University Press, 1980), pp. 69–138. Unfortunately, this book was not available to me until after I had finished most of my work—that is why my study only rarely acknowledges it. It is primarily an ideological study ("no work of cinema, or any other imaginative form, is ideologically innocent") and an attempt to compare Kubrick's work with that of certain other American film makers (mostly Welles and Ford). Kolker's book seems to promise more than it delivers. His most penetrating comments are those on *Paths of Glory, Dr. Strangelove,* and *Barry Lyndon*; his evaluation of *2001* is rather disappointing (especially in light of his book and chapter titles), and his brief critique of *A Clockwork Orange* is a complete misreading of the film.

9. Stanley Kubrick, "Words and Movies," *Sight and Sound* (Winter 1960/ 61)): 14. Brief but valuable.

See also "Kubrick Dissects the Movies," *Newsweek*, 2 December 1957, pp. 96–97. Refers to Kubrick, following the release of *Paths of Glory*, as the leading "boy wonder" who has Hollywood "by the horns." It is interesting that after this Kubrick had trouble finding work in Hollywood until Kirk Douglas brought him in to replace Anthony Mann as director of *Spartacus* (1960). This brief interview reveals that Kubrick formulated much of his film-making theory very early.

10. Philip Strick and Penelope Houston, "Interview with Stanley Kubrick," *Sight and Sound* (Spring 1972): 62–66. Good interview, mostly about *A Clockwork Orange.*

11. V. I. Pudovkin, *Film Technique*, enlarged ed., trans. Ivor Montagu (London: George Newness, 1933). In interviews from the early 1960s onward, Kubrick has repeatedly mentioned his admiration for this book. On p. 7 of *Film Technique*, Pudovkin says that "the film is yet young, and the wealth of its methods is not yet extensive." As a result, he feels, a limitation must be imposed on the "scale of theme," and in fact, he faulted Griffith's *Intolerance* for its thematic overreaching, characterizing the film as "ponderous," with a theme too deep for the film's "superficiality of form." Kubrick too has often expressed a similar concern for the complementary demands of form and content, and like Griffith, he has struggled with an epic subject matter. If Pudovkin were alive today, I think he would recognize in Kubrick's *2001* and *Barry Lyndon*, for instance, signs of that development in film language which he felt was necessary and inevitable.

12. André Bazin, "The Evolution of the Language of Cinema," in *What is Cinema?*, vol. 1, trans. Hugh Gray (Berkeley and Los Angeles: University of California Press, 1967), pp. 23–40.

13. "Words and Movies," p. 14.

14. "Director's Notes," *The Observer* (London).

15. "Kubrick Dissects the Movies," p. 97.

16. Walker, *Stanley Kubrick Directs*, p. 45.

17. For more on these subjects see: Max Planck, *The New Science*, trans. James Murphy and W. H. Johnston (New York: Meridian Books, 1959); Martin Gardner, *The Ambidextrous Universe* (New York: Basic Books,

1959); Richard Poirier, *The Performing Self* (New York: Oxford University Press, 1971), pp. 86–111; Erving Goffman, *The Presentation of Self in Everyday Life* (New York: Doubleday, 1959); R. D. Laing, *The Politics of Experience* (New York: Pantheon Books, 1967); Maz'ud Zavarzudeh, *The Mythopoeic Reality* (Urbana: University of Illinois Press, 1976), pp. 3–67.

18. See the following studies:

Thomas Allen Nelson, "Through a Shifting Lens: Realist Film Aesthetics," *Film Criticism* (Fall 1977): 15–23. Comparison of "humanist" and "modernist" film theory, including a discussion of film technology since Bazin.

Thomas Allen Nelson, "Film Styles and Film Meanings," *Film Criticism* (Spring 1979): 2–17. Expands earlier essay and applies Mitry's ideas to the films of Antonioni and Kubrick.

Brian Henderson, "Two Types of Film Theory," *Film Quarterly* (Spring 1971): 33–42. This essay contains an interesting comparison of Bazinian ("relation to real") and Eisensteinian ("part-whole") theories; Henderson believes that developments in film since the late 1950s have gone far beyond the explanatory capacities of the classical film theories.

J. Dudley Andrew, *The Major Film Theories: An Introduction* (London: Oxford University Press, 1976).

19. Dudley Andrew, *André Bazin* (New York: Oxford University Press, 1978), p. 121.

20. Penelope Houston, "Kubrick Country," *Saturday Review*, 25 December 1971, pp. 42–44. An interview with Kubrick after the release of *A Clockwork Orange*.

21. Seymour Krim, *Shake It for the World, Smartass* (New York: Dial Press, 1970), p. 349.

22. Andrew, *The Major Film Theories*, pp. 185–211. I am indebted to Andrew's fine description and analysis of Jean Mitry's work, which, as far as I know, has not yet been translated into English.

23. Louis Giannetti, *Understanding Movies*, 2d ed. (Englewood Cliffs, N.J.: Prentice-Hall, 1976); Leo Braudy, *The World in a Frame* (Garden City, N.Y.: Anchor Books, 1977).

24. Isaac Asimov, *Today and Tomorrow and . . .* (Garden City, N.Y.: Doubleday, 1973) and *The Collapsing Universe* (New York: Walker, 1977). Both these books provide excellent summaries for the layman of recent discoveries and theories in the sciences, especially physics and astronomy.

25. Eric Norden, "Interview with Stanley Kubrick," *Playboy* (September 1968), p. 85. One of the most extensive interviews; mostly about *2001*.

2. In the Beginning

1. For production notes and history on Kubrick's first four features, see the accounts in Gene D. Phillips' *Stanley Kubrick: A Film Odyssey* and Norman Kagan's *The Cinema of Stanley Kubrick*. A critic who responded very early to Kubrick's promise as a film maker was *Sight and Sound's* Gavin Lambert. See his three separate reviews of *Killer's Kiss* (Spring 1956, p. 198), *The Killing* (Autumn 1956, pp. 95–96), and *Paths of Glory* (Winter 1957/58, pp. 144–45).

2. James Naremore's analyses of *Touch of Evil* and *Psycho* warrant reading; see *The Magic of Orson Welles* (New York: Oxford University Press, 1978) and *A Filmguide to Psycho* (Bloomington: Indiana University Press, 1973).

3. Jim Thompson, author of *The Getaway*, which Sam Peckinpah updated and made into a film, released in 1972, is given screenplay credit for *Paths of Glory*, along with Kubrick and novelist-screenwriter Calder Willingham.

4. In Cobb, the chateau is first mentioned on p. 135, but not described until pp. 203–4, just before the court-martial. Assolant's (Mireau's) headquarters is located in the *mairie* of a nearby town.

5. Cobb's pre-attack account begins at "zero minus thirty minutes" and takes up nine pages (121–29), while the description of the attack, which lasts thirty-five minutes, takes up less than two pages (130–31).

6. Cobb's novel provides very little description of the ambiance of the court-martial, which is presented in the form of a question-and-answer transcript (pp. 207–22).

7. None of these scenes between Dax and Broulard has a source in Cobb, nor does the last scene of the film. The novel ends with the execution and a description of Sergeant Boulanger shooting each of the already dead soldiers in the head.

3. Lolita

1. For an informative description of Hollywood in the 1950s, one that discusses the impact of television, the rise of independent production companies, and the blacklist years, see Arthur Knight, *The Liveliest Art*, rev. ed. (New York: Macmillan, 1978), pp. 241–54.

2. Kubrick discusses the *Spartacus* experience in the following sources: Gelmis, *The Film Director as Superstar* ("I was disappointed in the film. It had everything but a good story," p. 314); Renaud Walter, "Entretien avec Stanley Kubrick," *Positif* (Winter 1968/69): 19–39; and in Phillips, *Stanley Kubrick: A Film Odyssey* ("the only film over which I did not have absolute control. I have since involved myself in the administrative side of film production because it is in this area that many artistic battles are won and lost," pp. 65–66).

3. In describing his postponed *Napoleon* project, Kubrick comments on his interest in historical battles:

> I think that it's extremely important to communicate the essence of these battles to the viewer, because they all have an aesthetic brilliance that doesn't require a military mind to appreciate. There's an aesthetic involved; it's almost like a great piece of music, or the purity of a mathematical formula. It's this quality I want to bring across as well as the sordid reality of battle. . . . There's a weird disparity between the sheer visual and organizational beauty of the historical battles sufficiently far in the past, and their human consequences. [Gelmis, pp. 296–97]

4. Kubrick, to his credit, avoided Cobb's Christ symbolism in the execu-

tion scene in *Paths of Glory*. Cobb has Langlois say, "Those posts make it look like the Crucifixion, don't they? And if we keep in this order, it will be Ferol who will play the role of Christ. That's the proper touch of irony, all right."

5. Alvin Toffler, "Interview with Vladimir Nabokov," *Playboy*, January 1964, pp. 35–45.

6. Vladimir Nabokov, *Lolita: A Screenplay* (New York: McGraw-Hill, 1974). See also Vladimir Nabokov, *Strong Opinions* (New York: McGraw-Hill, 1973). A collection of his "occasional English prose" (interviews, essays, etc.), with some comments on Kubrick's film.

7. Alfred Appel, Jr., *Nabokov's Dark Cinema* (New York: Oxford University Press, 1974). See especially the section on the "Making of *Lolita*," pp. 228–45. Appel, I think, overrates Nabokov's screenplay and underrates Kubrick's film; he is disappointed that Kubrick did not imitate or adapt the style of the American *noir* road films. See also Brandon French, "The Celluloid *Lolita*: A Not-So-Crazy Quilt," in *The Modern American Novel and the Movies*, ed. Gerald Peary and Roger Shatzkin (New York: Frederick Ungar, 1978), pp. 224–35. French, like Appel, regrets the lack of a visual style the equal of Nabokov's prose style: "There are a number of directors whose obtrusive, highly visible styles might have provided such an equivalent: Orson Welles, Bernardo Bertolucci, Luchino Visconti, Roman Polanski . . . but the best directorial equivalent . . . is Josef von Sternberg" (p. 233).

8. In 1970, Kubrick again clarified why *Lolita* was filmed in England and in the studio for MGM: "I would have done it at the time if the money had been available in America. But as it turned out the only funds I could raise for the film had to be spent in England. There's been such a revolution in Hollywood's treatment of sex over just the last few years that it's easy to forget that when I became interested in *Lolita* a lot of people felt that such a film couldn't be made—or at least couldn't be shown. . . . And filming in England we obviously had no choice but to rely mainly on studio shooting" (Gelmis, p. 299). Kubrick's discussion of how he prefers the studio to actual locations for a psychological film can be found in "Stanley Kubrick, Movie-Maker," *The Observer* (London), 4 December 1960.

9. Pudovkin, in *Film Technique*, pp. 105–20, discusses his concept of the role of the actor. Like Griffith, he relied on editing and the close-up for emotional effect, something which is only an occasional technique in Kubrick's work.

10. Konstantin Stanislavsky, *Stanislavsky, on the Art of the Stage*, trans. with introductory essay by David Magarshack (New York: Hill and Wang, 1961). His description of the three types of actor (the creative, the imitative, and the stagehack) has interesting applications to film acting. Translate "creative" as method actor, "imitative" as a conventional studio type, and "stagehack" as character actor—Nikolai M. Gorchakov, *Stanislavsky Directs*, trans. Miriam Goldina (New York: Funk and Wagnalls, 1954). This book came out between *Fear and Desire* and *Killer's Kiss*, but as has been mentioned in the text, Kubrick did not have the money to hire actors trained well enough to put his reading into practice.

For a helpful and informative summary of film acting and the history of acting styles, see James F. Scott, *Film: The Medium and the Maker* (New York: Holt, Rinehart, and Winston, 1975), pp. 209–59.

11. Obviously, I keep seeing parallels between Kubrick's films and Buñuel's which, as far as I know, have not been widely discussed. Buñuel himself has said the following about Kubrick: "I'm a Kubrick fan, ever since *Paths of Glory*. Fabulous movie; that's what it's all about: codes of conduct, the way people behave when the codes break down. *A Clockwork Orange* is my favorite. I was very predisposed against the film. After seeing it, I realized it's the only movie about what the modern world really means." See Carlos Fuentes, "The Discreet Charm of Luis Buñuel," in *The World of Luis Buñuel: Essays in Criticism*, ed. Joan Mellen (New York: Oxford University Press, 1978), p. 65. Mellen provides a description of Buñuel's style which, in some ways, could apply as well to Kubrick's *Lolita*: "Not content to play about the surfaces of reality, Buñuel would bring the unconscious into view by so integrating it with everyday life that the film itself renders it empirically real" (p. 5).

12. Jonathan Stang, "Film Fan to Film Maker," *New York Times Magazine*, 12 October 1958.

13. For Kubrick's comments about changes made to satisfy the Production Code and the Legion of Decency, and why he began the film with the murder of Quilty, see Gelmis, pp. 300–301.

4. Dr. Strangelove

1. Helpful biographical and production information on the making of *Dr. Strangelove* can be found in Kagan, *The Cinema of Stanley Kubrick*, pp. 111–13; Phillips, *Stanley Kubrick: A Film Odyssey*, pp. 107–9; Gelmis, *The Film Director as Superstar*, pp. 301–2, 309–11. The quotation from Kubrick can be found in Walker, *Stanley Kubrick Directs*, p. 158.

2. Peter Bryant, *Red Alert* (New York: Ace Books, 1958). George's "Foreword" tries to impress the reader with the topicality of his novel: "It is a story that could happen. It may even be happening as you read these words. And then it really will be two hours to doom." Each chapter is titled by a reference to one of the three settings and three different times (Greenwich, Moscow, Washington). The novel ends this way: "The President sank into the seat he had used during the action. He was very weary, but he felt that his biggest effort was still to come. Yet he looked forward to it. He felt, like Zorubin [the Russian Ambassador], that no-one who had lived through that time could ever again take any action which might lead to war" (p. 191).

See also Peter George, *Dr. Strangelove* (New York: Bantam, 1963). George's novelization of the screenplay; helpful for much that it includes from the released film (mostly some dialogue), but, overall, not very revealing and poorly written.

3. Gelmis, p. 309.

4. At the time, Terry Southern's claim to fame was a comic novel about Southern Californian mores called *Flash and Filigree* (1958).

5. For a good discussion of the "mythopoeic" in recent fiction, see Maz'ud Zavarzudeh, *The Mythopoeic Reality*, and John W. Tilton, *Cosmic Satire in the Contemporary Novel* (Lewisburg, Pa.: Bucknell University Press, 1977). The latter, incidentally, briefly compares Burgess's *A Clockwork Orange* with Kubrick's 1971 film.

6. Alexander Walker, in particular, has some interesting things to say about the actors and acting styles of *Dr. Strangelove* in *Stanley Kubrick Directs*, pp. 158–217. Originally, Peter Sellers was to have played the Kong part, but because he was injured just before the filming of the B-52 scenes, Kubrick turned to Pickens.

George C. Scott has recently described his portrayal of Buck Turgidson as his best film role. Another notable performance of his—as Patton—involved another general officer and a certain degree of caricature.

7. Quoted in Kagan, p. 111.

8. See Gelmis, p. 309.

9. Quoted in Walker, pp. 176–77.

10. F. Anthony Macklin, "Sex and *Dr. Strangelove*," *Film Comment* (Summer 1965): 55–57; George W. Linden, "*Dr. Strangelove*," in *Nuclear War Films*, ed. Jack G. Shaheen (Carbondale: Southern Illinois University Press, 1978), pp. 59–67. See Kagan, pp. 136–37, for another list of sexual allusions.

5. 2001: A Space Odyssey

1. *The Making of 2001*, ed. Jerome Agel (New York: New American Library, 1970), includes reprints of interviews, reviews, production notes, special effects information, stills, and a wide assortment of commentary and trivia; it also anthologizes Clarke's "The Sentinel," pp. 15–23. Needless to say, it is invaluable.

Some of the more interesting technical features of *2001* are: (1) It was the first to use large-scale front projection—for "The Dawn of Man," a front projection screen covered with highly reflective materials measured 40′ X 90′. (2) For the moon excavation set, Kubrick had constructed a 60′ pit, 60′ by 120′, containing sand washed to resemble the color of the Moon's surface. (3) *Discovery's* fictional size was 770′ long; in actuality, it was a 54′ model and the exterior detail was done by hand so that in close-up it would look authentic. (4) *Discovery's* centrifuge cost $300,000, was 38′ across with 8′ interior, and rotated at speeds up to 3 mph. (5) Douglas Trumbull's slit-scan special effects for the Star-Gate were a major innovation at the time.

See *American Cinematographer*, June 1968, for essays on the technical effects of *2001*, especially those by Douglas Trumbull and Herb A. Lightman. Material here has been incorporated and summarized in several chapters and articles on the film, such as Agel's collection and Carolyn Geduld's *Filmguide to 2001: A Space Odyssey* (Bloomington: Indiana University Press, 1973).

2. Kubrick's statement quoted from Phillips, *Stanley Kubrick: A Film Odyssey*, p. 148. In the *Playboy* interview, still one of the best background sources for *2001*, Kubrick discusses the scientific reading and philosophic speculation that went into the making of the film.

3. Arthur C. Clarke, *The Lost Worlds of 2001* (New York: New American Library, 1972). Contains script material and ideas not used in the final film; something of a grab-bag, and not as helpful as one might hope. Kubrick, it appears, kept his own counsel during much of the time he collaborated with Clarke. Clarke breaks down the "authorship" of *2001* in this

way: 90 percent Kubrick, 5 percent special effects crew, 5 percent Clarke.

4. Arthur C. Clarke, *2001: A Space Odyssey* (New York: New American Library, 1968). Based on a screenplay by Stanley Kubrick and Arthur C. Clarke. According to Clarke, Kubrick declined to share co-authorship of the novel.

5. Because his special effects crew could not come up with a credible Saturn model (the rings were the problem), Kubrick decided on Jupiter.

In the novel, Floyd is identified as the Chairman of the National Council of Astronautics and a widower. In the novel, he does not sleep in either *Orion* or *Aries*, and when he talks over the Picturephone in the novel, he talks with his housekeeper.

6. Kubrick, in the Gelmis interview, defines some of his intentions regarding character: "One of the things we were trying to convey in this part of the film is the reality of a world populated—as ours soon will be—by machine entities who have as much, or more, intelligence as human beings, and who have the same emotional potentialities in their personalities as human beings" (p. 307).

These psychological and symbolic patterns resemble the folklore and literature of the Sleeper Awakened (i.e., *The Arabian Nights*, Shakespeare's *A Midsummer Night's Dream*, the Rip Van Winkle story), indicating that even in the futuristic settings of *2001*, elements of the fairy tale, a form Kubrick is interested in, have been incorporated.

7. The scene of Moon-Watcher and the bone is the only episode in *2001* filmed outside the studio. It was shot on a lot at the Boreham Wood studio. Clarke says that as Kubrick walked back to the studio after finishing the scene, he kept tossing bones into the air and shooting them with a handheld camera.

In Clarke, HAL's name is explained as an abbreviation for *H*euristically programmed *AL*gorithmic computer; he is the "brain and nervous system of the ship" (p. 95). The fact that the name is one letter displaced in the alphabet for IBM was, according to Kubrick, a happy coincidence.

8. After a preview before an audience in New York City, Kubrick trimmed *2001* from a running time of 161 to 141 minutes. Before that, he had deleted the prologue material (mostly prepared statements by leading scientists), which is printed in Agel.

9. In Clarke, Floyd does not appear suddenly on a screen in HAL's "brain." There, after disconnecting the computer, Bowman talks with Mission Control and Floyd, who then explains the purpose of the mission (the reader has been told by the narrator earlier). Three months then pass before he arrives at Saturn and goes through the Star-Gate. Kubrick alters and compresses these events and develops associative effects not found in the novel.

10. On the subject of language, Kubrick once said the following: "Perhaps it has something to do with the *magic of words*. If you can talk brilliantly about a problem, it can create the consoling illusion that it has been mastered" (in Walker, *Stanley Kubrick Directs*, p. 251).

11. Here is an example of what Clarke refers to as Mission Control "Technish," which occasionally is duplicated in the film: "Mission Control, this is X-ray-Delta-One. At two-zero-four-five, on-board fault prediction center in our niner-triple-zero computer showed Alpha Echo three-five unit

as probable failure within seventy-two hours. Request check your telemetry monitoring and suggest you review unit in your ship systems simulator" (p. 121).

12. While shooting, Kubrick tried to create a working "mood" or atmosphere by playing classical music, even though at the time he had hired veteran Hollywood composer Alex North (who did the music for *Spartacus*) to score the film; sometime later, he decided on the now famous classical selections for *2001*. He once remarked that the von Karajan version of "The Blue Danube" is ideal for "depicting grace and beauty in turning. It also gets about as far away as you can get from the cliché of space music" (in Agel, p. 88).

13. For a discussion of how motifs from "The Dawn of Man" (waterhole, bone, etc.) inform later sequences, see Don Daniels, "A Skeleton Key to *2001*," *Sight and Sound* (Winter 1970/71): 28–33. Other essays on the film are listed in the bibliography.

14. Two interesting visual parallels come to mind during the Moon monolith scene. The shape of the excavation resembles the horseshoe table in the conference room (where a man also photographs Floyd); and when the five figures line up for the photograph, with Floyd centered, it recalls the five judges of *Paths* who face the prisoners from across a marble floor on another Kubrickian gameboard.

15. On the subject of machines as man's children, consider this comment by Kubrick: "All man's technology grew out of his discovery of the tool-weapon. There's no doubt that there is a deep emotional relationship between man and his machine-weapons, which are his children. The machine is beginning to assert itself in a very profound way, even attracting affection and obsession. Man has always worshiped beauty, and I think there's a new kind of beauty in the world" (in Phillips, p. 126).

According to Clarke, he and Kubrick decided that the shape of *Discovery* should be a matter of "aesthetics rather than technology" (*The Lost Worlds of 2001*, p. 124). In his novel, Clarke describes the spaceship as being shaped like an "arrow," which may explain the symbolism of Bowman's name. Kubrick evidently decided on the film's version (the fossilized appearance of an extinct mammal or reptile) sometime after Clarke had finished his work.

16. In Clarke, HAL detects the "fault" in the AE-35 unit just after Poole's birthday celebration; in the film he detects it during a conversation with Bowman about his drawings and the secret preparations for the mission (a scene not found in the novel).

17. Carolyn Geduld's *Filmguide* study of *2001* contains a very extensive analysis of the "uterine" imagery in the film. In places, her discussion is quite good, but elsewhere she exhibits an unexplained hostility toward the film.

18. The subject of "normality" appears once again in a Kubrick film, this time just before HAL is disconnected. HAL assures Bowman that he is all right: "I know I have made some poor decisions lately, but everything is now back to normal." The most touching moment of the film comes when Bowman is disconnecting HAL. HAL's refrain, "I can feel it, I can feel it," provides a haunting, emotional prelude to Bowman's eventual death and rebirth.

19. In Clarke's novel, Bowman's last transmission to Earth as he is being sucked into the Star-Gate reads: "The thing's hollow—it goes on forever— and—oh my God!—*it's full of stars!*" (p. 191).

20. Here is how Kubrick explains his problems with the ending: "The ending was altered shortly before shooting it. In the original, there was no transformation of Bowman. He just wandered around the room and finally saw the artifact. But this didn't seem like it was satisfying enough, and we constantly searched for ideas until we finally came up with the ending as you see it" (Agel, p. 157).

21. The title of the Walter Tevis novel refers to the fall of Icarus, a mythological analogy the reverse of the Homeric pattern of Kubrick's *2001*, for the superior alien in the novel descends to Earth and failure, never to return home. The film *The Man Who Fell to Earth*, directed by Nicolas Roeg, was released in 1976.

22. Quoted from Gelmis, p. 304.

23. It may or may not be significant that Bowman is wearing a *green* helmet when he disconnects HAL.

24. In Clarke, the Star-Child looks on Earth as a toy and brings death before giving life:

> A thousand miles below, he became aware that a slumbering cargo of death had awoken, and was stirring sluggishly in orbit. The feeble energies it contained were no possible menace to him; but he preferred a cleaner sky. He put forth his will, and the circling megatons flowered in a silent detonation that brought a brief, false dawn to half the sleeping globe.
>
> Then he waited, marshaling his thoughts and brooding over his still untested powers. For though he was master of the world, he was not quite sure what to do next.
>
> But he would think of something. [p. 221]

6. A Clockwork Orange

1. For comments and information about the production of *A Clockwork Orange*, its economics (a budget of less than $2 million) and its technology, see the following sources: Norman Kagan, *The Cinema of Stanley Kubrick*, pp. 167–69; Gene Phillips, *Stanley Kubrick: A Film Odyssey*, pp. 157–70; Philip Strick and Penelope Houston, "An Interview with Stanley Kubrick," *Sight and Sound* (Winter 1971/2): 62–66; Michel Ciment, "Entretien avec Stanley Kubrick," *Positif* (June 1972): 23–33; Penelope Houston, "Kubrick Country," *Saturday Review*, 25 December 1971, pp. 42–44; and Andrew Bailey, "A Clockwork Utopia," *Rolling Stone*, 20 January 1972, pp. 20–22.

2. Houston, "Kubrick Country," p. 42.

3. Bailey, "A Clockwork Utopia," p. 22.

In the novel, Dr. Branom provides a definition of Alex's Nadsat: "Odd bits of old rhyming slang. . . . A bit of gypsy talk, too. But most of the roots are Slav. Propaganda. Subliminal penetration" (p. 114, American edition).

4. From "Interview with Anthony Burgess," *Playboy*, September 1974,

pp. 69–86. In this interview and in Anthony Burgess, "Juice from *A Clockwork Orange*," *Rolling Stone*, 8 June 1972, pp. 52–53, Burgess comments on his intentions in *A Clockwork Orange*. Although brief, the *Rolling Stone* article is excellent.

5. Here is how Kubrick explains why he felt it unnecessary to seek Burgess's collaboration on the screenplay of *Clockwork*:

> I wasn't particularly concerned about this because in a book as brilliantly written as *A Clockwork Orange* one would have to be lazy not to be able to find the answers to any questions that might arise within the text of the novel itself. I think it is reasonable to say that, whatever Burgess had to say about the story was said in the book. [Strick/Houston, "Interview with Stanley Kubrick," p. 63]

Burgess, on the other hand, had this to say about Kubrick's film:

> very much a Kubrick movie, technically brilliant, thoughtful, relevant, poetic, mind-opening. It was possible for me to see the work as a radical remaking of my own novel, not as a mere interpretation and this— the feeling that it was no impertinence to blazon it as 'Stanley Kubrick's *A Clockwork Orange*'—is the best tribute I can pay to the Kubrickian mastery. [Anthony Burgess, "Author Has His Say on 'Clockwork' Film," *Los Angeles Times*, *Calendar* section, 13 February 1972, p. 1]

In the British edition of Burgess's novel (London: Heinemann, 1962), Alex—in a chapter not included at the end of the American version— comes to the conclusion that Youth itself is nothing more than a clockwork toy: "But Youth is only being in a way like it might be an animal. No, it is not just like being an animal so much as being like one of those malenky toys you viddy being sold in the streets, like little chellovecks made out of tin and with a spring inside and then a winding handle on the outside. . . . Being young is like being like one of these malenky machines" (p. 195).

6. A good source for Burgess's theological and philosophical ideas are his essays collected in *1985* (Boston: Little, Brown and Co., 1978). In one titled "Cacotopia," he discusses the polarity of "Pelagian" and "Augustinian" thinking.

7. About the violence in *A Clockwork Orange*, its negative impact (i.e., aversive) on an audience, and art's responsibilities, Burgess and Kubrick, respectively, have said the following:

> Art never imitates. It merely takes over what is already present in the real world, such as violence, and makes an aesthetic pattern out of it, or tries to explain it, or tries to relate it to some other aspect of life. [*Playboy* interview with Burgess, p. 72]

> Art consists of reshaping life but it does not create life or cause life. [Strick/Houston, "Interview with Stanley Kubrick," p. 63]

In the novel, Alex reads aloud from F. Alexander's book (the "other"

Clockwork Orange) the overly ripe passage cited in my text. He calls it a "very high type preaching goloss" and Dim rewards his recitation with a Bronx cheer (pp. 21–22, American version). Later, Alex describes how he understands the meaning of Alexander's book: "The name was about a clockwork orange. Listening to the J. S. Bach, I began to pony better what that meant now, and I thought, slooshying away to the brown gorgeousness of the starry German master, that I would like to have tolchocked them both harder and ripped them to ribbons on their own floor" (p. 34).

8. See B. F. Skinner, *Beyond Freedom and Dignity* (New York: Alfred A. Knopf, 1971), especially pp. 150ff. A comment particularly appropriate to a study of Alex's mindscreen is Skinner's belief that "it is the environment that acts upon the perceiving person, not the perceiving person who acts upon environment" (p. 188).

9. Bailey, "The Clockwork Utopia," p. 22. For more on the same subject, see Ciment, "Entretien avec Stanley Kubrick," pp. 24–25.

10. Houston, "Kubrick Country," p. 42.

11. In the novel, Alex talks about how the "Bad" comes from the self and that the self is created by God, which prompts this analysis of the State: "But the not-self cannot have the Bad, meaning they of the government and the judges and the schools cannot allow the Bad because they cannot allow the self" (p. 40, American version).

12. Kagan, *The Cinema of Stanley Kubrick*, p. 167.

13. Throughout chapter 6 I have made use of Bruce F. Kawin's extremely useful terminology and definitions on the crucial subject of first-person film aesthetics (see *Mindscreen*, particularly pp. 3–22). Here is how he summarizes the three ways of signifying subjectivity within a first-person narrative film, all of which involve distortion: (1) through what a character *says* (voice-over); (2) what a character *sees* (subjective focus, imitative angles of vision); and (3) what a character *thinks* (memory, fantasy, emotion, etc.). By "mindscreen," he means the last category. Significant to this study, of course, is that *A Clockwork Orange* exhibits all three, while it requires an audience to perceive the "mindscreen" of its creator, the film maker himself. Within this authorial subjectivity, "the image does not simply *appear*, but gives the audience the impression of having been *chosen*."

14. An invaluable source of study for Kubrick's *Clockwork* is the published screenplay (New York: Ballantine Books, 1972), which was assembled by Kubrick and staff members after a frame-by-frame analysis; it contains over 700 stills from the film.

15. Here is what Kubrick says about Walter Carlos' electronic music: "I think Walter Carlos is the only electronic composer and realizer who has managed to create a sound which is not an attempt at copying the instruments of the orchestra and yet which, at the same time, achieves a beauty of its own employing electronic tonalities. I think that his version of the fourth movement of Beethoven's Ninth Symphony rivals hearing a full orchestra playing it, and that is saying an awful lot" (in Strick/Houston, "Interview with Stanley Kubrick," p. 64).

16. The huge heads of the laughing dummies on the derelict casino stage recall the "mannequin" imagery common to earlier films, i.e., the factory scene in *Killer's Kiss* and Johnny Clay's mask in the robbery scene of *The*

Killing. In *Clockwork*, of course, the performing styles of Aubrey Morris (Deltoid) and Patrick Magee, in particular, suggest that of animated but decidedly mechanical toys. In several ways, Magee's performance recalls Sellers as Strangelove. In contrast, the dehumanized "maskies" worn by Alex and his droogs during the first HOME sequence resemble the activity of clowns from the *commedia del l'arte* or figures out of a George Méliès' magic-show film like "The Magic Lantern."

17. First a musical play (1973), now a midnight horror-camp phenomenon of the first order, *The Rocky Horror Picture Show* (directed by Jim Sharman) parodies horror films in general, and especially those from the Hammer Studio. One scene is a take-off on the very scene from *The Curse of Frankenstein* (1957) that appears on a drive-in movie screen in Kubrick's *Lolita* (it shows the monster unwrapping himself). *The Rocky Horror Picture Show* also pays homage to *Dr. Strangelove*—a character named Dr. Scott, with a German accent, appears in a wheelchair. Two recent essays that discuss the film and the subject of midnight audiences are: Kenneth von Gunden, "The RH Factor," *Film Comment* (September–October, 1979): 54–56; and Jonathan Rosenbaum, "The Rocky Horror Picture Cult," *Sight and Sound* (Spring 1980): 78–79.

18. When Alex is expelled from his own home by the presence of Joe the lodger, Pee and Em's new "son," the mournful sounds of the slow movement from the "William Tell Overture" return as an accompaniment to both his piteous solicitations and thoughts of suicide on the Thames Embankment.

19. In response to a question about his interest in Napoleon as a film subject (in Strick/Houston interview), Kubrick made the following backhanded reference to *Spartacus*: "First of all, I start from the premise that there has never been a great historical film, and I say that with all apologies and respect to those who have made historical films, including myself" (p. 66).

20. Alex's comment about the first Ludovico film—that "it was a very good like professional piece of sinny"—comes directly from the novel (p. 102, American edition), while the added phrase "like it was done in Hollywood" is Kubrick's interpolation. In the novel, the sinny-cinema pun can be appreciated more easily than in the film.

21. Someone pointed out to me an interesting parallel between Alex's last vision and the Ascot musical number in the film version of the Lerner-Loewe musical play, *My Fair Lady* (1964, George Cukor), both of which are adaptations of Shaw's *Pygmalion*. When one thinks about it, *A Clockwork Orange* is a kind of upside-down version of the Pygmalion legend as are countless other fairy tales, a version that involves in its popular form the "awakening" of Eliza's full human potential by the misogynist Dr. Henry Higgins. Also, it concerns the pros and cons of "conditioning," develops a linguistic theme (i.e., phonetics), and comments on the shallowness of social distinctions (the primitive and her civilized detractors). As an element in Kubrick's cinematic self-references, it would have to be considered in the same company as "Singing in the Rain," which, incidentally, returns as musical accompaniment to the endtitles, only this time in its original form with Gene Kelly singing the lyrics.

7. Barry Lyndon

1. Recommended readings on *Barry Lyndon's* production, its economics, technology, and aesthetics include: John Alcott (who was the Director of Photography), "Photographing Stanley Kubrick's *Barry Lyndon*," *American Cinematographer*, March 1976, p. 268; Ed DiGiulio, "Two Special Lenses for *Barry Lyndon*," *American Cinematographer*, March 1976, p. 276; Richard Schickel, "Kubrick's Grandest Gamble," *Time*, 15 December 1975, pp. 72–78; Colin L. Westerbeck, Jr., "*Barry Lyndon*," *Commonweal*, March & April, 1976, p. 208. For a sampling of initial review opinion, see Penelope Houston, "*Barry Lyndon*," *Sight and Sound* (Spring 1976): 77–80; Michael Dempsey, "*Barry Lyndon*," *Film Quarterly* (Fall 1976): 49–54; Pauline Kael, "Kubrick's Gilded Age," *The New Yorker*, 29 December 1975, pp. 49–52; Andrew Sarris, "What Makes Barry Run?," *Village Voice*, 29 December 1975, pp. 111–12. Highly recommended as a summary of negative opinion is *Mad Magazine's* spoof, "Borey Lyndon," September 1976, pp. 4–10, listed under the "Kubrick-A-Brac Dept." For more extensive coverage, see: Hans Feldmann, "Kubrick and His Discontents," *Film Quarterly* (Fall 1976): 12–19; Alan Spiegel, "Kubrick's *Barry Lyndon*," *Salmagundi* (Fall 1977): 194–208; Thomas Allen Nelson, "*Barry Lyndon*: Kubrick's Cinema of Disparity," *Rocky Mountain Review* (Winter 1978/79): 39–51; and Robert Phillip Kolker, *A Cinema of Loneliness*, pp. 123–38.

2. All references to Thackeray's *The Luck of Barry Lyndon* come from the critical edition prepared and edited by Martin J. Anisman (New York: New York University Press, 1970). In addition, I am indebted to the discussion by Robert A. Colby, in *Thackeray's Canvass of Humanity: An Author and His Public* (Columbus: Ohio State University Press, 1979).

3. *The Luck of Barry Lyndon*, p. 351.

4. Ibid., p. 47.

5. Ibid., p. 49.

6. Ibid., p. 315.

7. Ibid., p. 167.

8. The film's *Epilogue* reads as follows: "It Was in the Reign of George III That the Aforesaid Personages Lived and Quarrelled. Good or Bad, Handsome or Ugly, Rich or Poor, They Are All Equal Now."

9. Quoted comment from Richard Schickel, "Kubrick's Grandest Gamble," p. 76.

10. In several places, Kubrick's camera and the narrator's commentary *are* in perfect harmony, especially when slow zooms move in for close-ups of Barry's face as the narrator explains or interprets what he is thinking or feeling (e.g., while Barry stands by a campfire and ponders his disappointment with military life, or as he decides to desert the British army by stealing an officer's horse and identity). This method of psychological penetration, however, tends to be less prominent in Part II, as the narrator's authority diminishes.

11. In a particularly revealing passage, Thackeray's Redmond Barry describes his father's death:

> At length, after his great day of triumph before his sacred majesty at Newmarket, Harry's fortune was just on the point of being made, for the gracious monarch promised to provide for him. But alas he was

taken in charge by another monarch, whose will will have no delay or denial,—by Death, namely, who seized upon my father at Chester races, leaving me a helpless orphan. Peace be to his ashes! He was not faultless, and dissipated all our princely family property; but he was as brave a fellow as ever tossed a bumper or called a main, and he drove his coach-and-six like a man of fashion. [p. 51]

12. Kubrick's casting for *Lyndon* deserves some comment, especially in light of the critical snickers occasioned by the selection of Ryan O'Neal and Marisa Berenson. Besides looking the part (a man/boy), O'Neal has a strongly emotional acting character and face (e.g., *Love Story*), as well as a talent for light comedy (e.g., *Paper Moon* and *What's Up Doc?*); Marisa Berenson is not only a professional model who wears clothes well (a not unimportant aspect of Lady Lyndon's characterization), but her face possesses a naturally sad expressiveness. Elsewhere, Kubrick uses first-rate performers (mostly English character actors), some of whom, like Philip Stone, Patrick Magee, and Anthony Sharp, have frequently appeared in his films.

13. Quoted comments can be found in Strick/Houston, "Interview with Stanley Kubrick," p. 65.

14. Here is how John Alcott (in the *American Cinematographer* essay cited earlier) explains the film's visual style from his position as Director of Photography: "Each composition is like a painting by one of the Old Masters, and they link one onto the other like the tiles of a wondrous mosaic" (p. 270). "As I saw it, the story of Barry Lyndon took place during a romantic type of period—although it didn't necessarily have to be a romantic film. I say 'a romantic period' because of the quality of the clothes, the dressing of the sets, and the architecture of that period. These all had a kind of soft feeling" (p. 274). Ed DiGiulio, who helped devise the still-camera lens used for the candlelight scenes, says that Kubrick wanted "to preserve the natural patina and feeling of those old castles at night as they actually were" and that they were not intended as a "gimmick" (in "Two Special Lenses for *Barry Lyndon*," p. 318).

15. Except for the 1789 reference, which has a clear importance to the film's thematic/structural intentions, the other dates do not seem historically significant. The marriage date (June 15, 1773) differs from that in Thackeray's novel (May 15, 1773), which could mean that Kubrick was shooting the early scenes of Part II during the summer or that he decided to suggest a form of seasonal progression—if so, Part II goes from the mythological height of Barry's fortune (Summer) to the discontents and death of Winter (11 December 1789). Or, heaven forbid, it may mean nothing at all.

8. The Shining

1. Stephen King, *The Shining* (New York: Doubleday and Co., 1977).

2. Quoted in Jack Kroll, "Stanley Kubrick's Horror Show," *Newsweek*, 26 May 1980, p. 99. For a sampling of other reviews and reactions, see the following: Richard Schickel, "Red Herrings and Refusals," *Time*, 2 June 1980, p. 69; Richard T. Jameson, "Kubrick's Shining," *Film Comment*

(July–August 1980): 28–32; Pauline Kael, "Devolution," *The New Yorker*, 1 June 1980, pp. 130–47; John Hofsess, "The Shining Example of Kubrick," *Los Angeles Times, Calendar* section, 1 June 1980, pp. 1, 25; Paul Mayersberg, "The Overlook Hotel," *Sight and Sound* (Winter 1980/81): 54–57.

3. Robin Wood, "Return of the Repressed," *Film Comment* (July–August 1978): 25–32.

4. Diane Johnson, who teaches literature at a California university, has written five novels and a biography of George Meredith's first wife, Mary Ellen Peacock (*Lesser Lives*). Her work examines character with Gothic wit and humane understanding, and it could be that Kubrick sought her assistance not only with plot/character ideas (since the film changes so much from King's novel) but with the problem of giving the film a contemporary American sound (dialogue) and ambiance. After all, he has been away for a long time.

5. Production details on the making of *The Shining* ($18 million budget) and comments by Stephen King can be found in: Jim Alberton and Peter S. Perakos, "*The Shining*," *Cinefantastique* (Fall 1978): 74; Peter S. Perakos, "Interview with Stephen King," *Cinefantastique* (Winter 1978): 12–15; David Chute, "King of the Night: An Interview with Stephen King," *Take One* (January 1979): 33–38; Harlan Kennedy, "Kubrick Goes Gothic," *American Film* (June 1980): 49–52. Of particular significance are the comments about the film's remarkable lighting and extensive use of the Steadicam by John Alcott (Director of Photography) and Garrett Brown (Steadicam Operator) in *American Cinematographer* (August 1980): see Herb Lightman's interview with Alcott ("Photographing Stanley Kubrick's *The Shining*"), p. 780, and Garrett Brown, "The Steadicam and 'The Shining'," p. 786.

6. For a helpful summary of mazes and labyrinths, see W. H. Matthews, *Mazes and Labyrinths: Their History and Development* (London: Longmans, Green, and Co., 1922). It may be only a coincidence, but in some ancient maze legends the emblem of a *double-ax* plays an important role. See especially the stories in Jorge Luis Borges, *Ficciones*, trans. Anthony Kerrigan (New York: Grove Press, 1962).

7. For a discussion of Navajo sand paintings, their mythology and symbolism, see Leland C. Wyman, *The Windways of the Navaho* (Colorado Springs: The Taylor Museum, 1962). Jack's passion for the enclosed order of the maze resembles the Navajo circle that protects one from malevolent outside forces, except that Kubrick's films usually reverse that mythology and characterize such worlds as entrapping, while outside space offers both uncertain exploration and hope. Like the maze, however, the Indian circle has an opening (the East) for both entrance and escape. Throughout the film, Danny is associated with circles. These, although they recall the Navajo circle of protection from outside evil, ironically enclose rather than banish the evil that exists *inside* his home (the circle/maze of Jack's madness).

ACKNOWLEDGMENTS

Sources for the stills used in this book are listed below.

Fear and Desire, p. 22: Joseph Burstyn.

Killer's Kiss, pp. 23 and 26: United Artists. Courtesy of United Artists.

The Killing, pp. 33 and 36: United Artists/Harris-Kubrick. Courtesy of United Artists.

Paths of Glory, pp. 40, 45, 48, and 50: United Artists/Harris-Kubrick. Courtesy of United Artists.

Lolita, pp. 54, 65, 67, 68, 70, 74, and 76: Metro-Goldwyn-Mayer/Harris-Kubrick.

Dr. Strangelove, pp. 79, 82, 86, 90, 93, and 97: Columbia Pictures/Hawk Films. Courtesy of Columbia Pictures.

2001: A Space Odyssey, pp. 11, 18, 99, 109, 115, 123, 124, 126, and 127: Metro-Goldwyn-Mayer/Stanley Kubrick.

A Clockwork Orange, pp. 133, 137, 141, 148, 152, 158, 160: Warner Brothers/Hawk Films. Copyright Warner Brothers, Inc.

Barry Lyndon, pp. 5, 165, 169, 178, 180, 181, 185, 186, 190, 192: Warner Brothers/Hawk Films. Copyright Warner Brothers, Inc.

The Shining, pp. 107, 206, 210, 215, and 221: Warner Brothers/Hawk Films. Copyright Warner Brothers, Inc.

The frontispiece, the still on p. 1, and the jacket photograph were used by permission of Warner Brothers, Inc. Copyright Warner Brothers, Inc.

INDEX